MY LIFE AS A
SKATEBOARDER JUNKIE
INMATE PASTOR

HOSOI

HarperOne

An Imprint of HarperCollins*Publishers*

HarperOne

HOSOI

MY LIFE AS A SKATEBOARDER JUNKIE INMATE PASTOR.

HarperCollins books may be purchased for educational, business, or sales promotional use. For information please write: Special Markets Department, HarperCollins Publishers, 10 East 53rd Street, New York, NY 10022.

HARPERCOLLINS WEBSITE:
HTTP://WWW.HARPERCOLLINS.COM

HARPERCOLLINS®, ®, AND HARPERONE™ ARE TRADEMARKS OF HARPERCOLLINS PUBLISHERS.

FIRST EDITION

DESIGNED BY JAMES IACOBELLI

Library of Congress Cataloging-in-Publication Data

Hosoi, Christian.

Hosoi : my life as a skateboarder junkie inmate pastor / by Christian Hosoi.

p. cm.

ISBN 978—0—06—202430—5

1. Hosoi, Christian. 2. Skateboarders—United States—Biography. I. Title.

GV859.813.H67A3 2012

796.22092—dc23

[B] 2012002475

12 13 14 15 16 RRD(H) 10 9 8 7 6 5 4 3 2 1

DEDICATION

To my loving mother, who is in heaven,
my wonderful father, my beautiful
wife and adorable children, and to all my
friends and fans who have supported me
throughout my life

TABLE OF

CONTENTS

FOREWORD

CHRISTIAN HOSOI HAS ALWAYS HAD STYLE. THE FIRST TIME I EVER SAW HIM WAS IN A MAGAZINE, BLASTING A FRONTSIDE OLLIE TO DISASTER IN A SMALL BOWL. HE LOOKED ABOUT MY AGE (TEN AT THE TIME), BUT HAD LONG HAIR AND COLORFUL PADS. MOST IMPORTANT, HIS BODY FORM WAS THAT OF A VETERAN PRO SKATER LAUNCHED INTO THE AIR. I WAS IMMEDIATELY INSPIRED TO LEARN THAT TRICK, WHICH I EMULATED IN THE OASIS SNAKE RUN ON MY GIANT SIMS ANDRECHT BOARD. I KNEW I WOULD NEVER LOOK THAT STYLISH, BUT I HAD TO TRY. EMULATING CHRISTIAN TO NO AVAIL BECAME A CONSISTENT THREAD IN MY SKATING OVER THE NEXT DECADE.

CHRISTIAN AND I BECAME FRIENDS NOT LONG AFTER, AND EACH OTHER'S TOUGHEST COMPETITORS FOR YEARS TO COME. BUT THE BIGGEST CHALLENGE OF BEING COMPARED TO HIM WAS THAT HE COULD MAKE THE MOST BASIC TRICK LOOK *GOOD*. SO WHEN HE LEARNED SOMETHING NEW, HE DID IT LIKE NOBODY ELSE. HE DID IT IN A WAY YOU WISHED YOU COULD, BUT KNEW YOU WOULD NEVER ACHIEVE. A PRIME EXAMPLE IS WHEN WE BOTH LEARNED 540S: MINE WERE MECHANICAL, SPINNING FLATLY AND PRECISE. HIS WERE FULLY FLIPPED, AT LEAST SIX FEET HIGH, AND SEEMED TO BE SUSPENDED IN A SLOW-MOTION MIDAIR dance. In order to compete with such style, the only defense was to learn more tricks than anyone. And that wasn't always enough.

Eventually, skate fans in the '80s divided themselves into two groups: style versus tech. You can guess which side of the fence I landed on. But I always took cues from Christian to figure out how to give my latest tricks a little more flair. The only drawback to that approach is that if he learned the trick, it would become his because he did it in a way that was much more fun to watch. It was an amazing time of innovation and experimenting for both of us; we were young and seemingly invincible.

As skating's popularity waned, he and I both had struggles. We desperately wanted to continue our careers as pro skaters, but the industry was changing . . . meaning that the preferred *style* of skating was morphing into street-inspired moves. Even though we both had a hard time adapting, Christian managed to keep up and pull some of the hardest stuff with his ever-stylish ways. But in the early '90s, it became very difficult for either of us to make a living solely from our skating skills.

I lost touch with Christian in the following years but heard secondhand stories of his

TOUGH TIMES INCLUDING HEAVY DRUG USE. I DIDN'T
WANT TO BELIEVE THE RUMORS, BUT MY FEARS
WERE REALIZED WHEN I HEARD THAT HE HAD
BEEN ARRESTED AND PUT IN JAIL. AS HIS TRIAL
AND SENTENCING NEARED, I WROTE LETTERS OF
SUPPORT TO THE DISTRICT ATTORNEY, HOPING THAT
CHRISTIAN'S TALE COULD BE ONE OF CAUTION FOR
YOUTH TODAY, AND THAT HE COULD TELL HIS STORY
PERSONALLY IF HE WERE RELEASED. I HAD FAITH
THAT HE WOULD COME OUT ON THE OTHER SIDE WITH
STYLE, AND RETURN TO THE SPORT THAT CAME TO
DEFINE BOTH OF US. HE HAS SINCE DONE THAT AND
MORE, AND WE (AS SKATERS AND PEERS) ARE LUCKY
TO HAVE HIM BACK. THIS BOOK IS PART OF THAT
PROCESS. ENJOY THE STORIES OF SUCCESS, EXCESS,
AND DEBAUCHERY. BUT LEARN FROM IT, AND REALIZE
IT IS TOO EASY TO TAKE YOUR OPPORTUNITIES FOR
GRANTED AND LOSE YOURSELF IN THE PROCESS.

CHRISTIAN'S REDEMPTION IS INSPIRATIONAL,
AND HIS SKATING CONTINUES TO EXUDE THE BEST
STYLE; I'M STILL JEALOUS OF HIS FRONTSIDE OLLIE
DISASTERS . . . BUT I'LL KEEP WORKING ON THEM.

—TONY HAWK

STREETWEAR

JIMMY'Z AD CAMPAIGN, LATE 1980S. *COURTESY OF JIMMY'Z.*

INTRO

CHRIS AHRENS

They called him Christ, and his legions of disciples would follow him anywhere. Now, years past his competitive prime, the name Hosoi continues to inspire many dedicated followers. He was one of the top athletes in the world through most of the 1980s, but few beyond his chosen sport knew much about him in that era. That's because skateboarding was only decades old at the time and riding well beyond the margins of polite society. It's also because he disappeared right at the peak of his power. Rumors flew suggesting everything from his having lost his mind to his simply having lost interest in the sport he'd helped create. Nobody who knew him well would have been surprised if he'd turned up dead as a result of a drug deal gone south or his heart giving out from pushing too hard for too long. What is surprising is that he landed in one piece and lived to tell the tale. And what a tale it is.

At this writing there are more kids learning skateboarding than there are entering Little League baseball. In the early '60s, however, skateboarding—or sidewalk surfing, as it was often called—was an undisciplined activity practiced almost exclusively by teenage surfers in their off-hours. About that same time, the boy who would one day become a man, and eventually Christian's father, Hawaii-born Ivan Hosoi was surfing the biggest waves he could find on Oahu.

van soon imported his island style to the U.S. mainland, where he joined kids in risking their necks on homemade skateboards after nailing metal roller skates onto two-by-fours. Next came molded plastic foot-long skateboards with clay wheels. While clay led to newer, better tricks, hitting even the smallest pebble could warrant a trip to the emergency room.

It took urethane to rocket skateboarding into the future: the soft stickiness of the new wheels allowed riders access to steep walls, empty swimming pools, vertical movement, and flight. The wheels also, inadvertently, moved youth culture forward as kids around the world imitated the lives of punk-rock saints Jay Adams and Tony Alva, who had fallen under the influence while blasting to new heights and redefining what it meant to be young and wild in America.

In 1967, Ivan and his wife, Bonnie, had a son they named Christian Rosha Hosoi. The family soon moved to Berkeley, California, where Ivan attended graduate school in art. By the mid-'70s the Hosois had relocated to Los Angeles, where punk rock had proven a backlash against the generally passive hippies and had composted perfectly into skateboarding.

While a synthesis of the L.A./ Berkeley art scene, surfer cool, street smarts, and the psychedelic revolution, Christian was also his own person——a blend of ideas born in his own brain from a massive collage of experiences. The result was to turn the act of riding a skateboard into high-level performance art. Eventually the act would be performed far above

EARLY 1967. MOTHER, BONNIE, WHILE FATHER, IVAN, HOLDS FRAME. MY FIRST OF MANY PORTRAITS. *HOSOI FAMILY COLLECTION.*

thousands of gasping fans who realized that levitating at such altitudes could prove lethal. Everywhere he went, from Hollywood to London, he was celebrated as the best vertical and aerial skateboarder in the world.

That unofficial and underground title wouldn't mean much to anyone but the few thousand hard-core skaters who lived and died by his every move, if Hosoi hadn't also been a factor in a bigger world. He was, as anyone on hand will tell you, the sport's first and most enduring "rock star" and its most charismatic entertainer to date. It is well established by skate historians (yes, there is such a thing) that '80s skating belonged to Hosoi and his only real rival, Tony Hawk. Hawk readily admits, "When Christian was on fire, he was unbeatable." With a seemingly endless variety of his own rapid-fire tricks, Hawk emerged victorious more than anyone, including Hosoi. Yet it was the newly anointed high-flying Christ, bad-boy flag waving in the face of conformist patriotism, who often won the crowd. Where Tony was technical innovation, Christian was aerodynamic soul, sometimes trumping Hawk's amazing new "finger-flipping" tricks with dramatic moves of his own, like his signature Christ Air. His electrified performances caused him to stand out like Jimi Hendrix at a folk music festival.

I first saw Hosoi and Hawk skate a demo at a San Diego tradeshow in the mid-'80s. Tony was rifling off his quick-fire tricks, while Hosoi flew faster and higher with an immaculate style. As would happen each time they faced off, the crowd was split nearly equally in their favoritism. Later, partisan passions would bleed into the stands as fans clashed over the love of their favorite idol.

Hosoi's worshipful followers, the twenty-four/seven drug pipeline connected directly to his brain, and more money than a teenager should ever possess could deceive anyone into thinking he might just be some sort of fast-rolling messiah. It would take the slamming of a prison door to silence such nonsense, forcing him to face life soberly for the first time in his life.

I first met Christian Hosoi personally in 2004, when I interviewed him for *Risen* magazine in Nellis Federal Prison Camp, on the outskirts of Las Vegas, Nevada. He had the same cocky strut I had observed from afar and in skate films as he approached the empty prison cafeteria accompanied by a single armed guard. Like every prisoner there, he wore a pressed khaki uniform, though he was distinguished by his own style of short, spiked hair. He had been forgotten by the masses and he knew it. Yet he was neither bitter over nor jealous of the rising fame and fortune of Tony Hawk. I found Hosoi open, warm, and joyful, displaying no signs of the deterioration that often lingers after a lifetime of drug abuse.

He was a couple years into what was expected to be a ten-year imprisonment for trafficking narcotics over state lines. As a representative of skateboarding he had been a failure. As a messiah he was a bad joke. With reality pounding at the door, he was forced to confront some dark and empty spaces that no drug, sexual conquest, or screaming crowd could ever fill. Just as he always had, he was about to fly higher than anyone had ever thought possible. ✺

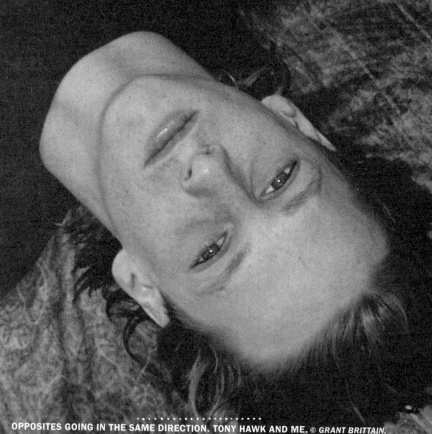

OPPOSITES GOING IN THE SAME DIRECTION. TONY HAWK AND ME. © *GRANT BRITTAIN.*

HUNTINGTON BEACH. OP PRO SURF CONTEST, 1986.
JUST BEFORE A MAJOR RIOT BROKE OUT. © *IVAN HOSOI.*

RISEN
SON FALLEN

When you're blasting air, it's not the going up that's the rush, but the coming down. Everything slows down up there. It takes forever because you're thinking of what you've got to do, calculating your projectile, your landing, everything. All of a sudden you start picking up speed, coming down fast. Once you hit, it's like you've been floating and you realize you can do whatever you want. I always loved doing whatever I wanted.

—CHRISTIAN HOSOI

CHAPTER01

I'm five years old and out pursuing my first love, climbing trees. The scene of this activity is Play Mountain Place, an alternative preschool off La Cienega and Washington Boulevards in Los Angeles. I'm way out on some limb, and nothing my teachers or anyone else can say or do will get me to come back down. I just keep climbing higher and higher, swinging from branch to branch, hearing the cracking sounds that eucalyptus makes just before it snaps. But I'm not worried; I'm stoked and wondering why the other kids in my class don't join me. Years from now I'll make a lot of money doing things nobody else wants to do with me.

In that case it's to blast the world's highest aerials on a skateboard. A lot of people said I was the best in the world in the late '80s. The record books show otherwise—that I often beat the world's best, but more often took second place to a guy named Tony Hawk. But record books don't tell the whole story. They don't say that I was known to be the most popular skateboarder of my time, and the highest paid. They don't say that my nickname was Christ and that I was the inventor of the Christ Air. They don't say that I was an outlaw and have lived in defiance of most laws, including gravity, most of my life. Everything has been one big experiment to see how far I can push things. And I pushed them further than anyone thought possible. I thought I got away with everything, but I was wrong. In January 2000, at thirty-two years old, I would find out just how wrong.

BUSTED

It's one of those classic clear Southern California mornings. It'll probably be even nicer where I'm headed, Hawaii. But I'm not going there for vacation or for the weather. I'm going because of the substance I'll be carrying beneath my clothes: crystal methamphetamine.

I've used other drugs since I was a child, but for the last seven years I've been snorting, smoking, and even shooting meth every day. Everything about meth—from scoring it, to lighting the torch, to blowing glass pipes as smoke fills my hungry lungs—is addicting. But I've done enough for a dozen people and I plan on quitting soon. I'll shock the world and be bigger than ever when I make my comeback in skateboarding.

But that will have to wait, because I don't want everybody to know where I am, not right now. I've been living underground for about five years, fleeing misdemeanor bench warrants after being busted three times for possession. Being on the run is just another rush—fun and crazy. The way I like it.

The guy at the hotel in L.A. gives me the dope to transport. I smoke some of it—for quality control purposes, of course. Just as he promised, it's killer. It's been iced up, meaning cooked down into rock form to be distilled for purity. I'm a courier—what they call a mule—so I pay nothing for the ice. I put everything into a hip sack, fasten it to my body, and conceal it all beneath my baggy clothes.

As arranged, a girl picks me up at the hotel and speeds me to the airport, where I'll use my one-way ticket to Honolulu, on the island of Oahu. Once there I have an address where I'll drop off the pound and a half of quality ice. The street value of this in the Islands is around $60,000, about four times what it is in California. My take is a fraction of that amount, about $2,500—not much, considering I'm taking most of the risk. Still, it's not bad since I thrive on risk and haven't collected a paycheck in some time. Ten years earlier I could have made this much for skating a couple of demos.

I could still get paid well from a number of sponsors if I cleared up my warrants, but to do that I'd have to serve at least thirty days in jail. Thirty days is a long time for someone like me, used to doing whatever I want.

I've been through a million airports and never once been searched, so with the meth tucked into my hip sack, today should be a walk in the park. I stroll through security and nobody even blinks. Glad to be through that stress point, I go to McDonald's for a snack before boarding. As I'm eating, I get a weird feeling and begin to sweat. Nothing like this has ever happened to me before; only later will I realize that it was an inner warning signal telling me something wasn't right. At the moment, though, instead of heeding it as a warning, I fight through the feeling and talk myself down. I pat my forehead with a napkin, take a deep breath, and am fine again.

After an uneventful flight, I exit the plane carrying a skateboard, something I always have with me. It's midday and the terminal is almost empty. As I head toward baggage claim, I notice a guy watching me. Even on drugs I've never been the paranoid type, but something's up with this guy. Despite the lack of uniform, he gives off cop vibes.

I hustle past him but can sense him following me as I continue beyond the baggage claim area. I consider ditching my luggage as I aim toward the nearest exit, repressing the urge to sprint. As I reach the sidewalk the guy says, "Excuse me, sir; can I talk to you for a second?"

I turn around and say, "What is it?"

"I have a suspicion you're carrying narcotics, and I want to see your ID."

"I don't know where you get that idea," I say defensively. "You can search my bags if you like."

"Actually," he counters, "we need to search *you.*"

BLOWING A RING OF METH. THIS PHOTO SPARKED A LIFELONG LOVE AFFAIR. © AMBER STANLEY.

"Sorry, but that's illegal; you don't have any reason to search me."

As he's talking, I'm scanning the area for someplace to run and dump the stuff. I'm looking along the sidewalk when I see two guys watching me. Then, off to the side, I notice two more guys. I'm surrounded by chain-link fences and plainclothes cops in tennis shoes. There's got to be some way out of this; there *always* is. Think, think, think!

Running won't work, but talking just might. Friends say I could have been a lawyer, given the way I can spin words when I need to. I put on my most innocent face and lie straight to the cop's face about my reasons for being in Hawaii. He's not buying it, though—not for a second. "I'm gonna get the dog," he says.

"Go get the dog," I agree, trying to call his bluff.

This all happens on the curb, just outside the airport. By the time the dog arrives and circles my bag, everyone nearby is watching the scene. The dog doesn't do anything unusual that I can see, but the cop says that it's given some sort of sign and that they now have the right to search me inside. I shrug and go with them.

The back room they lead me to is stark white with fluorescent bulbs flickering overhead. The place is immaculate except for a Styrofoam plate with partially eaten fried chicken and potato salad making a meal for flies. The cop who's apparently in charge is a thick-necked jock with gelled hair.

To me this is no big deal; something will work out. I'm not busted yet. Six or seven more cops cram into this little room, and one of them asks again to search me. I repeat, "No, that's illegal." This guy must have seen every old detective movie ever made. "We can do this the easy way or the hard way," he says. I'd laugh in his face, but this has quit being funny.

When he asks yet again, I say, "Okay, whatever." At his command I raise my hands. He pulls up my shirt and rips out the hip sack, holding it up like a trophy. "Oh, look what we found," he says cheerfully. He reads me my rights.

Now I really *am* busted, but I won't do much time. People do only six years for murder, four for manslaughter. I've got no felonies on my record, so I'll probably get probation and be on the streets again in months. Even if I do get a long sentence, I'll never rat on anybody. You do the crime, you do the time, right?

All of a sudden, the cops turn our friendly little get-together into an interrogation. One says, "Christian, tell us where you're taking the meth." I don't answer, of course. Next thing you know, the agent will be shining a light in my face and slapping me around, if they remain true to the movies.

When they ask again where I'm taking the drugs, I roll my eyes and answer, "Hawaiian Brian's," which is a pool hall in downtown Waikiki.

"Really, who you taking it to?"

"Brian."

They want a story, so I give them one. Of course the officer knows I'm lying, so he says, "Christian, if the guys you're going to meet were in your shoes, they'd turn *you* in."

"I don't know what you're talking about," I answer. I'm thinking that if somebody turned me in, he'd have some serious problems.

It's like the cop knows what I'm thinking. He says, "Christian, 98 percent of people who turn someone in don't suffer any retaliation."

"Well, I fit into that 2 percent. Maybe they don't do it that way in Hawaii, but that's how we do it where I'm from, in L.A."

"Christian, that's the movies. We know you're not the guy behind all this; we know you're just a mule. Tell us where you're taking the drugs and instead of ten years, you'll do two."

Talk about the movies—he's the one doing the Academy Award–worthy acting job. I'm not gonna do two years to turn somebody in. I'm not doing two years anyway, so why should I buy his story?

All along I'm picturing the guy I'm taking the meth to. He's a nice family man with children, and he doesn't even use drugs. He's not like me, an addict cruising around from drug house to drug house, from craziness to more craziness. I mean, I've been there blowing torches with parents while their babies cry for them in back rooms. I've seen guys turn blue after taking a big hit. I've seen guys OD from taking one hit too many, and guys that look like they're gonna die if they don't get another hit quickly. But I'm not going to turn in my connection; that would go against everything I stand for. I'd kill myself before I ever did anything like that.

Some of the plainclothes guys leave and two DEA agents walk in. The one who's apparently supposed to be "good cop" says, "Look, we know where you're going. Why not just be honest with us so you can get less time?" Somehow they know all about my plans, it turns out. It didn't occur to me then, but six months later I figure out that I was set up. Again I reply, "I don't know what you're talking about. I'm going to Hawaiian Brian's to meet Brian."

"Bad cop" leans over and says to me, "This is your last chance, Christian: tell us where you're taking the drugs." When I sarcastically reply, "That's my story and I'm stickin' to it," he cuffs me, marches me back out to the curb, and stuffs me in the backseat of an unmarked car.

All I can think is that I need to call my girl so she can get ahold of my dealer, so he can get me a lawyer. Obviously, when you do time for somebody, that person is going to take good care of you and your family, right? I'll have my rent paid probably, get money on my books, get a good lawyer, and get probation, or at least the best time possible. No big deal.

In the car, the detective comes on like a high-pressure used-car salesman. The problem is he's got nothing I want to drive home in. "This is the last time," he says urgently, pointing his finger at my chest. "If you don't talk to us now, you're going to do all ten years." I'm thinking, Okay—whatever, Danno; talk all you want, but I'm not telling you anything.

They take me to Honolulu's police headquarters and put me in a cell with just a bed—no sheets, nothing. I've been sitting there for hours when suddenly someone strolls in and slaps down a tray with a bologna sandwich, a cup of Kool-Aid, and an apple. He snaps, "Here's your lunch." I used to dine at the best restaurants and buy dinner for half a dozen friends almost every day of the week. But all that seems like a lifetime ago as I eat alone and quietly. I eat everything and sip the Kool-Aid slowly, hoping that if I keep busy, I'll also keep my mind occupied. It's not working.

The next day they take me to Oahu Community Correctional Center, OCCC. It's an old jail and they process me really slowly—you know, Hawaiian style. They issue me green jail clothes with black slippers and process me through, the iron door slamming behind me. All the while the news stations are broadcasting, "Professional skateboarder Christian Hosoi was arrested at Honolulu International Airport for interstate trafficking of narcotics." Both my mom and my dad hear about me from family members who've been watching the news. It tears them to pieces.

When I arrive at the holding tank, all these guys are stoked, almost cheering like I'm at a skate demo. Someone says, "Christian Hosoi, no way! We saw you on the news last night. You're my idol." I'm sure I'd be signing autographs if the guards would allow it. I'm thirty-two years old and these kids are like nineteen, maybe in their early twenties, and some of them are facing life in prison. When I ask what they're in for, it's all major crimes like murder. I don't want to kill anyone; I just want to get high. What am I doing here?

One of the older guys says he once saw me skate and used to own one of my boards. He seems friendly enough so I ask him, "What are you here for?" "Oh, murder," he says, casually. When he asks what I'm in for, I tell him about my meth bust, expecting him to say I'll get a light sentence. Instead, he replies, "Oh, *brah*, you're lookin' at ten years; it's mandatory." He says *he's* doing double life and will never be going home. "Ten years is a walk in the park—gravy, *brah*, gravy."

All these guys are really casual about spending the rest of their life behind bars. They hang out and play cards and watch TV for hours. Am I the only one who wants out of here?

I desperately want to head home and forget about all this, but it's not looking good: after inquiring further, I learn that the detectives and the guy in the holding tank were telling the truth about a probable ten-year sentence. The truth hits me like my own life sentence, or more like a *death* sentence. This *can't* be happening to me. But I get assigned a cell and settle in, left to myself in the quiet, and eventually the full weight of my situation hits me: I'm in to stay.

Three days after my arrest I appear before a judge, and the DA convinces him that I'm a danger to the community and a flight risk. There's no bail granted. I don't think I'm a danger to anyone but myself, but I'm certainly a flight risk; and if I fly, they're never gonna find me.

Every other day we're given ten minutes to talk on the phone. If you call someone and there's no answer, you can't call back for two more days. I ring Jennifer, my girlfriend, who was staying in Hawaii, but she doesn't answer. Because I have nothing to do, time crawls by. Back on my bunk I think of some questionable people I know on the outside. Why am I here and they're not? I'm a good person, but they beat people up, shoot people, rob people—and they're still on the street. One good thing is that for the first time in my adult life I'm not doing drugs.

JENNIFER AND ME. *HOSOI FAMILY COLLECTION.*

Within three days I fall into a routine: sleep, walk to chow, eat, get locked down for the night. I start smoking cigarettes, something I've always had a strange relationship with. Once, years earlier, I actually tried getting addicted to cigarettes just so I could figure out why so many of my friends enjoyed them. I would also use cigarette ashes on my homemade aluminum-can crack pipe. In jail I smoke because we get extra time outside if we light up.

Amazingly, I don't have any drug withdrawal problems, but I've got lots of time on my hands. It's not like I'm off to meet my girl, get high, party, or skate. All I think about is how to escape.

Each day we're marched outside to the rec area and I look up at the razor wire on top of the fence, wondering how I can break out of here. If I get over the fence, maybe I can run and never be found. If I manage it, will I ever skateboard again? I'm on an island, after all—where will I go? I can probably climb the wall, push the razor wire aside, and jump to the ground. But once on the street, what will I do? Will I take off my uniform and cruise around in boxers? It's Hawaii and residents don't always wear a lot of clothes, so it might not seem that strange to anyone. I've never been a thief, but sooner or later I'll have to steal some clothes.

I mentally rehearse a variety of escape scenarios whenever I'm out in the yard. I think through my escape plan the same way I think through a new skateboard trick. Before I skate up, I rehearse the motions mentally. This will be my most dangerous trick of all, but I believe I can pull it off. I sometimes even *start* the process of escape: act like I'm going to do it, but not follow through yet. All my life I've forged my own way, cut an uncharted path, and arrived at a place everyone said was unreachable. I've made a living doing the impossible, and this will be no different. The days and weeks and months pass, though, and before I get a chance to attempt my great leap, I'm transferred to a jail on the mainland.

But I'm getting way, way ahead of myself. Still in Hawaii, after a few days at OCCC, I finally get through to Jennifer on the phone. Turns out she's been trying desperately to reach me too—by now I'm way overdue getting home—but of course I no longer have my cell phone. Now that we're finally connected she's crying, and I'm trying *not* to cry because there are a bunch of killers surrounding me.

After filling her in on everything, I inform her that I'm looking at ten years. "I don't know if I'm going to make it," I conclude, my voice breaking.

That stops her. She says, "I love you, and we'll get through this. We've just got to trust in God."

I doubt even God can get me out of this one, so I reply, "What's God gonna do for me? I need a lawyer, babe!"

FIRST EVER PUBLISHED PHOTO OF ME, IN *SKATEBOARDER* MAGAZINE.
TAKEN IN 1979. PUBLISHED IN JUNE 1980. © *TED TERREBONNE.*

FLIGHT
PATHS

I was thinking that we had done everything there was on a board. Then Christian comes along and starts blasting out of the pool. I remember seeing him when he was about ten years old, and even as a little kid his style was already perfect. I couldn't give him any advice, except, "Come up to the big bowls and skate with us." A few months later he was doing just that. He is seriously my all-time favorite skater.

—JAY ADAMS

CHAPTER 02

My dad sets the carved wooden box on the kitchen table, opens it, pinches a large amount of weed, breaks it up with his fingers, and sets the leaf fragments on the table. Next he takes a rolling paper from the box and lays it on the table, next to the weed. Scooping the weed into his palm again, he sprinkles it onto the paper strip, saying something about not making the joint pregnant as he evens out a bulge. This makes my best friend Aaron Murray and me laugh. "Be sure to roll everything up tightly," my dad adds, rolling the joint and licking the edge of the paper before pressing the thin cigarette firmly between his fingers. "That's how you roll a joint," he concludes proudly, lighting it, taking a big hit, and passing it to me. I take a hit, cough, and pass the joint on to Aaron, who also takes a hit and coughs. We smoke the joint down to ash, and by then we're really high and I'm laughing so hard it's ridiculous. Aaron and I are eight years old, and from then on we roll our own joints and get high all the time.

Don't be too rough on my dad. He doesn't think like anyone you've ever met. He reasons differently: he used to say that I was a hyper kid and that pot settled me down. Even now, after all those years, he defends his weed solution for hyperactivity, saying it was better than what they prescribe now, Ritalin. I'm not sure about that one, but believe it or not, he and my mom have taught me some great values, mostly by example. From them I learned loyalty, honesty, not to steal or cheat, and always to try my best. They've always told me that I can accomplish nearly anything I put my mind to if I give it my best shot. And I always *do* give it my best shot, no matter what the odds. I don't blame anyone but myself when I fall, but I have to thank my parents for the rise.

THE BEST DYSFUNCTIONAL FAMILY EVER

Everyone calls him Pops, and everyone *I* know knows *him*. Take a look at those old films of me skating against Tony Hawk and you'll spot him—that Hawaiian-looking Japanese man at the edge of the pool, probably holding a camera. He was one of the few parents there to watch his kid skate. He was there for me when I was winning, but also later, when I lost everything. I'm an only child, and he gave all of himself to me. He was so cool that every kid I knew wished he was their dad. But there was nothing normal, traditional, or patterned in the way he raised me—or should I say, in the way he let me raise myself. From the beginning our lives were over the top.

When I'm eighteen months old, we all live in an apartment in the Bay Area. My parents leave me alone for a moment and I half-crawl and half-walk out a window and onto the roof of the apartment. When he hears a woman scream that there's a baby on the ledge, Pops runs out to get me. By the time he arrives I'm looking over the edge. He coaxes me into crawling over to him and then he grabs me by the arm and lifts me to safety. Apparently I smile the entire time as he carries me back into the house. I don't recommend anyone trying it, but hanging from a steep ledge must be good training for blasting high airs. Maybe that's why I'm never fearful skateboarding.

I have another advantage as a skater: I'm skating before I can even walk. I'm just a newborn when our family friend Jim Ganzer brings a skateboard by our house in Beachwood Canyon, Hollywood. He and Pops roll me over the kitchen floor on that board, holding on to my hands.

I can't tell you exactly what my first skateboard was, because that memory is buried in my childhood, like another kid's recollection of his first rocking horse. Pops says I was around five years old when a friend sent us a set of the new urethane wheels by Cadillac and a pair of Chicago trucks—the metal mechanisms that a board sits on and that wheels ride under.

Hawaiian surfing legend Gerry Lopez was my idol at the time. I once saw a surf movie with Pops where it looked like the entire ocean was falling down around Lopez at Pipeline, and he was standing in the barrel as casually as if he was standing on the sidewalk, waiting for the light to change. In the movie, he rode a red board with a silver lightning bolt. Pops makes me a fiberglass skateboard, a miniature version of Lopez's surfboard, red with a silver lightning bolt. The skateboard has a kicked-up nose like a surfboard and is turned down in the tail—something Pops thinks will work well for braking. I ride the board in reverse, so it works like a kicktail skateboard, something that won't be invented for another few years.

I'm no older than six when several cute girls my age run over to my house, giggling in their floral bikinis, asking me to come out and skate. One of them stands guard to make sure there aren't any cars coming while I bomb the hill, and the rest of them cheer me on as I speed past them.

Girls cheering me on while I ride a skateboard—I can almost think that was some sort of premonition of things to come.

My first store-bought board is a G&S with OJ wheels. I love that board so much I keep it in my room, right next to my bed. One day I'm out playing hide-and-seek and stash that board in the bushes. When I return, it's gone. That sucks big-time.

There's no pro skateboarding yet; I'm just a little kid in search of big heroes. Aside from surfers, my influences aren't skateboarders, but musicians and martial artists. I want to be Led Zeppelin's Jimmy Page and blast out those big power chords of his. The only thing I want more than that is to be martial arts legend Bruce Lee. At an age when other kids are reading comic books, I have everything in Bruce Lee's books underlined and even memorized. I take his sayings to heart—things like, "Be water, fast and fluid." Since I can't actually *be* Bruce Lee, I want to beat him and every other martial artist in the world, someday. My dad practices martial arts, and he drives me to the studio with him, where we do kung fu together.

Whenever there's a new kung fu movie in town, we go to the Mar Vista Theater in Chinatown. We don't just *watch* the movies; we absorb every frame in Bruce Lee's pictures, sometimes watching them two or three times. Bruce Lee isn't like all the other action movie heroes. He doesn't tell his opponents what he's going to do to them; he simply does it. By then it's too late for them. He's overwhelmingly fast, powerful, stylish, and confident—and that's just how I'm going to be.

BRUCE LEE ON WHEELS

There aren't many kids my age skateboarding in my neighborhood, but Aaron, the kid I smoked that first joint with, is one of them. Aaron "Fingers" Murray will become a legendary skateboarder, and one day he'll own a skateboard company called Koping Killer.

We've always had a lot in common. Like me he's part Asian, and his parents are really liberal. Both his parents attended Chouinard Art Institute with Pops. Aaron is adventurous and curious and desires to be the best at whatever he does. By the time we begin hanging out, his parents are separated and so are mine. Whenever we're at one of our dads' houses, we hang out together all day and long into the night. During the day we skate.

At night we tear around the house, leaping over couches and chairs and playing games while our dads jam the blues on guitars and drink Rémy Martin cognac and smoke cigarettes and fat joints that we take hits from.

I gradually discover that a lot of parents who survived the '60s carry that experience over as they experiment with unique ways of raising their kids and continue to use drugs. Smoking weed is no big deal to them; they consider it harmless. Such parents are different than most parents today—but even back then, nobody is as different as Pops. He's radical in his approach to everything, especially raising a child, even for those times.

Initially I think all parents are like mine. When I visit most other kids' houses, however, I see that it isn't so. Most kids have to hide when they get high. They live in massive houses crawling with brothers and sisters. Nobody plays or even talks together, and they all seem to hate each other. The kids hang out quietly in their separate rooms, probably smoking weed, while their parents politely talk about things not worth the words.

When I'm with my mom or my dad, they don't hide a thing from me, and they let me and my friends in on the discussion if we're interested. They tell me that if I want to be like Jimmy Page or Bruce Lee, all it takes is practice. Not like, "Get real, kid—*nobody* will ever achieve that, much less you." As a little kid you immediately think either *I can* or *I can't*. All I ever hear is "You can." Maybe it would be good to hear what I can't or shouldn't do once in a while, but that never happens in our family.

Aaron and I jump around the house until we're too tired to stay awake, playing like most other eight-year-olds, except that we're stoned out of our minds on the best weed a person can get. Being high makes it easy to imagine that we're Bruce Lee, throwing around nunchakus, acting it all out, jumping from one table to another, daring each other to jump further, saying, "Okay, I'll bet you can't do *that*." Once we both land a jump, we pull the tables wider and wider apart, leaping further and further. When we finally miss a jump, we know just how far we can or can't go. (It's like Clint Eastwood says: "A man's gotta know his limitations.") We're totally free to push the limits of possibility as we become crazy acrobatic daredevils, something that will soon translate into our skateboarding.

There are times we're maybe thirty feet up in some tree, saying, "I'm gonna jump from here and land on that bush." When we suddenly realize how high up we are, occasionally we're like, "All right, I can't do that after all," but usually we don't back down. In the martial arts movies people say things like, "Your tiger claw is no match for my praying mantis." Once skateboarding gets us in its grip, that becomes, "My ollie is higher than your ollie." We want to do things our own way, be the best, jump the furthest, and reign supreme as king of the mountain.

MY FATHER. THE ARTIST EVERYBODY CALLED POPS.
HOSOI FAMILY COLLECTION.

DEEPER AND HIGHER

Nobody stays together forever in L.A., and my parents are no exception. They split up around the time I'm eight years old. When I get older, Pops eventually tells me that my mom once threw all his possessions out the window, onto the street. He doesn't mention what led up to that, but knowing him, I suspect it was at least partially his fault. It always takes two, right?

He tries to shield me from things like that, and I guess it works, because I don't remember things being too bad. There's a lot of arguing at home, but nothing crazy or violent or anything—just the day-to-day disagreements that for some people lead to court proceedings and for others, like my parents, separation. They never seem mad at each other after their separation; they simply quit living together. As far as I can tell they're close friends and everybody's happy. They never do get divorced except as a formality, years later, so my mom can remarry. Together or apart, they are always there for me.

You might think I got into drugs as a result of my upbringing or my parents' breakup, but that's not true. As a child I never had that deep longing for my parents to get back together that you sometimes hear about, and I never felt that something was broken or missing in my life. I'm the type that would have found drugs whether my parents were together or not, even if they didn't smoke weed, which is hard to imagine. When you feel entitled, as I did, you're never satisfied. You want more. In my case, that meant running deeper and getting higher.

THICKER THAN WATER

My father's full name is Ivan Toyo Hosoi. He's full-blooded Japanese. He was born on Oahu on September 26, 1942. As a child he stole the family car and drove it through Honolulu, getting out and peering into various bars in search of his dad. Even after being punished, he continued taking the car to town now and then.

Eventually he was shipped off to the "Big Island" of Hawaii to work on the Parker Ranch as a cowboy. Because of being sent away, he thought for a long time that he had been adopted. That hurt, but being Japanese in the 1940s, Pops also suffered racism, and one of his uncles was actually sent to an internment camp in California.

My mom, who passed away last year, was part Hawaiian; she was born on Maui. Before she married my father, her name was Bonnie Puamana Cummings.

I was born Christian Rosha Hosoi in Good Shepherd Hospital in Los Angeles on October 5, 1967. Pops once told a friend that my name represented three religions: Christian for Christianity, Rosha for Judaism, and Hosoi for Buddhism. I don't know, but it sounds good.

In 1974, when I'm six years old, the family is still together, and we move to Oahu. Pops has been a surfer since the 1950s, so we go to the beach every day, all day, whenever I'm not in school. I mess around, riding some little waves, but I never really hook up with surfing the way he does.

After a year on Oahu we move back to L.A. because the teaching job he was promised at the University of Hawaii doesn't pan out. The other reason we move is that I have a bad kidney infection, made worse by all the mosquitoes that forever buzz the Hawaiian Islands. The first house we rent in California is in Beachwood Canyon, Hollywood. Later we rent a big studio on Washington Boulevard and Vermont Avenue, in L.A.'s Koreatown.

My parents first moved from Hawaii to L.A. before I was born so that Pops could refine his art skills at Chouinard. My mom helped put him through school and he ended up transferring to and graduating from U.C. Berkeley, where he received a master's degree in fine art.

Picture us in Berkeley in the late '60s: I'm being pushed in a stroller when the Berkeley riots go down. How crazy is that? I'm already a rebel at two years old!

Besides being birthed into rebellion, I'm born into music and art. Pops often has his paintings displayed in a gallery where he also plays music. When I get sleepy, he simply lays me down in the soft velvet of his guitar case, behind the amps, with nothing but my legs sticking out. When he isn't working on his own projects, he assists famed artists Sam Francis and Ron Davis. Whatever those guys want he builds for them. At other times he does his immaculate custom woodwork on people's mansions.

From a young age Pops whispers in my ear that surfing and skate-boarding are art forms, and I learn to see all creative expression from an artistic point of view. I want to express my art through skateboarding and do things no skateboarder has ever done before. I want to fly higher than anyone ever has and put on a show while doing it.

While Pops is a free spirit, my mother is a lot more regimented, and I can honestly say I've never met anyone like her. She has a strong family foundation, embodied in the aloha spirit of Hawaii, and is just over the top with things like family reunions and sending out cards for every-one's birthday. She dresses right for every occasion and is well spoken, business-minded, and organized. Even as rambunctious and rebellious as I am, when she says, "Christian, you gotta keep your head on straight," I respond right away.

When we move back to L.A. from Hawaii, my mom works as a secretary for a big company in Beverly Hills. She tells me to do my homework, and she's probably the only person in the world who could get me to do it. But she isn't *all* business; she's also a '60s girl, into art, wine, and weed. A friend of mine remembers sleeping over once when we were young teenagers. He says that I was yelling at my mom to find my roaches and she told me where they were. He claims he saw her take a hit from a joint before walking out the door to go to work. Like most kids of the time, he'd never seen adults be so casual about weed.

Like Pops, my mom really doesn't care so much what I do. Unlike Pops, she insists that I keep things together when I do them. I learn about business and working with people who are different from me, from her.

My parents teach me a lot about life, but in skateboarding I'm on my own, at least for the time being. There are no videos to rewind again and again; all we have are the skaters we see on the streets and the still photos we cut from the mags. We memorize those stills and have to imagine what happened before and after the shots were taken. We study each shot so carefully that we can tell you what boards and wheels everyone rides. We know who took the shot, where it was taken, and more often than not who's standing in the background. Having only magazines for reference stimulates the imagination far more than any video ever could.

In 1978 I'm eleven years old and Pops and I build a ramp in our backyard. Aaron also builds a ramp in his father's warehouse, and together they move that to my backyard. Now we have a bank ramp and a quarter-pipe right there at home, any time we want. I make it sound like *we* build them, but of course our dads are the ones who do all the work. We act like we're helping, which really amounts to nothing more than telling them to hurry up. ✿

SKATE
AND DESTROY

Christian skated the
way you're supposed to skate.
—STEVE CABALLERO

CHAPTER 03

GENESIS OF A REBEL SKATER

The only thing Aaron and I think about is that the Marina Del Rey Skatepark will soon open. For months we have eyed the construction crews laying down iron bars and digging deep holes. Soon the cement trucks will pour out a concrete paradise. The place is nearly done one day when Pops drives us there to check it out. Skaters are hanging out in the parking lot, just waiting, though opening day is still a couple weeks away.

At first Aaron and I wait with everybody else, but being fidgety, we soon begin exploring. We sneak in past the NO TRESPASSING signs until we see a gate cracked open a little. When we hear the sounds of skateboards, we inch forward and peek in to see Tony Alva and Jay Adams skating right in front of us. Wow! The whole Z-Flex team is there with them: guys like Shogo Kubo, George Wilson, Dennis "Polar Bear" Agnew, and Marty Grimes are all taking their turns, ripping hard. But we recognize only Tony and Jay, because they're prominently featured in every skate magazine. We've never seen famous skateboarders up close before, and there they are, the most famous skaters in the world, close enough to touch. We didn't know it at the time, but the bowl they're riding is called the Dog Bowl, and it's soon to become the gold standard of the skate world.

All of the bowls at Marina are trimmed with perfect coping and clean, light-blue tiles, with one white tile placed every ten feet or so. That's how we recognize the park in the photos. But we've never seen skaters blast with such speed and power before. I can still see and hear Tony Alva—TA, as he's often called—carving a frontside air and planting a perfect tail tap. Next up, Jay Adams drops in and snaps back off the lip, hands behind his back, before moving into a long and loud frontside grind. TA's long frizzy hair is sticking out beneath his helmet and flowing as he rides. Jay has a black-and-gray beanie pulled on over the top of his helmet—something I will soon come to realize is typical of his unorthodox way of approaching *everything*.

They're moving higher and faster now, doing tricks we've never seen, not even in magazines. To be there and to see it with our own eyes, to grow up during that time of skateboarding, to experience that moment in history—this lights a fire in my heart that has never burned out. At that moment Aaron and I commit ourselves to skating every day for the rest of our lives and to becoming professional skateboarders.

Soon it's opening day at Marina! We arrive before the skatepark opens. Pops pays, and Aaron and I run in to be among the first ones ever to ride the smaller bowls. This place is a dream—perfect for learning all the basic tricks. We skate for hours, attempting all the tricks the big guys do. Within weeks Marina becomes a second home to us. Pops is stoked for us, but he's like, "Oh boy, this is getting expensive." We run wild at Marina, smoking weed and skating day and night. Inside, they have some of the first video games, like Space Invaders and Asteroids, along with a Playboy pinball machine and other cool old-school games. But we never *pay* to play; we learn to cheat the machines. I pluck out one of my long hairs and attach a quarter to it with a small piece of tape from a sticker. Holding on to the hair, I drop the quarter into the slot and bounce it up and down, the continuous dinging sound announcing that we have tons of free games coming. Aaron stands guard to make sure nobody busts us. Finally I pull the quarter out, pocket it, and we play as many games as we want.

Pops is dedicated to his art, but even more dedicated to his son. He puts his art career on hold and takes over as the manager of Marina. This is a huge step in supporting me as a skater. Now I'm there all day—at least whenever I'm not in school—and long into the night. I even have a little job. Each morning I sweep out the pools before anyone gets to the park. I ride through the bowls on roller skates, making sure everything is free from litter and whatever might have blown in overnight. One time I fall really hard on my butt: that's the last time I'll ever wear a pair of roller skates in my life.

Just as in surfing, if you're at a spot often enough you're a local. I'm a Marina Del Rey Skatepark local, one of the originals. I'm still just a kid, though, and I never venture beyond the little bowls—what they call the brown bowls or the rust bowls. Aaron is a surfer at heart and is soon spending more time surfing than skating. That leaves me on this mission alone. My goal is simply to blow away anyone who rides the little bowls. Mission number one is accomplished before age eleven.

People come from everywhere in L.A. County and beyond to skate Marina. It attracts kids like Aaron and me who have grown up skating, listening to Bob Marley and the Rolling Stones, and smoking weed. Most of these guys are from broken homes, and skateboarding and rebellion are what binds us all together. While everyone is from different backgrounds, you never see anybody's parents, except sometimes when they pick their kids up or drop them off. From hundreds of kids who skate Marina regularly, only Pops and Mike Smith's dad are there with their kids on a consistent basis.

After skating the park all day, some friends and I skate over to the supermarket and steal the plastic guards off the handlebars of shopping carts. We cut them up at home and snap them onto our skateboard trucks, using them for copers. (Copers are plastic half-tubing that protect the axles of a skateboard's trucks, allowing the rider to grind long distances.) Our copers might not be as good as store-bought ones, but it's more fun swiping them than buying them. With all the skateboarders in the area, a lot of shopping carts in our neighborhood are missing plastic guards!

Skateboarder magazine is like our Bible, and we live on every word, every photo, and every ad. Marina hasn't even been open a year when someone shows me the new issue of *Skateboarder*. For the first time, I see a full-page color photo of me in a magazine. It says it was taken by *Skateboarder* staff photographer Ted Terrebonne. Wow! That's me, doing a frontside ollie in a rust bowl. Seeing myself in *Skateboarder* at age ten sets me on a course that directs the rest of my life.

That's my first big exposure, and because of my long hair a lot of people think I'm a girl. Tony Hawk, the guy who will become my biggest competitive rival, tells it this way: "Because of that first photo in *Skateboarder* magazine I thought Christian was a girl for two years. The long hair threw me off, but at the same time, I thought, This girl rips! Seeing a photo of someone so young blasting airs is what made me want to fly."

I don't care what people think, and I won't cut my hair for them or anyone else, no matter what they say. They'll find out soon enough that I'm a boy, when I smoke them all in the contests.

I think my friend Eric Dressen is one of the only skaters to be featured in *Skateboarder* at a younger age than me. Eric's half a year older than I am, and a phenomenal skater for his age, or for any age. In 1979, at the age of eleven or twelve, he beats guys twice his age in the Gyro Dog Bowl Pro contest at Marina, which inspires the rest of us kids greatly.

In the late '70s skateboarding is basically surfing done on land, and some people still call it sidewalk surfing. We rip down sidewalks and imitate getting barreled on waves, ducking beneath overhanging bushes that line the streets as they curl over us. We spray dirt when we slide out, the way a surfer throws spray while cutting back. Jay, TA, Shogo, and Polar Bear are all excellent surfers and the top pool skaters in our area (and therefore probably in the world). As surfers they want to throw cutbacks and hit the lip, not spin 360s in endless circles, like the top freestyle skaters do in the contests. When a surfer skates, he wants to slam the top and grind the coping as hard and as loud as possible. That aggressive style is in our blood, growing up as we do in or near a surf town like Venice Beach.

There are very few skate movies, so we do the next best thing by attending every surf movie that premieres at the Santa Monica Civic Auditorium. I'm usually there with Jay Adams and my original skate hero, Shogo Kubo. We openly fire up joints in the front row of the theater and watch Hawaiian surfer Larry Bertlemann on the screen, breaking all the rules with a rad new style. Bertlemann is the biggest thing in surfing at the time, and his skate influence runs deep also. He forms a strong link between Hawaii and California. When he visits Southern California, he surfs and skates with TA and Jay. His impact on Jay runs so deep that Jay alters his entire method of skating and begins skating like Bertlemann surfs and skates, in that cool, low rotational style he becomes known for. Bertlemann is the fastest thing on water and the first guy we see blast an aerial on a wave. People have been catching air on skateboards for a while, but when we see Larry flying on waves we're honored. Surfing may have spawned skateboarding, but skateboarding is now paying back its debt to its big brother by teaching it some new tricks.

The skate contests aren't geared toward the surf style of skating, though. They're all freestyle events with everyone high-jumping over limbo bars and doing pirouettes, 360s, tick-tacks, and walk-the-dogs, all on flat surfaces. Stacy Peralta is a Dogtown skater—Dogtown is one of the hilly L.A. neighborhoods where surf-style skateboarding got its start—and his movie, *Dogtown and Z-Boys*, reveals how he, Jay, TA, and some of their crew break down the status quo. It's a good thing they do, because freestyle has gotten to the point where you barely need a skateboard to perform your tricks. We think it's lame for guys to be frozen in one position, balancing

their boards on two wheels. Most of us from Venice or Dogtown relate to what the late Dogtown legend Bob Biniak said: "We were like a hockey team showing up for a figure skating competition." I can't sum it up any better than that. And while it's all about winning for us, it's not just winning for *ourselves*, but for Venice and Dogtown. These are more than names on some tourist map; they're revolutions of culture and attitude.

It's April 28–29, 1979, and the first Dog Bowl Pro contest is on at Marina. The best skaters in the world have come to our park, and of course Aaron and I are there too—not as competitors, but as kids skating around and hanging out in and under the bleachers. Undercover, as it were. From beneath the bleachers we're as close to the action as can be, and we observe every little thing the pros do and say. There's a big gap between them and us, but we're taking notes not only on their skating but on how they live, which is way beyond the edge.

Everyone turns to see Alva show up in a stretch limo. He's always pulling something rad like that. Last year he arrived at the Skateboarding World Championships in a one-piece gold suit that Elvis's designer custom-tailored for him. What a rock star! Jay Adams is also a rock star, but low-key in his approach. Jay doesn't really like contests or the spotlight so he lurks in the shadows, letting TA bask in the light.

Our friend Polar Bear is ripping on everyone and leading on the first day of the competition, but a fall on day two ends his dominance. Bert LaMar ends up winning, followed by David Andrecht. A kid who would become a close friend, David Hackett, tears into third.

Polar Bear, who will die of a drug overdose many years later, is a close friend and one of the only older guys who skates the little bowls with me. I'm twelve and he's around seventeen. Most of the established guys are like seventeen or eighteen, and they skate only in the Dog Bowl or one of the other big bowls, like the Upper Keyhole. The big bowls are basically *owned* by Polar Bear, Shogo, Marty Grimes, Jay, and TA. TA is older, like twenty-two, and there's something about the way he cruises up to the park alone with his shades on and his beanie pulled down low, *cholo* style, in his blue-gray Toyota pickup. He's all business when he comes to skate. At other parks he pushes his way to the front of the line, but at Marina that's not necessary. Everyone gives him room and instant respect, and he skates hard, leaves his mark, and leaves. While his aggressive attitude sometimes gets him into trouble at other parks, at Marina he's a god and can do no wrong.

We younger guys don't know what real sponsorship is, but I begin getting a kind of secondhand sponsorship through Jay. At his stepfather's house Jay loads me up with new Z-Flex boards and wheels and real copers for my trucks. Jay's family has a shed in the backyard and we also load up on weed there, smoking out every time I stop by. I'm soon getting my first sponsorship as Tracker begins flowing me trucks and Vans flows me shoes. Now I'm set. I spend my time either at Jay's house, my house, or Marina. When Jay cruises over to my house, we smoke pot right out in the living room, where we also shoot pool and listen to Bob Marley, Gregory Isaacs, the Cars, or the B-52s.

One of the older guys offers me coke but I pass on it, because I don't think I'm ready for it yet. For some reason, I agree to smoke heroin once, though—but just enough to know that I hate it. Thank goodness it doesn't suit my style, because all anyone wants to do on heroin is sit around. Lagging is not for me. ✦

DEL MAR SKATE RANCH. THE YEAR I TURNED PRO.
© GRANT BRITTAIN.

BIRTH OF
A COUNTERCULTURE

Marina was
a lot more rugged.
—TONY HAWK

CHAPTER 04

> *I can't lag; I've got too much to do, like spend all my days and most of my nights skating the best skatepark in the world, Marina. Once the park closes for the night and everyone else splits, I turn on the lights for whatever bowl my friends and I want to skate—another perk of my dad's job—and we roll long into the night in private sessions.*

Marina Skatepark is located on the outskirts of L.A., sandwiched between the on- and off-ramps of a freeway and a baseball diamond, and surrounded by potted trees from a nearby nursery. The fence is lined with eight-foot-high murals Pops has painted of all the top skaters. By night the place is totally dark except for whichever one bowl we light up. It's like a stage at a rock concert, and we're both the main act and the audience. We fire up fat joints and blast air, hooting each other on as we invent moves that nobody has seen before but that will soon become famous.

Marina is like home to a lot of kids, and I realize that many of them are there all the time because they don't have much of a family to go home to. Sessions at Marina replace family time for many locals. I have a loving home, but that doesn't matter. Marina is where my heart is, and these skaters, along with Pops and my mom, are my family. We love the place so much that sometimes Pops and I sleep there, smoking weed until we fall asleep in the back of his Volkswagen van. In the morning it's up early to skate and start the process all over again.

Marina is not just everything to *us*; it's big in its own right. Film crews arrive every other month, it seems, and the documentary *Skateboard Madness* is filmed there. Big punk bands play there as well, and Devo's original "Freedom of Choice" music video stars Stacy Peralta, among others, skating at Marina. Commercials and educational movies are filmed there also, all using skateboarding to illustrate some moral about being a responsible young person and a good citizen. They never shoot a video on the dangers of drug abuse, but maybe they should, even though I suspect nobody would listen.

There are a lot of heavy drugs being used, but nobody considers pot a real drug. For skaters, weed is like the air we breathe. It makes sense to us to skate stoned, but not to some of the older guys—guys like Stacy Peralta.

I know now, looking back from the year 2012, that he's right when he says, "Why do you need to get high when you skate? Skating gets you high."

One of Marina's owners, Dennis Ogden, remembers how bad we were:

A LOT OF PEOPLE REEKED OF WEED WHEN THEY CAME TO THE ADMIS-SIONS AREA, AND IVAN AND CHRISTIAN HOSOI WERE SOME OF THE TOPS AMONG THEM. MY MOM IS KIND OF STRAITLACED, AND AT FIRST SHE'S AGHAST WHEN SHE SEES THE ENVIRONMENT THERE. BUT EVEN-TUALLY IT SEEMS NORMAL, EVEN TO HER. WITH KIDS LIKE CHRISTIAN, WEED IS JUST PART OF LIFE. HE'S BARELY IN HIS EARLY TEENS AND HIS DAD AND A LOT OF OTHER ADULTS DON'T SEE ANYTHING WRONG WITH HIM SMOKING WEED. CHRISTIAN IS BECOMING THE BEST GUY WE HAVE EVER SEEN, SO WHAT CAN ANYONE SAY?

Despite all the weed, drugs aren't the only important thing to me. My goal is to become like the big guys. Take Shogo Kubo, one of the great, now nearly forgotten skaters of his time. He's Japanese like I am, and at first I pattern my entire style after him. He's fast, fearless, and smooth. As I gain skills, Shogo, Jay, and some of my other heroes push me to leave the little bowls and skate the Upper Keyhole (nine-foot-deep pool with coping and tile) with them. All the big bowls look deep and dangerous to a little kid, but I finally suck up all my fear and follow them into their land of the giants.

The little bowls are four and six feet deep, while the Keyhole is nearly twice that. I'm used to the little bowls, where you have to pull off the wall super hard to not lock up on the lip. When I try skating that way in the Keyhole, it doesn't work. At first I bottom-land, but after a few tries, I finally pull it. By the end of that first day I'm blasting two-feet-out airs, one-foot-out frontside airs, and hand-on-coping inverts. I'm in solid with the main guys now. Once I've tasted the big bowls, the little bowls aren't interesting to me anymore. From now on, I'll leave little bowls to little kids, or use them for warming up. I can't wait to skate the big bowls in the big contests with the big boys.

THE BOYZ

Skateboarding is our art, and because I've grown up in an artist's home, I can never be just another follow-the-leader skater. Everything, from the way we dress to the way we skate, bears our own original stamp. There's never any discussion about school or where we're going to work when we grow up. The present and the future are all about skating with our friends in Venice and at Marina. We can't see it when we're in the midst of things, but both places are on the leading edge in creating radical social change in youth culture. And leading that culture shift are TA and Jay.

Everything about TA is attitude, and we memorize his every move. He's not your typical surf/stoner guy. He's really smart, and he has a presence like nobody else, always doing his own thing in his own way. He's one of the first pros with his own company, Alva Skateboards. Guys like TA and Jay are forging their own identity, something that will later translate to the identity of the thousands of kids around the world who look up to them. But nobody has any idea that they're birthing a new culture right then and there. It's always been a toss-up to me as to what is cooler, TA's step-aside style, or Jay's go-with-the-flow approach. These guys are my heroes, and even though they're several years older than me, we have a lot in common. Since TA is fading from the scene, Jay and I hang out all the time.

Without even wanting to be, Jay's at the forefront of the revolution. He's a natural though reluctant leader: everybody wants to copy what he does. Since the beginning he's been a naturally blond surfer dude who leads everyone in that style. Then one day he shows up with a Mohawk and everyone tries to copy *that*. Well, they can *try*, but there's only one Jay Adams.

For a young skateboarder, hanging out with Jay is like a novice musician hanging out with Mick Jagger. He's like the coolest guy ever, placed in a bullet-proof young-adult body. He's mischievous, funny, and willing to try anything. I learn everything I need to from Jay; he's a free-spirited, soulful skater, a legend in his own right. He's never won a skate contest that I know of, but he's still one of the most highly revered skaters of his day.

This one guy at Marina has a chip on his shoulder about Jay. He's kind of a *vato* gang guy and a crackhead who's extra spun cuz he also smokes PCP. The guy says every time he's reminded of Jay, it makes him want to fight him. That's a crackhead for you, right? One day TA's had enough and he finally punches the guy, knocking him back over the bicycle rack. That's the last we ever see of him.

The American hard-core punk scene is coming on strong in L.A. Skateboarding and punk together are a match made in heaven—or some might say hell. Black Flag plays a lot of our contests, and the Circle Jerks, Fear, and other famous punk groups rock Marina regularly. When live music isn't being pumped in, we skate to recordings of the Meteors, the Ramones, the Cars, the B-52s, Devo, Selector, the Specials, Madness—all that. If you get a chance, check out some of the underground footage of us skating at that time. When you do, listen to what's being played in the background; you'll probably hear the Ramones singing, "I wanna be sedated," which is ironic since, in fact, almost all of us were.

Tony Hawk isn't from Marina, but he's been there nearly from the beginning and will remain there all the way to the end. These are some of his early memories of our park:

THE FIRST TIME ANYONE EVER OFFERED ME WEED WAS AT MARINA SKATEPARK. I WAS ELEVEN YEARS OLD AND I QUICKLY TOLD THE GUY NO. HE LOOKED AT ME IN AMAZEMENT AND SAID, "WOW, A STRAIGHT SKATER." NOT THAT THERE WASN'T WEED AT OTHER PARKS, BUT MARINA WAS A LOT MORE RUGGED.

I REMEMBER ONCE THAT THESE HORDES OF PUNKERS STARTED POURING INTO MARINA. THIS WAS LIKE '79 OR '80. I HAD SEEN PUNKS BEFORE, BUT THIS WAS A LEGIT CREW. I ASKED SOMEONE WHAT WAS HAPPENING AND THEY TOLD ME THAT THE CIRCLE JERKS WERE GOING TO PLAY. THAT NIGHT THE COVER FOR THE CIRCLE JERKS ALBUM, *GROUP SEX*, WAS SHOT THERE. THAT KIND OF THING NEVER HAPPENED AT THE OTHER PARKS. NO WAY! HONESTLY, MARINA WAS PRETTY INTIMIDATING IF YOU WEREN'T A LOCAL.

I'm twelve years old when I'm introduced to acid by two seventeen-year-old girls who work at Marina Skatepark. I'm at one of their houses, high

as a kite. But I don't remember seeing anyone's face melting or having any hallucinations or out-of-body experiences. I've done acid hundreds of times since, and I never really do hallucinate. All I do is laugh, skate, and rage.

Every day's an adventure at Marina. With all the punk bands playing there, a lot of punkers start hanging out. Punkers and skaters usually mix pretty well. The skate punk thing is starting to take off, so a lot of the time the two groups overlap: they're the same people. But both punk and skateboarding are about aggression, and when a large crew of punkers get together, trouble's gonna break out for sure.

One day these punk bands, the Circle Jerks and Fear, play. This big Indian guy has been hired for security. As big and tough as he is, even he can't stop trouble from starting. One fight starts out small but escalates into a gang-style brawl that spills over into the parking lot—it's basically the skinheads against the skaters. TA is standing next to the security guard, cuz they're friends, when suddenly, out of nowhere, this kid runs up and socks the Indian guy. TA turns and socks the kid and begins pounding him against the trunk of a car. Meanwhile, this little skinhead comes up and just blindsides TA. He hits hard for a little guy, and TA spins around and slinks back inside the park. I follow him inside and by then his eye is swollen shut. I'm like, "Dang! You got rocked, bro!"

Everybody knows that skateboarding is rowdy, but no park is ever as rowdy as Marina. It erupts like this from time to time and that's part of what we love about it. Once we even see this massive girl-fight that seems to last forever. I never had so much fun as a spectator!

As I've said, skateboarding is performance art to me, and while it's about winning, I'm even more interested in expressing myself to the crowd. Doing big airs is my favorite expression, so getting higher and higher is just a natural progression for me. The more the crowd cheers,

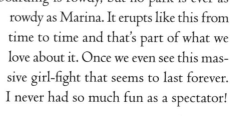

FIRST MAJOR CONTEST WIN AT THE MARINA DEL REY SKATEPARK GOLD CUP SERIES. TWELVE YEARS OLD. 1980. © *GLEN E. FRIEDMAN*

the higher I fly—simple as that. I feed off people's responses, just as they feed off mine: by the end of the show they're screaming and I'm flying. My reward comes in attracting the cutest-looking girls I can find, and lots of them. My strategy's been working pretty well so far. It's actually been working since the age of nine, when I made out with a girl of eleven at the Renaissance Faire, behind the archery area.

"DON'T GET CAUGHT, STUPID"

I'm always holding weed, but somehow I get busted only twice for minor possession. The first time I get picked up I'm in eighth grade. Some friends and I are cutting class and smoking a joint in the alley behind the school. Suddenly a pair of undercover cops spring from the bushes and order us to raise our hands. I comply, but I won't toss the joint because it contains some really killer weed. One hand remains closed around it, hoping to protect it from inspection. No such luck: one of the cops is like, "Okay, what's in your hand? Open it." What can I do? I open it and show him the joint. He confiscates it and I'm thinking the hypocrite will probably smoke it later.

The cops handcuff my friends and me and drive us out in front of the school. When the car pulls up, everyone—including our teacher—races to the window and peers out at us. I'd wave, but I've got these metal bracelets on that keep my hands pretty still. So I just smile and shrug my shoulders at my classmates. The cop uncuffs the others right there and lets them go.

I'm not so lucky. Since I'm the one with the joint, one officer forces me back into the car and drives me to the station, where Pops is called. When he swings by to pick me up, he plays the game for the cops, saying something like, "I'm sorry, officer. I can assure you nothing like this will ever happen again." He signs me out and we get into his car. On the way home, he chuckles and says, "Dude, why you gettin' busted?" When I tell him about the undercover cops, he's like, "Yeah, just don't get caught, stupid." At home we fire up a fat joint and life goes back to normal for a while.

A year later a friend and I are strolling through Veterans Park in Westwood with a chunk of hash that we're about to smoke in a ceramic pipe of mine. Suddenly my friend says, "Dude, what are those people doing in the bushes over there?" As we jog away, knowing that *whatever* they're doing could mean trouble for us, I throw the hash but hang on to the pipe. My friend's following close behind, and for some reason he scoops up the hash again.

Then we hear, "Police! Hold it right there." We turn and watch as two officers close the distance. "Are you guys doin' drugs?" one asks. "No," I respond, which isn't exactly a lie, since we haven't smoked anything *yet*. They tell us to raise our hands. Before we do, my friend, who looks about to cry, chucks the hash toward them, and it lands right at one cop's feet. The cop picks it up and then notices that we haven't followed orders. "Okay, hands on your head," he says.

While they're searching my friend, I toss the pipe into the bushes. One of the cops sees me do it and retrieves the pipe. He brings it over and says, "Is this yours?" When I deny it he hits me on the head with the pipe. Then he hits me in the ribs and asks again, "Is this your pipe?" Again I say no and he hits me in the ribs again and asks again if it's my pipe. This could get old fast, so I say, "Yeah, I guess so."

My friend's crying as they shove us into the car. Me, I'm just chillin', thinking that the car looks familiar as I check the side of the driver's face and recognize the cop who busted me at school a year earlier. He looks in his rearview mirror and asks, "Didn't I bust you once before?" Making my face blank, I answer, "I don't know, dude."

Now my friend is howling and pleading, "No, please—*please* don't take me in." I know this kid's family, and they're not gonna be happy. Me, I'm all good; I'm just gonna be told I'm a dummy for getting caught again, and then Pops and I are gonna spark up another fatty.

COMING OF AGE

I spend endless hours on my skateboard each day, and it pays off when I win the Gold Cup amateur series. I'm twelve years old and have beaten the top amateur skaters of all ages. I start the season slowly, in twenty-eighth place at Oasis. Then I move up to ninth at Big O, and at Colton I score sixth. I finally end up winning the contest and the entire series at my home park, Marina. I feel I'm improving so fast there's nothing left to do but turn pro. I'm riding for the biggest skate company in the world as the top amateur of the prestigious Powell-Peralta Bones Brigade.

Top pro Stacy Peralta is retired by then, and co-owner of Powell-Peralta. After my Gold Cup victory I tell him of my plans to turn pro, but he says

I need to wait a couple years. "A couple years!" I reply. "There's no way I'm waiting that long." To a twelve-year-old, two years is an eternity. I reason with Stacy, saying, "Look, I'm doing more advanced tricks than most of the pros; I can place in the pros right now." When he doesn't budge, I quit

LAKEWOOD SKATEPARK CIRCA 1981. (FRONT ROW: LEFT TO RIGHT) **LESTER KASAI, LANCE MOUNTAIN, STEVE CABALLERO, BILLY RUFF, MICKE ALBA, TONY HAWK, MARK "GATOR" ROGOWSKI, AND ME.** (BACK ROW: SECOND FROM RIGHT) **STEVE KEENAN.**

the team. Later, when Pops is asked why I left Powell-Peralta, he replies in his usual poetic fashion, "The bird has flown." Problem is I didn't fly *into* anything better for a long while.

Once I leave Powell-Peralta, Denise Barter of Dogtown Skateboards asks me to ride for them. She sponsors Tony Hawk, Mark "Gator" Rogowski, and Mike Smith. My affirmative reply is instant. "Dogtown: the team

that Shogo Kubo rode for! And I'll get my own Dogtown Hosoi model!" "Yeah and I'll turn you pro right away," she says. Once I agree to ride for Dogtown, I have my graphics made up for my new model. Unfortunately, Dogtown goes out of business before my model ever gets released.

Stacy has this to say about my leaving his company:

IT WASN'T BECAUSE HE WAS TOO YOUNG; I WANTED ALL MY SKATERS TO BECOME THE BEST THEY COULD AS AMATEURS, SO WHEN THEY TURNED PRO, THEY WOULD IMMEDIATELY MAKE A SPLASH. BUT IT WORKED OUT: WHEN DOGTOWN WENT UNDER, I HIRED TONY HAWK. SO I LOST ONE GREAT SKATER AND REPLACED HIM WITH ANOTHER GREAT SKATER.

I was just starting to come into my own and get more vocal at the time. Prior to that, I was pretty quiet with people I didn't know, as Stacy recalls:

WHEN CHRISTIAN WAS REALLY YOUNG, AROUND TEN OR ELEVEN, I DON'T RECALL EVER HEARING HIM SPEAK. I THINK AT ONE POINT I ACTUALLY WONDERED IF HE WAS MUTE. IT WASN'T UNTIL AFTER HE TURNED PRO THAT HE REALLY STARTED TO PROJECT, NOT JUST IN HIS SKATING, BUT WITH HIS PERSONALITY. I NEVER UNDERSTOOD HOW A KID SO QUIET COULD DEVELOP THIS ROCK-STAR PERSONA.

I don't think Stacy understands me at all as I'm entering my teen years, even though he's watched me skate since I was a little kid. He knows I've got the ability, but he's seen me coming out of smoke-filled vans at the contests, hangin' out with some of the wilder guys like Jay, TA, Duane Peters, and Ray "Bones" Rodriguez. It will take years for me to see Stacy as an individualist, with the courage to swim against the tide. As a kid, however, I'm too immature to understand. We simply look at guys who don't smoke as barneys, kooks, straightedges—you know. My thinking is,

You're over there; we're over here. That's your scene; this is our scene. Later.

As I mentioned, whenever I skate an event I focus on the girls in the crowd. I can have a hot chick any time I want, but if I win the contest it's a slam-dunk guarantee that I'll get the best one of all, and sometimes more than one. I'm like a kid in a candy store with nobody guarding the register. I'm thirteen when I have sex for the first time. The girl is cool and she's a virgin, like I am. But I don't have to sneak around or anything to have sex. In fact, Pops drives me over to her house to pick her up and then drives us back home, where we do it in my own bedroom. I actually think Pops is kind of proud of me, like, Yeah, my kid's becoming a man. Years later I hook up with that same girl again, and one day she calls to say I got her pregnant and she had an abortion. I ask if she needs any money and what her mom thinks. She says her mom just laughed. Exactly what I feel is lost to time, but the experience doesn't cause me to slow down any.

Having sex makes you cool with your friends, but it's like a powerful drug: I want more of it all the time. No wonder a popular expression links sex, drugs, and rock 'n' roll. They all tie together, since rock 'n' roll (or punk) and drugs help get girls—the types of girls I want as I'm starting out, anyway. I'm just a kid, but I've developed this adult, rock-star lifestyle and high style. ✳

ONE OF A KIND, PAINT PEN GRAPHIC BY POPS. CIRCA 1985. © *CHUCK KATZ*.

THEY
CALLED ME CHRIST

We were at this ramp contest
in Nebraska, and when Christian
appeared, you would have thought it
was Mick Jagger. People went crazy,
and afterwards he took off his shirt
and threw it to a girl in the crowd.
It was like he was getting
off the stage in Woodstock.

—STACY PERALTA

CHAPTER05

WEED AND OTHER CLOSE FRIENDS

It's 1980 and I meet this guy Eddie Reategui at Lakewood Skatepark. We hit it off right away. Eddie's a good skater and well on his way to becoming one of the top guys. I still have really long hair, and he recently told me what everybody tells me at that time—that the first time he saw me skate he thought I was a girl. Apparently he told his friend, "Look at that chick—she's ripping." The friend replied, "That's not a girl; that's Christian Hosoi."

Eddie and a friend have stolen a pot plant the size of a Christmas tree. Later some other guys steal it from them, but not before Eddie and his friend trim off most of the leaves and put them into a garbage bag. He has a burrito wrapper, and we use it to make a giant Cheech & Chong–size joint that we smoke with Pops in his car.

Eddie and I hang out all the time and enter the same contests together. Pops drives us down to Del Mar for a contest, and when we stop in the parking lot, Eddie gets out of the van, grabs his stuff, and begins walking toward the nearby hotel. When I ask him where he's going, he looks back and says, "I'm going up to the hotel." Then I tell him, "No, dude, *this* is the hotel," meaning the van. Things are pretty ghetto in skating still, and we sleep in the van a lot. It's actually great fun. Grant Brittain, who works at the Del Mar Skate Ranch at the time and will later run the place, remembers us staying there and recalls seeing billows of smoke pouring out of the van's doors.

Grant talks about that time:

I STARTED WORKING AT DEL MAR IN 1978. THERE WAS A HOTEL RIGHT UP THE STREET, BUT EVEN IF YOU COULD AFFORD IT, IT WOULD BE LIKE TWENTY PEOPLE CRAMMED INTO ONE ROOM. SO A LOT OF SKATERS SLEPT IN THEIR CARS, IN THE PARKING LOT. ONE OF MY FRIENDS LIVED IN THE PARKING LOT IN HIS PLYMOUTH DUSTER FOR LIKE SIX MONTHS. A LOT OF BUSINESSPEOPLE HATED SKATERS, AND THAT'S ONE OF THE REASONS THEY BULLDOZED THE DEL MAR SKATE RANCH IN '87. THEY WERE BUILDING A HILTON AND DIDN'T WANT TO HAVE THESE GRUBBY SKATERS AROUND.

OVER THE YEARS I SAW ALL THE BEST SKATERS PASS THROUGH DEL MAR, AND I CAN HONESTLY SAY THAT HOSOI WAS ONE OF THE BEST OF THEM ALL. DEL MAR WAS TONY HAWK'S HOME PARK, AND HE WAS AMAZING THERE. SO WAS CHRISTIAN, BUT COMPARING HAWK AND HOSOI IS LIKE COMPARING PAUL MCCARTNEY AND MICK JAGGER.

In the morning Eddie and I barge into Micke Alba's hotel room. Micke and his older brother Steve are among the top skaters at the time. Micke is there with some girl, and even though he's only a little older than us, he doesn't want us around. He throws us his car keys and snaps, "You guys beat it," before he slams the door on us. We have girls of our own, and we're delighted to drive them down to the beach in Micke's car.

Eddie's driving until he gets scared and tells me to take over. I don't really know what I'm doing, but I fake it, saying my usual, "I've got this." Except for the few times my dad has let me drive his van up and down the driveway or around the block, I've never driven a car. Leaving the beach I back up, smack into the car behind us, go forward, and hit the car in front of us. A few broken taillights later we somehow make it back to the park alive.

Later, back in L.A., Eddie and I brag to Pops that we know how to drive. He says, "Oh, cool," flips us his car keys, and we're off. I tell Eddie to drive and we cruise around L.A. before slipping into one Hollywood young-adult club or another.

My friend Mofo (Morizen Foche) is the photo editor of *Thrasher* magazine. I think he's the first one to call me Christ, and when he tags me with that in print, it sticks. I have no idea what the name really means, other than what I hear—that Christ is supposed to be God. That's cool, cuz I'm looking to be the god of skateboarding. Besides, it fits perfectly with the move I'm known for, the Christ Air, where I launch and then form a cross with my hands held out to the sides, my board in one hand. Yup, Christ is a killer nickname.

According to Mofo,

I FIRST MET CHRISTIAN WHEN HE WAS ABOUT TWELVE YEARS OLD. EVEN THEN HE WAS HIP AND HE COULD HANG WITH AN OLDER CROWD. SOCIALLY AND CONVERSATIONALLY, HE WASN'T THAT DORKY, AWK-WARD KID. THAT WAS PROBABLY DUE TO HIS UPBRINGING, CUZ HIS DAD'S REALLY HIP TOO. WHEN I WORKED FOR *THRASHER*, I WOULD WRITE EVERYTHING OUT BY HAND. IF SOMEONE'S NAME WAS ROBERT, IT OF COURSE BECAME BOB. DAVID BECOMES DAVE. THAT'S WHEN I STARTED WRITING CHRISTIAN'S NAME AS CHRIST. THIS WAS ABOUT THE TIME THAT THIS BAND CRASS CAME OUT WITH AN ALBUM CALLED *CHRIST THE ALBUM*. IT WAS THEN THAT I DESIGNED THE *THRASHER* COVER THAT SAID "CHRIST" ON IT. AFTER THAT, EVERYONE STARTED CALLING HIM CHRIST. BUT CHRISTIAN WAS ONE OF THOSE GUYS THAT MADE MY JOB EASIER. HE HAD SO MUCH TALENT; ALL WE HAD TO DO WAS CAPTURE IT.

I'm one of approximately thirty-five legit pro skaters in the world. Most of them barely make a living. Nobody cares, though, because we're all about having fun and living in the moment. Our lives are all skate, skate, skate, party, party, party. It won't be money, money, money for a few years. When we're on our boards, nothing else matters; we're just innocent and free to create.

I concentrate on the art of skateboarding and lay the groundwork for the moves I'll become famous for, like the patented Christ Air I just described, plus the Rocket Air and a one-footed air, all performed as high and stylishly as possible. By then Tony Hawk is finger-flipping and making up new tricks almost weekly. But I don't hang out with him personally, only at competitions. I mainly hang around with hard-core stoners and old-school skaters like Jay Adams.

The best skateboarders in the world have passed the torch to my generation and me, and it's now up to us to keep things burning. It's just days before my fifteenth birthday, and I'm champing at the bit to prove myself against the top pros. The time finally arrives, but even without Stacy to hold me back, it's taken over two years. I'm a pro skater and riding my own Sims Rising Sun model. We're skating Pipeline Skatepark in Upland, California, and I'm a combination of stoked and nervous as I face the empty pool. The new pros—Tony Hawk, Gator Rogowski, Lance Mountain, and Neil Blender—are all there, and we're like a pack of hungry dogs, ready to rip into raw meat. But the established pros aren't gonna just lie down and die. Guys like Steve "Cab" Caballero, Eddie Elguera, and Duane Peters are still ripping hard and locked in these heavy battles for the top spot. Other skaters who have also rocketed to legendary status in the sport are Upland local boys Chris Miller and Steve and Micke Alba.

A lot of the major tricks in skateboarding are being invented at this generational transition, and if I miss a beat I'll fall behind and everyone will say, "You should have been there; you really missed out." History is being made, and I intend to write some history myself.

From the first, everyone is just blasting at Upland, and that's when I break out my first original trick, the Tweak Air. I earn the respect of my new peers and end up getting fourth place. Cab, being his usual phenomenal self, wins that one. Lester Kasai flies into second by blasting high airs. He's riding my model, so that's not a bad showing for my boards and me. I've fulfilled one of my dreams—that of competing with the pros—but neither Tony Hawk nor I is near our full potential yet. We're more blending in than dominating. But blending in is *not* what we came to the party for.

SCHOOL DAZE

Only one thing interferes with having the best life ever: school. But I'm not gonna let anything so trivial as an education screw up my life. I don't want to be stuck in a classroom when there's so much to be learned on the street, so I don't really take school seriously. I wear whatever clothes I want, including Bob Marley shirts that I top off with a pot leaf necklace. It doesn't bother me that people know I'm stoned, and when my teachers comment on it, I laugh and admit it, saying, "Okay, you got me; I'm stoned." Weed permeates my entire world. In fact, it's the smell I most associate with my upbringing. Just fun for the whole family. After a rough day at school, I return home, light up a joint. On the days I ditch school, I hang out and watch reruns of *Bewitched, The*

REACHING INTO A BAG OF STICKERS TO STOKE THE KIDS. © GRANT BRITTAIN.

Family, The Honeymooners, and *Get Smart* in the front room, laughing my head off. Nothing wrong with that.

The school I attended at Hamilton High in L.A. was called Westside Alternative School, but everyone knew it simply as "Area D." Suddenly the school changes locations, and that new spot couldn't be any better—directly across the street from the Venice pier! My school is now situated in surf/ skate central. Am I the luckiest kid in the world or what? Studying anything out of a book is the last thing on my mind. I'm getting the education I need

on my skateboard, doing drugs in the street. Venice is like a trip around the world any day of the week, but on the weekends it's a carnival of clowns, musicians, jugglers, street vendors, tourists, drug dealers, surfers, and the world's best skateboarders—all competing for the crowd's favor, in one place. It's a lot gnarlier than most of the other skate towns of the time, and that works for us.

Neither my mom nor my dad lives in Venice. Pops lives in midtown L.A. and my mom lives in Koreatown, which is only about fifteen miles from Venice. Still, with L.A. congestion, it can easily take half an hour to get there. My mom drives me to school every morning and then fights traffic back to Beverly Hills, where she still works as a secretary. I skate the boardwalk before and after school, until Pops picks me up in the evening.

Considering the amount of weed I smoke, I'm a fairly good student. Amazingly, I have a good memory, and thanks to my mom I have pretty strong organizational skills. Occasionally my competitive nature works to my advantage, in that I like to get better grades than other people. I cheat only once, when I haven't studied for a test. Then, in lieu of actual preparation, I write some crucial info on a tiny piece of paper, then tape the paper to the Converse star on the side of my shoe. Crossing my legs, I can look down and see all the answers and copy everything down. Guaranteed A. Usually, though, I get my grades the old-fashioned way: I earn them. When the top student in our class is caught copying off my paper, all my little stoner buddies feel kind of proud.

I'm sick of school and look for ways to get out of class. I hit on the idea of asking my teacher if I can skateboard on my own and get a PE grade for it. She agrees, on the condition that I write down all the hours I skate. I skate far more than I ever attend class, and if I wrote down the real number of skate hours, she wouldn't believe me. I record half my skate time and it still equals three hours a day. That satisfies the PE teacher and I ace that class. Next I ask my art teacher if I can do all my art assignments at once.

She gives me all the assignments for the semester, and I complete them in a single week. With two fewer classes, I'm out of school by noon. Even with such a light schedule, though, I still cut class as often as possible.

My skating career is starting to kick into high gear, but my teachers won't let me take my schoolwork on the road. One day when I'm in tenth grade Pops picks me up and I tell him, for the umpteenth time, "School is lame. I wanna quit." He says, "Okay, quit—but *you've* gotta tell Mom!" That sounds funny now, but not surprisingly, my mother freaks when I tell her. Even so, I'm granted the freedom to make my own choice, and from that day forward I stop attending school.

My newfound freedom allows me to skate and hang out in Venice full-time. Anything goes in that town, and I fit right in, partying hard, wearing wild clothes, and dying my hair different colors—even trying

WESTMINSTER RAMP. ROCKET WHEELS PHOTO SHOOT. © *GRANT BRITTAIN.*

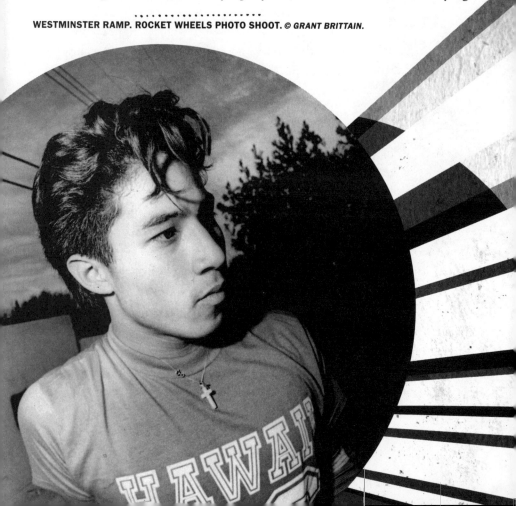

green polka dots once. My friends and I basically run the streets.

ROLLING IN THE FAST LANE

I win my first big pro contest in Vancouver, Canada, in 1984. Eddie and I are kind of like a tag-team, where he dominates the amateurs and I begin to dominate the pros. Everything's going as planned, and we both win our divisions in Vancouver. Shortly after Vancouver we fly to Arizona together for the next event. Eddie's brother lives in Arizona and has offered Eddie a car to keep if he'll pick it up there. I have a round-trip ticket for Arizona, but after the contest Eddie talks me into driving home to L.A. with him. The second we get on the road, however, the car starts sputtering. The heap won't go over fifty miles per hour. To make matters worse, Eddie is so tired that he keeps falling asleep behind the wheel.

I know how to drive for real by then, but I don't yet have a license, so I decide to let Eddie continue the driving while I serve as copilot. We work out a system where he sits in the driver's seat and does most of the driving, but I keep my foot on the gas, and when he nods off to sleep I steer. As needed, I yell "Brake," and he comes to long enough to get us stopped. This works pretty well: he sleeps for hours while I steer the car from the passenger seat. This is cool on the empty roads in the desert, but when we approach the L.A. freeways, it gets downright insane. I finally have to wake him up so he can get us home.

We somehow make it home to L.A. without dying and drag into my place, where we both crash for a while. When we wake up, Pops makes us breakfast and tells Eddie how to get home via the freeways. Eddie drives off, though we later learn that his car dies on some freeway

VENICE BEACH JUMP RAMP DAYS. *HOSOI FAMILY COLLECTION.*

OJ II AD. WAIKIKI BEACH. CIRCA 1985. *COURTESY HOSOI FAMILY COLLECTION AND SANTA CRUZ.*

interchange, miles from his house. He's stranded there until a cop pulls up and rescues him. It's a good thing the cop doesn't search the car, because we always have weed on us.

Drugs are skateboarding's open secret, as I guess you've gathered by now, with tons of weed for daily use and acid and mushrooms for special occasions. Cocaine is around too, and big for those who can afford it. There's even some heroin, but you don't see that out in the open. I'm smoking about an ounce of weed a week and do acid, XTC (Ecstasy), or 'shrooms every other week or so. We travel from contest to contest, do a few practice runs, maybe score mushrooms or acid, and drop it for our entertainment at night.

Skateboarding is my ticket into nearly every home, and one day I go visit my friend Vanessa Vadim. Vanessa's a cool kid who just happens to be the daughter of Jane Fonda. Jane isn't home, and Vanessa and I end up in her mom's bedroom, where I spot a pair of fluorescent-orange high-top Reeboks in the closet. This is at a time when sneakers are pretty basic, mostly solid black or white. I try the high-tops on and they fit perfectly, and I'm like, "These are sick!" Vanessa tells me to keep them, so I wear Jane Fonda's Reeboks all that day and into the night.

That same night Alan Losi, Micke Alba, Gator Rogowski, Eddie, Eddie's best friend David Duncan, and I drive out to a famous ramp in the desert. We take mushrooms and skate the ramp late that night in pitch darkness, with no lights anywhere. Six of us are on the ramp, riding together, switching sides while skating blindly at high speed. This is insanity, but insanity's our true drug of choice, and we're just cracking up, laughing the whole time—me in those rad orange Reeboks.

I've taken my time starting coke, but I make up for lost time and soon find myself with more than I can handle. There's a kid my age (who ends up doing a reality TV show) from Beverly Hills High. His dad's a doctor with a cabinet containing a big cookie jar filled with the finest pure cocaine. The kid steals the key to his father's cabinet, has a copy made, and puts the original key back. He then fills an economy-size aspirin bottle to the top with pure coke, calls me, and says, "Dude, I got the coke. Get some buds and let's party." I score an ounce of killer weed and we meet back at my house. My dad's there, working on some art project while we kids

break out the Deering two-gram scale and weigh the coke out, some to snort and some to sell. We take hits of coco puff (weed laced with coke) from the bong, do lines of coke, and amp up to party for the next few days.

By age fifteen I'm a famous skater and becoming well known in the L.A. club scene. My friends and I make money at the clubs by selling methaqualone, a powdered form of Quaalude that everyone eats and smokes. It's the latest trend in the L.A. club scene. We also buy jars of stimulants known as pink hearts and 20-20s through ads in *High Times* magazine.

We sell the pills one at a time. Buck apiece! Another source of a good time and a little income is balloons that we fill with nitrous oxide and sell for three bucks (or two for five). (P.S. Just in case you were wondering, I do drugs with some really famous people who cannot be mentioned in this book. Have to respect their privacy.)

I hang out with a lot of major drug dealers. Naturally they always have the best coke and often the hottest girlfriends. When they're not around, their girlfriends like to hang out with me, but I have enough integrity not to sleep with them, no matter how tempting it is. Still, I enjoy the expression on a dealer's face when I tell him that I've done all the blow he gave to his girlfriend and *didn't* sleep with her.

Ever since I was a child my mother has taught me to tell the truth, no matter what. "It will save you a lot of heartache," she says. When I hook up with girls, I tell them honestly that I have no plans of settling down with them. I don't want to have one single girlfriend. Telling the truth always opened the door for an open relationship.

I like my way of doing things. I meet a girl, hang

MAX PERLICH "MENTO" HAND-DRAWN GRAPHIC BY POPS.
© IVAN HOSOI.

JIMMY JAM, ME, AND MAX PERLICH. NEW YEAR'S EVE PARTY. *HOSOI FAMILY COLLECTION.*

out for a while, get what I want, and quickly move on to the next one. As touring skaters, we stop in towns all over the United States, Canada, and Europe. At each stop I write like sixty-five postcards to different girls I've gone out with and send them all out. I say the same thing each time. If I ever went out with *you*, you probably got a postcard that said, "See you soon. Love, Christian." Forgive me. I've changed.

A GATOR IN FLORIDA

My first big paid trip as a pro skater is to Kona Skate Park in Florida. This is also my first time alone on a plane. As we fly over Alabama, we encounter a gnarly storm and the plane jumps around in the sky like a feather in a hurricane. The wing out my window is swaying three feet up and down, and I'm thinking that it's gonna snap off any second. I'm thinking, If this plane crashes, I'm gonna die all alone. I look over and see that the flight attendant is reading calmly in her seat. When I express my concerns to her, she says, "Don't worry. I've been in far worse; we'll make it okay." I suck it up and trust we really will be okay, though we end up dropping in for an emergency landing in Birmingham, Alabama. A few hours later we're in Florida.

Once in Florida I find out that Gator is my roommate at the hotel. That's cool with me. Gator, a close friend, is becoming famous as one of the best skaters in the world. Sadly, he will become more famous than ever after the brutal murder he commits several years later. Back then he's just a great skater, into kooky teenaged pranks like we all were. At the hotel he decides we should throw everything from our room into the bathroom: dressers, beds, TV, everything. This is back before everything was all bolted down like it is now. You can thank guys like us for that. As we run around the hotel room, ollying off the walls, Gator starts breaking lightbulbs, lamps, and whatever else he can find. He's wild and a little strange, but to me he's just another typical crazy skateboarder.

These are the punk-rock days, and we're all thrashers. We skate, do drugs, and mess with people. That's what skateboarding is all about for us at the time. The owners of the hotel eventually bang on the door of our room, presumably alerted by our neighbors. After they look at the mess we've made, they say, "You guys are out of here." They call the owner of the Kona Skate Park, where the contest is to be held. He storms over and demands, "What are you guys doing?" We answer, "Oh, we're just messing around." He wants to kick us out of the contest, but we're a pretty big draw so he decides to let us compete. We offer him and the hotel owner a weak apology and are allowed to stay in the hotel and compete in the event.

We *say* we're sorry, but we're not sorry at all. Later that evening Mike Smith (another top pro) and I hit the mall. We're not shopping; we're just being our normal, rebel selves. My favorite look these days is double boxer shorts, one pair forward and one backward. That wouldn't be weird enough, though, so Mike and I decide to wear nothing but bath towels to the mall. We get toothpaste, shaving cream, and anything we can find and lather it in our hair to make it all crazy and spiky. Florida is really conservative in 1982, and we're at the mall, naked except for our towels, with our hair looking really crazy. Everybody does double takes; they look at us like we're nuts as we blast through major department stores where people are trying on suits and ties while we hold our towels up with one hand. Soon we've got security guards bolting after us. We ditch them out a side door, get in the car, and peel out for the hotel.

I'm not sure, but I think I got fourth at that contest. I clearly remember one run where I slammed really hard doing a move called a sweeper. I still remember the pain of that fall, and that's the reason I don't do sweepers, even to this day.

You could say we were just being kids, but there's something more to it. We're beyond anyone's rules and do whatever we want, whenever we want. ✺

HUNTINGTON BEACH OP PRO SURF CONTEST. INSIDE THE CAGE. © IVAN HOSOI.

DIFFERENT METHODS TO GET TO
THE TOP. ME AND TONY HAWK.
MID-'80S. © GRANT BRITTAIN.

TOO HIGH

WE WERE YOUNG
AND WE FELT INVINCIBLE.

—TONY HAWK

CHAPTER 06

Skateboarding is my day job, but after dark I'm all about the clubs. I'm only fifteen, but I attend young-adult nightclubs for ages eighteen and up more nights than not. Pops drops my friends and me off at whatever club we request, and I kick him back some buds by way of a thank-you. Then later—much later— I call him to swing by and pick us up. Since those clubs don't serve alcohol, they stay open until 4:00 a.m. I often call him shortly after that, and he's in a good mood when he gets there, laughing and joking with us before he drops my friends off. Pops is rad, more like a buddy or a cool older brother than a dad.

ops rarely gives advice directly. Rather, he asks me questions and tries to get me to think. Then he basically accepts whatever answer I give him. He has a type of wisdom, and when he does give advice it's usually worth taking—things like, "Don't let fame go to your head; just skate and do what you do." When I start making money, he asks, "Do you wanna save it or spend it?" I tell him, "I'm gonna spend it all," and he says, "All right, spend it all, but don't wonder where it all went when it's gone." Money and fame are in endless supply. The train is just leaving the station, and I can't see this trip ever ending.

PARTY GODS

Just traveling to Brazil can be risky, and that's one reason I love it so much. I'm sixteen years old and my only regret is that I've missed Mardi Gras by returning home a week too early. I've heard that Mardi Gras began as a religious holiday, one where you get everything out of your system before denying yourself for the forty days leading up to Easter. It's nice not being religious, because I never have to deny myself anything.

When I return to Brazil a few years later I'm with some of my friends, including this friend we call "Block," Cesario Montano. He's a talented photographer and artist, and even though he's Catholic there are few restrictions in his life. He talks about that time:

WE CALL CHRISTIAN CHRIST AND I TAKE A CLASSIC PHOTO OF HIM IN FRONT OF THE CRISTO IN RIO. HE HAS HIS ARMS OUT, HOLDING A SKATEBOARD IN ONE HAND, LIKE HE DOES WHEN DOING A CHRIST AIR.

PHOTO SHOOT AT THE FOOT OF CRISTO IN RIO DE JANEIRO. © CESARIO "BLOCK" MONTANO.

© CESARIO "BLOCK" MONTANO.

© CESARIO "BLOCK" MONTANO.

IT SEEMS WE ALL HAD SOME RELIGIOUS TRAINING, BUT CHRISTIAN IS ONE OF MY FEW FRIENDS THAT I DON'T RECALL EVER SAYING ANYTHING ABOUT RELIGION OR GOD.

We may have missed Mardi Gras that first visit, but that doesn't stop us from partying like carnival is on—there's live music day and night, and the parties in Brazil never stop. This is one place where I can get hot and cold anything—what I want, when I want it: great food, beautiful women, and all kinds of different drugs. There's this one substance I don't get the name of, but we whiff it off a handkerchief. It's kind of like a nitrous high. I do coke constantly. Why not? Though super cheap, it's of such good quality that I smuggle some back home in my pocket, just to show everybody. Because it looks like pink chips of abalone, I call it pink champagne. Of course, the way I *show* people back in L.A. is by using it with them, so it doesn't last very long.

Everything about Brazil appeals to me. I especially love how Brazilians live life to the fullest. They party like skaters—actually, harder than most skaters I've ever known; they party like tomorrow will never come. The weather is perfect, as in Hawaii, and when I'm interviewed for Brazilian TV, I tell them I wish I could stay another week. Maybe it's a good thing I can't stay; the way I'm partying, I might not have survived carnival.

Brazil's really wild, but there are other places in the world where a riot can break out just by someone giving out a few T-shirts to a crowd. Block recalls one such incident in the Dominican Republic:

THIS GUY HAD A GUN ON THE PLANE AND I ASKED HIM WHAT IT WAS FOR. HE SAID, "OH, I'M A BANK COURIER." IT'S LIKE THREE IN THE MORNING WHEN WE LAND IN THIS SUGARCANE FIELD. IN THE AIRPORT, IMMIGRATION RECOGNIZES US AS PRO SKATEBOARDERS. WE ALL HAVE OUR SKATEBOARDS WITH US AND THEY TELL US TO SKATE, CUZ THEY'LL ALL BE WORKING WHEN WE PERFORM AT THE STADIUM ON THE COMING SUNDAY. WE'RE ALL SKATING ON THE FLOOR AND THE

BENCHES, AND THEY'RE APPRECIATIVE, BUT THERE'S NOBODY THERE
TO PICK US UP. THE GUY WITH THE GUN COMES OVER AND WE TELL
HIM THE SITUATION. HE TELLS US TO FOLLOW HIM; WE PACK EVERY-
THING INTO HIS CAR AND WE'RE OFF, DOWN THIS DIRT ROAD, WITHOUT
A LIGHT ANYWHERE.

WE'RE GOING THROUGH THE GNARLIEST LITTLE SHANTYTOWNS
WHEN THE GUY PULLS OVER AND TELLS CHRISTIAN AND ME, "HEY,
FOLLOW ME IN HERE." HE LEAVES THE OTHER SKATERS—SCOTT OS-
TER, ANDY HOWELL, BO IKEDA, SERGIE VENTURA—IN THE CAR. HE
WANTS CHRISTIAN AND ME TO FOLLOW HIM INSIDE, BUT EVERYTHING
FEELS KIND OF SKETCHY. INSIDE, HE POURS US SHOTS OF RUM; WE
ALL TAKE A SHOT AND WE'RE OFF AGAIN. PRETTY SOON THE SHACKS
AND DIRT ROADS GIVE WAY TO A CASINO AND LUXURY RESORT, AND
THAT'S WHERE THEY PUT US UP.

The event goes well, with everyone a little more amped than usual as we skate. Then, when Block throws product like hats and T-shirts to the crowd, things begin to erupt. At first this is fun, but chaos soon breaks out and kids begin throwing chairs and knocking each other down. By the time security arrives and escorts us out of there, it's turning into a riot. Once outside we run onto the bus and are driven off to safety. That was the first time we felt like true rock stars.

At this point I've been skating and smoking for half my life. I'm starting to win regularly, but I wonder how I'd do if I weren't stoned. For the first time ever I decide to compete in an event without getting high. Ironically, the contest is at the Mile High Ramp in Tahoe. I don't smoke and have one of my worst showings in a long time, taking eleventh place. Naturally I figure it's because I didn't smoke weed. I get high in the next contest and get first place. After that it's first or second every time, and it seems obvious to me that I need weed to get into that zone.

It doesn't occur to me that that's an excuse I use so I can keep getting high. After all, if I had won at Tahoe, I might have had to quit smoking weed, which has become a psychological placebo that triggers me, sort of

like morning coffee. I may not drink a whole cup of java, but after I take even a sip—*bam!* I'm up.

So is it the weed that empowers? No, says the adult in retrospect. Does it give me confidence at the time? Absolutely.

Meanwhile, my biggest rival, Tony Hawk, is on a surer, steadier path to the top and in some ways plays it safer: he doesn't seem to have my need for weed to succeed. We're both becoming famous, though, and with that come endorsements, which lead to money.

Everyone calls Tony Alva "Mad Dog" because of his aggressive style and his attitude. (These days, even *he* will tell you he was arrogant as a kid, and he got socked from time to time because of it.) My model with Sims helps me launch my pro career, but I'm starting to gain my own identity aside from the company. TA isn't skating as much as he once did, and he hasn't done contests in quite a while. He doesn't need to; he's a hero to the skate world—the legend credited with being the first to launch an aerial in a pool.

He drives down from L.A. and shows up at Del Mar Skate Ranch at a contest I'm in. He mentions that he's bringing Alva Skateboards back and says, "Dude, you should ride for me." This is a great opportunity to do something out of the box, so I quickly agree to be on the team, which consists of just the two of us. With that, I go from a big corporate company with a big warehouse, to Alva Skateboards, which is located in a garage. It isn't exactly glamorous, but working closer to the source is more my style. I admire TA's stylish skating, of course, but also his individuality and his confidence, something he later admits often crosses the line into ego. Some people don't like him, but a lot more love him.

In the evenings TA and I hit the clubs, where I rage and he hammers out live music with a group he starts called the Scoundrels. We're just out partying and raging in the clubs and on the streets of Hollywood and San Francisco like a couple of stoned-out dirty cowboys looking for a gunfight.

HOLLYWOOD TO THE MAX

Max Perlich isn't a skate legend, but he can skate pretty well for an actor. I've known Max since we went to preschool together at Play Mountain

Place, the private preschool and elementary school off La Cienega and Washington Boulevards where I climbed trees as a kid.

By his teens Max is coming on in the movies and getting big in the Hollywood club scene. He's featured in such hits as *Ferris Bueller's Day Off, Can't Buy Me Love, Drugstore Cowboy,* and *Blow*. When we screech up to the clubs in his classic Lincoln Continental, everybody knows the party's on. Some friends of ours run Osko's, which is one of the biggest clubs in Hollywood at the time. Inside of Osko's is a private club called Funky Reggae. Max and I are both several years under age, but we stroll right in as the doorman unhooks the velvet rope and waves us through. It's like that at every club—just breezing past material girls and wannabe actors and even some celebrities, to the front of the line. For us it's red-carpet treatment all the way! One night I carry one of my Hosoi neon-pink Alva Fish boards to the owner of the club because he digs skateboarding. This greases the wheels further, and through him we meet all the bouncers. These guys also work as the bouncers of other clubs in L.A., and because we know them we never get hit for IDs anywhere.

Max is a blast to hang out with, but he sure takes a lot of heat from everyone. I mean, we all love the guy, but he can really get under your skin. He'll be saying something and you'll tell him to stop. He doesn't stop, but keeps it up and starts saying, "Okay, hit me if you don't like it. Hit me. Hit me." Nobody wants to hit him, but he keeps at it until somebody finally *does* hit him. Then he says, astounded, "Why did you hit me?" When they answer, "You asked me to," he replies, "Yeah, but I didn't think you'd *do* it." Then it starts up all over again.

One night Max and I hit the bar at Funky Reggae as Herbie Hancock's "Rockit" plays. There's a DJ scratchin', neon lights flashin', B-boys break-dancin'. Chynna Phillips floats by, nods and smiles, and Pauly Shore whispers something in my ear that's drowned out by the music. I reach for my wallet to pay for our drinks, but the bartender won't take my money. Max and I click glasses and down shots. Here's to being us!

I'm partying hard, but no matter how crazy I get, I take skating seriously. My main competition is, of course, Tony Hawk, but Lance Mountain, Gator, Chris Miller, Mike McGill, Cab, and a few others can finish either of us off if we fall or don't skate our best. We're at the top of the pack now, doing moves that few can keep up with.

While there are many great skaters, I think I enjoy Cab's skating the most at this time; he's known for high airs, radical skating, and making it all look easy. He has bleached hair and wears suspenders, punk style. We hang out at contests together, though he's three years older than me, and when we skate we have a blast. Cab's an idol to me, especially after he takes down the top pros of the time, Duane Peters and Eddie Elguera, and becomes recognized as the top skater in the world. (He would later tell me that he fell behind for a while when he didn't learn the 540. Still, nobody can say he isn't one of the best ever.) While I love Cab and all the other pros, I don't want to imitate any of them—not even Jay or Alva. I have it in my mind to develop my own style of skating.

Alva Skateboards fits me better than any other skate company, but in a way we're like a rock band with two leaders, both with their own ideas and both capable of being the front man. TA's not only a friend and the owner of the company; he's a good mentor, showing me how to create something that will last in skateboarding. Because of our age difference and because he's no longer skating competitively, there isn't really any competition between us. But we're both headstrong and bound to clash at some point.

When the clash comes, it splits us up. I design a swallowtail skateboard as my model. I choose that design because one of my favorite moves, the tail tap, has become more difficult to do since ramps started using PVC coping. With a swallowtail you can do a tail tap and it will hold in there. I launch that board with Alva while TA designs a diamond-tailed board with a dolphin nose. Then he does an ad in *Thrasher*, pointing to my design with *his* name on it instead of *mine*, along with the words, "Obvious superior design." TA remembers things differently, saying the swallowtail was a collaboration between us. But I'm so pissed that I don't even go to him; I go to his business partner and say, "How can TA disrespect me like this? Tell him I quit." Despite my anger, I realize that for TA to take credit like that is actually a compliment.

THE ORIGINAL SEED

Skate photographer and historian Craig Stecyk dubbed Jay Adams "the original seed." That makes sense to me. Ever since I've known him, Jay has seemed free from all the normal entanglements of life. He has what everyone else wants—natural ability, good drugs, and hot chicks. Whether he's skating or not, you know something crazy's going down when he's around. There isn't a lot of film of Jay skating; that's because he doesn't care if he's famous or not. Jay skates only for fun, and he thinks commercialism is causing people to lose control of their egos. He doesn't have much money, but if he doesn't think something is cool, he won't be a part of it no matter how much it pays. As an example, he's offered a Band-Aid commercial for TV. All he'd have to do is sing, "I'm stuck on Band-Aid, cuz Band-Aid's stuck on me," to get paid more than he usually makes all year. But his soul is not for sale: he turns the job down. Instead of cash, he earns something greater—the undying respect of his friends, because most other people would have sung that jingle and taken the cash.

Jay and I have been doing coke for weeks, and now I've been up all night before competing in a contest at the Eagle Rock ramp the next day. I haven't practiced at all, and when I skate my heat the next morning, I think I manage third place. Not bad, considering, but I could easily have won if I'd had even a little sleep. It finally hits me that coke isn't good for my career. No kidding, duh!

Does that stop me? No. Cocaine continues to fuel my party-till-dawn ambitions until the day I think it's literally going to kill me. When that happens I've been doing coke for days on end with some girls who have an endless supply of it. The party rages for what feels like weeks, all of us doing lines as long as your arm, all day and all night. We do so much blow for so long that we're delirious on the stuff. When I finally go home early one morning, after snorting coke all night, my heart is pounding so hard and fast it seems like it could explode out of my chest. I tell Pops that I think I'm about to pass out, and he casually asks, "Are you too high?"

"Yeah, Pops," I snap. "I'm too high."

"You'll be all right; just relax."

"This is serious."

"Don't panic," he urges. "You'll be all right."

I'm not convinced. "I'm afraid I'll stop breathing while I'm sleeping, and then I won't wake up tomorrow," I say. Then I beg like a little kid: "Please watch me while I sleep."

"All right," he says. "I'll make sure you're breathing."

I know he ain't gonna watch me forever, or even all the way until I wake up, despite what he says. I tell myself to calm down, calm down. I feel like I have to shut it down now or I'm not gonna make it; that's how far I've pushed things. Eventually, though, I do fall asleep.

I'm surprised to wake up the next day—actually surprised to be alive—and I decide then and there to quit coke. Just like that I'm done with it. I continue to smoke weed all day, every day, though, and I drink a little alcohol, do a little XTC, 'shrooms, and acid from time to time. By *my* standards, I'm drug-free. These remaining drugs seem so minor compared to cocaine that I never consider slowing down my party routine or actually training for an event. Why should I? My skating career is going through the roof, I'm making tons of money through sponsorships, and I'm having the time of my life. Besides, simply put, I love how drugs make me feel.

Showmanship is a little like a drug to me too; it gives me a rush. Style isn't always helpful in winning a competition, but to my crew it's everything, on the ramp or off. I want to do my tricks smoothly, yes— but also with flair. I'm an artist, an entertainer. I cut my hair short and dye it different colors every couple of weeks. Since a person can't have long hair and short hair at the same time, I wear hair extensions. That way I can feel the wind blow my hair back and can change up my look whenever I like. In the contests I'm totally stoned, sometimes smoking joints right there under the grandstand while they call my name for a heat. I like standing at the top of the ramp, laughing and dancing to whatever music is on, before blasting the biggest airs I can. I'm dancing and hooting and laughing, partying my way through each event and through life. What could be better?

540 DEGREES OF INSANITY

In 1983 the group Suicidal Tendencies releases its first album. David Bowie hits gold with "Let's Dance." *Flashdance* is every girl's favorite movie. McDonald's introduces the McNugget, and Mike McGill is preparing to serve up the McTwist. This is a move that will forever change skating. Also called the 540, the McTwist is a 540-degree turn accomplished in midair. While these days the 540 is a pretty basic trick, in the early '80s it seemed almost miraculous. I think Mike invented the trick while he was away, teaching skate camps in Sweden.

Now it's 1984, and Mike's got the McTwist ready for showtime. The skate world has been buzzing for some time with the rumor that he has a new trick—one where he flips upside down and twists into a 540-degree spin. Everyone is hassling him to try it from the moment he arrives at the Del Mar Skate Ranch. Then suddenly—*bam!*—he busts it out and blows everyone away. It's stunning! I realize I'll have to learn it immediately if I want to continue winning contests. From the first, the fans go nuts for the McTwist. They expect to see it at each demo, and I'll be on the ramp and all I can hear is "Twist, twist, twist, twist." By the mid-'80s, you have to do McTwists just to place.

When you're flying as high above the ramp as we are, you can find yourself lost in space with nowhere to go but down. Sometimes you have to bail your board from a great height and hope for the best. It can be a long drop from there, like twenty feet, and you can get injured either by falling or by being hit by your board as it rockets down on you like a brick. For me the McTwist is especially dangerous, since I don't want to do it like everyone else. I won't take any shortcuts by just spinning side to side, like some other skaters do. I'll flip end over end at maximum height and speed. I have the McTwist down for the very next contest, and because of it I win that one.

My rule when learning a trick is that I need to complete it three times in a row, right off the bat. My advice, especially if you get injured doing a trick, is to just get on the ramp and get it over with, so you're not a prisoner to that phobia. If I make a trick only once, I know I don't have it yet. With the McTwist, I fall a lot in practice because of how difficult my method of doing it is. This is one trick I don't stick every time, not for a while at least. But I'm one of those athletes who get better in competition. I can focus during the contest and make it when it counts. Pressure is like the glue that keeps me on my board, so I skate my best when it matters the most. ✺

SAD PLANT OFF THE EXTENSION. MID-'80S. © IVAN HOSOI.

CHRISTIAN

HOSOI

STREET MODEL

HAMMERHEAD

SANTA CRUZ SKATEBOARDS STREET
MODEL GRAPHIC. *HOSOI FAMILY
COLLECTION AND SANTA CRUZ.*

SKTBRDS

THE SHARKS AND JETS RIDE AGAIN

I'M A DAGGER!

—CHRISTIAN HOSOI

CHAPTER 07

A lot of my friends are actors during these years, and they tell me they could get me into the business if I want. I'm kinda thinking about it, and have even been contemplating various agents, but when it comes right down to it, I'm not willing to sacrifice my skateboarding for that or anything else. Anyway, my actor friends are always depressed, waiting for someone to call them with work. Who needs that? I can skate and party whenever I like, so I never have to wait for anything.

I get a chance to dabble, though. It all comes together in the movie *Thrashin'*. Now, this picture would never win an Academy Award. In fact, it's considered cheesy at the time, but over the years it will become a cult classic. (If you see the movie, I'm the skater with a green streak in his hair who flies over a car. I even have one line—one word actually, "Wimps!"—that I say to my crew's rivals during a breakdancing scene.)

The film is about a conflict between a street gang called the Daggers and another crew called the Ramp Locals. I'm a Dagger.

David Hackett reads for the role as the lead Dagger, but he butts heads with one of the "suits" and doesn't get the part. He would have been good as the bad guy, Hook, but that part is landed by an established actor who's about to become a close friend of mine, Robert Rusler. The film also stars Josh Brolin and Sherilyn Fenn, but the producer rejects Sherilyn's boyfriend, a young actor who's been hanging around named Johnny Depp. Also on the set is Catherine Hardwicke. This is Catherine's first job in the movies, and she works as the production designer. You might know her name from her later work as the director of movies such as *Lords of Dogtown* and *Twilight*.

Don't see *Thrashin'* for the plot, but if you've ever been into skating or punk rock, you've gotta check it out. *Thrashin'* features the best skaters in the world, including TA, Tony Hawk, Jesse Martinez, Alan Losi, Cab, Lester Kasai, Tony Magnusson, Mike McGill, Billy Ruff, Steve Olson, Kevin Staab, Dave Duncan, and Eddie Reategui. D. David Morin plays the announcer, a role he regularly plays at skateboarding contests. Also see *Thrashin'* for the punk music: the movie features Devo, Fear, the Circle Jerks, the Screaming Sirens, and the Red Hot Chili Peppers.

In May 2011 there was a cast-and-crew reunion to celebrate *Thrashin's* twenty-fifth anniversary, and a lot of the skaters from the movie showed up, including Steve Olson, an amazing skater who was injured performing a stunt for the movie. Producer/writer Alan Sacks was also at the screening, and it was fun to look back with him on that time. Catherine reminded us all how crazy it was, especially on the first day of shooting the race scene in Benedict Canyon. There's a scene in the movie where legendary skater Jesse Martinez is being hauled away by the paramedics. He's not acting in that scene. Those are real paramedics and he has a real broken leg. Jesse and nine other world-class skateboarders were rushed to the emergency room on the first day.

Another scene Catherine brought back to mind is one where the Daggers burn the ramp of their rivals, the Ramp Locals. I wasn't there for that, but I heard that people nearly got torched when the ramp was set ablaze. If you see the movie, watch TA running for his life in that scene. According to Alva, "There were so many fumes coming off that ramp that as soon as a match was lit, it just went up in flames. They're lucky the DP [director of photography] was ready and got it on film. They're even luckier that nobody got hurt."

Thrashin' is so much fun because the entire skate world is involved. Rusler remembers things this way:

I'VE ALREADY DONE A FEW MOVIES, LIKE *WEIRD SCIENCE* AND *NIGHTMARE ON ELM STREET 2.* AFTER BEING TOLD I HAVE THE PART IN *THRASHIN',* I WALK OUTSIDE AND CHRISTIAN AND STEVE OLSON AND THESE OTHER HOT SKATERS, MONDO AND MUNSKE, ARE THERE TO AUDITION. BACK INSIDE, TONY ALVA IS HAVING A CONVERSATION WITH THE PRODUCER, ALAN SACKS. THEY'RE DISCUSSING USING CHRISTIAN: SACKS IS APPREHENSIVE TO HIRE HIM CUZ HE ISN'T EIGHTEEN YET. I MET CHRISTIAN WHEN WE WERE KIDS AT MARINA SKATEPARK, BUT I DON'T REALLY KNOW HIM WELL YET. TA HAS BEEN HIRED AS A CONSULTANT AND ALSO AS ONE OF THE ACTORS FOR THE FILM. I TELL ALAN AND THE FILM'S DIRECTOR, DAVID WINTERS, "YOU'VE GOTTA HIRE THIS KID," SINCE CHRISTIAN IS ALREADY THE MAN. I TELL THEM HE NEEDS TO BE

MORE THAN A STUNT DOUBLE, BUT ONE OF OUR GANG, THE DAGGERS. ONCE THEY MEET WITH CHRISTIAN THEY REALIZE I'M RIGHT AND THEY HIRE HIM ON THE SPOT.

WE'VE BEEN FILMING A WHILE AND IT'S MY BIRTHDAY. ONE OF THE ASSISTANTS COMES TO ME AND SAYS WE HAVE ABOUT TWO AND A HALF HOURS BEFORE I HAVE TO WORK AGAIN. TA SAYS, "COME ON, THE CHILI PEPPERS ARE PLAYING THIS CLUB IN HOLLYWOOD AND YOU'RE COMIN' WITH US." I SAY, "YOU DON'T UNDERSTAND: I CAN'T JUST LEAVE A SET. IF THEY CALL FOR ME AND I'M NOT HERE, I'LL GET IN A LOT OF TROUBLE." TA AND THE OTHERS ARE EGGING ME ON, DUTCH-RUBBING ME, TELLING ME TO TAKE IT EASY. UNDER PRESSURE I AGREE TO CRUISE WITH THEM AND WE END UP AT CLUB LINGERIE, WHERE WE SMOKE AND DRINK AND DO MUSHROOMS. I'M HAVING A BLAST, THE TIME OF MY LIFE, WITHOUT A CARE IN THE WORLD. THIS IS ONE OF THE BEST SHOWS I'VE EVER SEEN: THE CHILI PEPPERS ARE JUST RAGING AND SO ARE WE, SLAMMING IN THE PIT.

BY THE TIME WE GET BACK TO THE SET, I'M PEAKING ON 'SHROOMS AND THE ENTIRE STAFF IS LIVID. TURNS OUT THE PRODUCTION CREW WERE GOING TO SURPRISE ME FOR MY BIRTHDAY BY HAVING A STRIP-PER JUMP OUT OF A CAKE. I FEEL BAD THEY WENT TO ALL THAT TROU-BLE, BUT I DON'T REGRET WHAT I DID THAT DAY. THAT DAY WAS UN-FORGETTABLE.

AFTER THE MOVIE WRAPS I CONTINUE HANGING WITH CHRISTIAN. I HAVE MY OWN HOUSE, BUT I LIVE AT HIS PLACE MORE THAN MY OWN. SOME OF THE MOST MAGICAL TIMES OF MY LIFE ARE HANGING WITH OL-SON, CHRISTIAN, AARON, BLOCK, AND ALL THOSE GUYS. EVERY NIGHT IT'S ONE OF THE LIVE MUSIC CLUBS LIKE LINGO, THE ROXBURY, FUNKY REGGAE, SATURDAY NIGHT FEVER, POWER TOOLS, SEVENTH GRADE, EGG SALAD, OR SCARLET LETTER. MONDAY IS ALWAYS THIS BLUES BAR CALLED THE KING KING. IT'S NEVER REALLY CROWDED, MAYBE LIKE TWENTY PEOPLE IN THERE. SOMETIMES BRUCE WILLIS WILL STOP IN AND PLAY HARP WITH THE BAND. I REMEMBER ONCE SEEING MICK JAG-GER CRUISE IN AND SIT IN WITH THE BAND.

KAHUNA RAMP IN HOUSTON, TEXAS. CIRCA 1986. © GRANT BRITTAIN.

In one scene from *Thrashin'*, I'm out with my gang chasing the Ramp Locals when I run dead-on into a street-sweeper. I hit that thing so hard that I actually put a dent in it. But I get paid an extra hundred bucks each time I do a stunt like that, so I do like three to five takes and exit with some extra spending cash for the day.

We earn our money and put in long days on the set—from six at night till six in the morning, or from six in the morning till six at night. On set everything is really controlled, as a movie set needs to be. Off set is the fun time. The director, David Winters, had played one of the Jets in the movie version of *West Side Story* and this is kind of *West Side Story* on skateboards, without the plot, singing, or memorable acting. Winters will be sittin' there with all these girls hangin' out, giving him neck rubs. Between takes, some skater will sneak in there, trying to swoop down on one of his girls. Winters wants me to do a full-on sex scene in *Thrashin'*. I'm stoked to do it, but at seventeen I'm a year too young to have sex legally on camera. Bummer, cuz I've got more experience than anyone in that department.

None of us will ever forget how much fun we had doing *Thrashin'*. Duncan and Eddie still have a company called Daggers as a tribute to the movie.

OFF-SCREEN DRAMA

I get over the disappointment of not having sex on screen fast by going to the clubs every night of the week and hooking up all the time. The clubs are like home to us, and we do whatever we want there. My friends are there all the time, and I see fellow Dagger and hot skater Johnny Ray Bartel at least once a week. Johnny's an amazing bass player who plays the King King all the time. A lot of big-time celebrities drop into the King King, and I know all the locals. If somebody famous shows up that we don't know, we always give them their space, cuz to approach them would be like, "Oh, let me get a photo with you." In my world you never ask anyone for an autograph or a photo, no matter who they are. They're more famous than we are, but that doesn't matter; to our way of thinking, they wish they were us. They're playing a stage role; we're not. We're doing something they can only pretend to do.

We always have the hottest girls, and it's obvious that everyone else, including the A-list celebrities, wants to be hangin' out with them. Even the most famous among them are like every other guy there: on the hunt. Prince is out there with his bodyguards. I don't know him, but I watch him cuz he's one of my favorite artists. I scan the crowd and there are all kinds of girls: white girls, Mexican girls, black girls, Asian girls. There are girls with crazy spiked Mohawks, girls with every hair in place, girls with makeup streaked under their eyes so that they look like coyotes or new-wave tigresses. Some are in sheer-looking lingerie; others are dressed in the height of fashion.

Standing out among them is Stacy Ice, a crazy-looking white girl with blond hair, spandex pants, and a super sexed-out look. She's dancing like a Vegas showgirl out on the floor. I notice her not only because she's my part-time girlfriend, but also because Prince is checking her out. That gives me a rush: Prince is checkin' out *my* girl. When Stacy also notices Prince watching her, I pull her toward me, laugh, and say, "Okay, him or me?" She laughs too and I know she's chosen me. This isn't the first time a celebrity has checked her out, and it won't be the last. Rusler and I have all kinds of girls, but even he'll tell you that "Stacy was the quintessential club trophy at the time."

I know that kids look up to me, but I have no concept of being a role model to them. It would never occur to me to pretend I'm someone I'm not in order to make an impression one way or another. A friend of mine, Kele Rosecrans, is one of many victims of my shortsightedness. Kele is a fifteen-year-old skater at the time. He sometimes tours with me. One evening when we're in Vegas he comes looking for me and finds me in my hotel room with six or seven girls in a hot tub. In my autobiographical movie *Rising Son,* he says that this and some of my other actions influenced his life so much that he nearly got kicked out of school. Sorry, bro.

Once I have money, I want to make an entrance at the contests, rather than just show up. The entrance always begins in a rented white Lincoln Town Car. This sure beats rolling up in some dented-up beater where the attention comes from a leaky muffler. My entrance was meant to be intimidating, and it worked. Tony Hawk remembers it this way:

ONE OF CHRISTIAN'S NICKNAMES WAS HOLMES, AND I SOMETIMES CALLED IT HURRICANE HOLMES THE WAY HE ROLLED IN. HE'S GOT STYLE, HE'S LOUD, HE'S CONFIDENT, AND HE'S GOT AN ENTOURAGE. I'M THE GUY HE'S SUPPOSED TO BE GUNNING FOR, AND THAT'S TOTALLY INTIMIDATING. LIKE MOST OF US, I WAS STILL THIS AWKWARD KID, BUT I DON'T THINK HE WAS AFRAID OF ANYTHING.

AND IT WASN'T JUST SHOW. HE COULD DELIVER: HIS STYLE OF SKATING WAS PERFECT. YOU NEVER HEARD ANYONE SAY THEY DIDN'T LIKE HIS STYLE, BUT WITH ME THEY'D SAY THAT ALL THE TIME. I HAD MY HATERS, AND I STILL HAD MY DOUBTS THAT WHAT I WAS DOING WAS LEGITIMATE, CUZ SOME CONSIDERED ME A CIRCUS-TRICK SKATER. IT WAS OBVIOUS THAT CHRISTIAN NEVER HAD ANY OF THOSE DOUBTS. I'D OVERHEAR SOMEONE SAY, "OH, HE'S THE BEST; HE'S THE MAN." HOW DO YOU COMPETE WITH THAT SORT OF REPUTATION?

Most everyone else just drives to the contest, skates their heat, goes to dinner, and goes back to the hotel. No matter where the contest is, my routine looks like this: skate till they turn the lights off and kick me out, meet all the locals and hang out with new and old friends at a backyard barbecue or local restaurant, and then hit the clubs for the night. By the day of the finals, the locals are good friends of ours, and they cheer for us, even though we live in a whole different county, state, or country.

FRIENDS BUT RIVALS

No matter how popular I am, the fans are split nearly evenly between Tony Hawk and me. While our different

SEQUENCE: STICKER TOSS. *HOSOI FAMILY COLLECTION.*

personalities play a big role in this, our styles of skating also contribute. From the beginning, Tony's skating is based on technical tricks. He's banging out tricks so fast that we all wonder what new one he'll pull out next. His style and mine are an obvious contrast to anyone watching. Where he's trick-oriented, my skating is driven by speed, power, and style. That's what fuels *my* fire.

Tony and I are perfect rivals—white knight, black knight. He has blond hair; mine is black. He's dressed pretty clean-cut for a skater; I'm dressed like Jimi Hendrix. We have one thing in common, though: we both want to win. I try Tony's tricks once in a while, and to me they feel uncomfortable because of how technical they are. They aren't very high, fast, or aggressive. You have to get up there, get the board back under your feet, and land it in a hurry. There's no hang time and no time for style when you're skating like that. Still, Tony is one of the best skaters of all time, and I understand why he has the reputation he does in our sport.

Most football teams don't hate each other, but sometimes their fans do. At times Tony's fans and mine clash with each other. When they erupt, we feed off all that energy in order to skate better. The media makes it seem like Tony and I don't like each other, but that's not true. He's not a huge partier like me, so we don't hang out often, but we respect each other and often do demos together. Sometimes it's just the two of us, in the same hotel for days—work the demos, hustle chicks, and play quarters.

By the time Tony and I are in our midteens, there's this north/south rivalry that has grown up around us. Without really trying, we both become figureheads for one direction or the other. By then I'm riding for Independent Trucks, which is from northern California. Tony's riding for Independent's main competition, Tracker Trucks, which is from Southern California. In the skate world it's basically Tracker versus Independent and *Thrasher* magazine versus *TransWorld Skateboarding*. Tony and I get heavily featured in both magazines, but he's more *TransWorld Skateboarding* and I'm more *Thrasher*.

Tony gets the worst of our so-called rivalry once when some Nor Cal guys boo him. Here's his recollection:

THEY WERE BOOING ME AND THROWING CRAP INTO THE POOL WHILE I WAS SKATING. AS A REACTION TO THEM BOOING ME, THERE WAS THIS CREW THAT WEREN'T NECESSARILY FOR ME, BUT BANDED TOGETHER AGAINST THE UP-NORTH GUYS AND ROOTED FOR ME. THE SKATE MEDIA PLAYED IT UP LIKE CHRISTIAN AND I DIDN'T GET ALONG, BUT I'D DROP IN AT HIS HOUSE AND WE'D SKATE HIS RAMP TOGETHER, AND WE SHARED ROOMS OFTEN ON THE ROAD. WE NEVER HAD ANY PROBLEMS, AND WE ALWAYS HAD GOOD TIMES TOGETHER. IT WASN'T LIKE WE HUNG OUT ALL THE TIME, BUT WE WERE AMONG THE FEW PRO SKATERS IN THE WORLD AND WE WERE FRIENDS.

IN THE END IT WAS TWO DIFFERENT TYPES OF SKATING. THEY WERE "SKATE AND DESTROY"; WE WERE "SKATE AND CREATE." I DIDN'T LIKE THE BOOING, BUT IT FIRED ME UP AND I THOUGHT, OKAY, I'M GONNA SHUT THESE GUYS UP WITH MY NEXT RUN.

Sometimes it's me who's getting booed, of course, depending on the crowd and the sponsorship. I'm like Tony, though: booing does nothing but make me skate harder. It kicks me into overdrive, so I fly higher on my next run. If I win after being booed by the crowd, I hold up the trophy and say into the microphone, "Thanks for booing me; this win's for you."

DRIVEN

By the age of seventeen I've graduated to adults-only, twenty-one-and-up clubs. I'm living at my mom's and own my first car, a Jeep CJ5. I could buy nearly any car I want, but I like this one because it has enough room to carry a few friends and the portable jump ramp we use on the Venice boardwalk. I drive everywhere, but I'm extra-cautious not to get pulled over by the cops. As I mentioned, I taught myself to drive at fifteen, but since I dropped out of school at that age, I never did driver's education and won't have a license for another year. Still, I'm a good driver. If I weren't, we'd be dead right now.

After my Jeep I buy a blue convertible '69 Mustang 302 Boss. That thing sounds killer jamming around L.A. to Venice Beach. By this point I have my license and don't have to be paranoid about the cops. I love the rush of using my Mustang like a skateboard, jumping lanes and screaming around each turn, blitzing onto the Santa Monica Freeway in rush-hour traffic. Sometimes I have two wheels on the sidewalk and two on the street, racing down the street. My passengers sometimes freak, but I'm always in control.

According to Rusler, my friend Scott Oster sometimes tries to simulate my driving style. That gets him in trouble sometimes. Like one day when we're all at Damiano's on Fairfax, sitting down to eat. Suddenly we hear brakes squealing, followed by the crash of metal and breaking glass. We

BIG SURF, TEMPE, ARIZONA. DRAINED THE FIRST WAVE PARK IN THE WORLD, FOR STREET AND VERT CONTEST. MID-'80S. © GRANT BRITTAIN.

ICING ON THE CAKE. MID-1980. © *GRANT BRITTAIN*.

sprint outside to see that Oster has piled up his car again. He was looking to see who was in Damiano's, then busted a U-turn. In the process, a girl T-boned him and dragged his car halfway down the street. Thank God he's a skater! He would have been dead otherwise.

I never really crash, but I come too close for comfort once. We're at a Long Beach tradeshow and I'm driving some of the guys in a rented Turbo Thunderbird to L.A. for Rusler's birthday party at the El Rey Theater. Suddenly somebody in the backseat distracts me and I turn around, letting the Thunderbird run up onto the center divider. The car carves up the divider, does a full ollie, and—*boom!*—comes back down so hard it flattens both tires on the passenger side. We're about to roll when I turn the wheel and pull out.

We manage to get the car to the side of the road, but it's in no shape to be driven anywhere. Our only form of transportation now is our feet and the single skateboard in the trunk of the car. We take turns skating from one telephone to another and then turn the board over to the next guy. Once we straighten everything out with the Thunderbird's car-rental company, I take the U-Haul truck we rented for the show and take off for Rusler's party. I don't get there till 1:15 A.M., and by then there's nobody around; the place is completely shut down. The next day I hear there was a big brawl started by one of our friends. Obviously.

TAKING CARE OF BUSINESS

From the time I'm about fifteen years old, I enjoy the business side of things. When my first checks begin to dribble in, they total like $1,500 to $2,000 a month. Not bad for a kid doing nothing but riding a skateboard! Contests don't pay much, but sponsorships are already proving lucrative. The business sense my mom passed on to me really pays off, and by age seventeen I'm getting pretty savvy. No matter what business I'm involved in, I inform any potential partners what's up, saying, in effect, "I want 51 percent of the company; otherwise, I'm taking my offer elsewhere." I do my homework before meetings, question friends in the industry as to what it costs to make a shirt or whatever, and they tell me. Same with skateboards, wheels, trucks, everything. So before we ever sit down to hammer out a deal, I know what everything costs—what it sells for,

what production and distribution costs are, and what profit margins are. Because of my age and my partying reputation, most people figure I'll be easy to manipulate. They have no idea that I've done my research and am prepared with whatever questions and answers might be called for. The result is that I always end up with lucrative contracts.

I'm soon ready to start my own company, Hosoi Skateboards. I can't think of any other pros except Tony Alva, Stacy Peralta, and Bruce Logan who have ever run their own companies. I'm not the first, certainly, but I'm the youngest, starting Hosoi Skateboards when I'm still just seventeen.

My mom helps me file all my paperwork and get everything else in order. I've got it all but the cash. I hit up a drug dealer I know and ask him to back me. No problem. He gives me all the start-up money I need. I hand a sack filled with $20,000 in small bills to a skateboard manufacturer to produce my boards. No doubt the man I'm dealing with surmises that the money has a dirty history, but who's going to turn down that much cash? He builds me two thousand Hammerhead skateboards, and once we pick them up Pops and I screen the artwork onto them ourselves at a house in Topanga Canyon. The Hammerhead is born!

At an age when most kids haven't yet had their first job at McDonald's and are struggling through basic economics in high school, I'm the president of a viable company. My dad is the vice president, and my mom's the treasurer and secretary. The new boards move like hotcakes: by the end of the first year I'm taking down a solid six figures on them. This is beyond what any other skateboarder has ever made before. But I never brag about my newfound wealth, especially not to adults. Instead, I just buy everyone around me dinner. Maybe that's why nobody ever tells me my skate career won't last forever. I never hear questions like, "What are you gonna do when you grow up?" They all act like it will never end, because they want to eat, drink, and go to the clubs. Nobody ever offers that necessary advice, saying, "Dude, you're getting out of control; you should save some money." It's cool, though. I don't want to own anything or have anything own me. That's why I don't buy a house. In fact, I'd rather rent three houses and move into them whenever I want than own one house and be stuck with it. How boring. I'm on the move.

I'm making around $20,000 a month, combined income from Hosoi Skateboards and sponsorships, and I easily spend three-fourths of that. I don't really know, though, cuz I don't keep close track. If I were to make a budget, it would start with something like $2,000 a month for necessities, including weed. Once rent is covered, the rest can go for

CAPITOLA CLASSIC STREET CONTEST. MID-'80S.
A SIMILAR SHOT BECAME THE COVER OF *THRASHER* MAGAZINE.
© MORIZEN FOCHE, COURTESY OF THRASHER MAGAZINE.

anything—maybe a motorcycle, a new car, a cool watch, a necklace, and of course clothes. I once spent $1,500 on a jacket, $800 on boots, and $500 on a Jim Morrison–type belt. That was at a place a friend of mine owns, where all the big stars shop. (Forgive my stoner's memory, but I just can't recall the name of the place.) The rest goes for things like trips to Hawaii with my team, buying breakfast, lunch, and dinner for whoever's around, and buying whatever else catches my eye. Lance Mountain remembers my buying white leather jackets for myself and my entire crew when we were in Japan.

The Hammerhead is at the heart of my financial success at this point. Generally speaking, except for the graphics no one can tell one skateboard from another back then. They're all identical—thirty inches long, ten inches wide, round in the nose and tail, kicked up in the tail. My new board incorporates the swallowtail from my model with Alva, a feature that I like, but what makes the Hammerhead unique is that it's cut out near the nose so you can grab it and easily hold on while doing aerial maneuvers.

The Hammerhead looks completely different than all the other shapes, but it performs so well that we can't keep them in stock. In fact, that board's so popular that a company in Canada begins counterfeiting it and I have to pay $40,000 to get them to cease and desist. The worst part is that the counterfeits are horribly made and fall apart, which sucks for the Hosoi name. I've sweated over the construction of our boards, to be sure they're the highest quality. We use the best Canadian hardwoods, while the counterfeiters use whatever scraps they can find. I actually get kicked out of Pipeline Skatepark when I go there and demand that the owner not carry counterfeit Hosoi boards anymore. Finally, in desperation, we run an ad in *Thrasher* exposing the ripoffs and warning our customers to buy the "real Hosoi" original Hammerhead, something they can get only from us.

As my popularity soars, I hate not being able to sign every autograph. I've always taken extra time out to be sure that my fans get what they came for. There's an art to interacting well with the public when you're famous. How you handle things can harm or help you artistically. You have to focus on your work, but you don't have to be a jerk and disconnect from the world around you. That balance has been on my mind ever since I've been in the public eye.

At the clubs it's different. I'm not Rolling Stones famous, so I'm not a household name. The club regulars all know me, but many others have no idea who I am or what I do. Because of the way I dress, they probably think I'm some up-and-coming rock star or something. I typically wear patent-leather cowboy boots, ripped Levi's, a vest with no shirt, rings on every finger, and necklaces, while most of my peers rock faded T-shirts, jeans, and torn-up skate shoes. I look like anything but a skater when I'm out for the night. Even during the day I don't look like any other skater you've ever seen. Good thing I've got lots of changes of clothes, cuz skateboarding is about to go through one of its own major changes. ✳

CHRIST AIR. PRAHRAN RAMP IN MELBOURNE, AUSTRALIA. LATE '80S.
HOSOI FAMILY COLLECTION.

BACK TO
THE STREETS

> SKATEBOARDING IS NOT A CRIME.
> —POPULAR BUMPER STICKER FROM THE 1980S

CHAPTER 08

If I have any spiritual thoughts, they're centered on karma. I figure if you're a good person, you'll have a good life—simple as that. I try to be good to everyone I know, and I share whatever I have. I figure the amazing life I lead is my payoff for being a good guy. But honestly, I don't think much about it. All I know is that, for whatever reason, the world is all gift-wrapped and handed to me like a birthday present.

I have everything—a successful company, solid sponsorships, magazine covers, the key to any club in Hollywood, and just about any girl I lay my eyes on. My career is going Richter, and all my childhood friends, my peers, and my family are with me to travel the world and toast my successes. I win, I party, and I have all the friends and money I want. But I still want *more*. I'm young, and with time on my side I push all negative feelings aside and keep racing toward the future. I'll figure out the details later.

There's money to be made as a pro skater if you know how to make it, as I noted in the previous chapter. By working as my own agent, I can hammer out agreements that truly benefit me, signing deals for thousands of dollars. When you ride for somebody else you don't have a lot of responsibility, but you don't call your own shots either. That means you and your image are controlled by the company. Owning my own company suits me, because now more than ever I do what I want, when I want. The world opens up to me like a stoked oyster: I take the best of life, share the spoils with my friends, and leave the rest for the others to divvy up. Lance Mountain sums it up in *Rising Son* by saying, "We [other top pro skaters] were all driving around the country in a station wagon, doing demos for free, while he was being flown to New York, picked up in a limo, and being paid a thousand bucks for it."

I'm having plenty of fun, that's for sure—but there's a dissatisfied feeling beginning to gnaw at me from deep inside.

JIMMY'Z

Jim Ganzer is a family friend who attended Chouinard Art Institute in L.A. with Pops. He's the guy I mentioned who first rolled me around on a skateboard when I was still in diapers. Now Ganzer has hit the big time

JIMMY'Z © 1984 ™

© JIMMY'Z 1988   TEAM: JIMMY'Z HAWAII

PHOTO: WARREN BOLSTER   SKATE: CHRISTIAN HOSOI

JIMMY'Z AD. GRANT'S RAMP IN KANEOHE, HAWAII. LATE '80S.
COURTESY OF JIMMY'Z.

W. C. FIELD'S HOUSE. CONVERTED THE MASTER BEDROOM INTO MY CLOSET.
© GRANT BRITTAIN.

as L.A.'s latest fashion guru. His company, Jimmy'z, is light-years ahead of its time, designing the coolest clothing ever—really different from anything else, and perfect for someone like me.

Jimmy is as unconventional as I am, so it's only natural he would become my first big clothing sponsor. I think he's the first to blend surf, skate, fashion, and art together. He gives it his own unique twist, and the result is pure art. While the clothes are already cool, I customize every T-shirt I wear, ripping them five different ways, using excess material as streamers while the sleeves become headbands. By the time I'm done cutting a shirt up, it looks nothing like what it started out being.

I never endorse a product I don't believe in, but the originality of Jimmy'z is the raddest, so I'm all in from the start. Though I never tell Jimmy, I would maybe wear his clothes for nothing. But this is business, and I've got bills to pay.

David Hackett, a pro skater himself, is multitalented; he works at Jimmy'z, where he wears a lot of hats. His main job there, however, is team manager. He brings a pair of hand-stitched prototype shorts to Del Mar Skate Ranch, where I'm competing. We all respect Hackett; he's never involved with anything lame. By the time Hackett's in his midtwenties and working for Jimmy'z, he no longer competes and is revered as a legendary old-school master. Same goes for our bro Steve Olson.

These guys skate with a style I've never grown tired of. They can still

blow away much of the competition in the style department, but they've moved on to other things in order to make a living. As one of the early pros, Hackett knows the pitfalls of being a pro skater, and I'm stoked that he's in my corner. I'm not yet sponsored by Jimmy'z that day Hackett brings the shorts out, but I'm so hyped on the product that I wear them in the contest that day. Later, I also wear them in a Hosoi Rocket Wheels ad for Santa Cruz Skateboards, where I make

AUSTRALIA RAMP RIOT. BELL'S BEACH.
HOSOI FAMILY COLLECTION.

sure the Jimmy'z logo stands out. I know how to market, promote, and place products, and since I'm at the top of my sport, my name and endorsement are making Ganzer money.

When I take Ganzer the ads I'm in, he's really stoked on what I've done. I tell him that I want to be featured in *his* ads, which so far mainly show Vince Klyne, a popular surfer, model, and actor from Hawaii. (Klyne will later make his name on the big screen by beating up Keanu Reeves in a scene for the movie *Point Break*. My friend Anthony Kiedis, a front man for the Red Hot Chili Peppers, also takes a few swings at Keanu for that flick.)

After brief negotiations with Ganzer we settle on a $40,000 salary for the first year, $60,000 for the second year, and $90,000 for the third. This doesn't sound like much in today's era of multi-million-dollar sports contracts, but it was an unheard-of sum for a seventeen-year-old skateboarder—*any* skateboarder for that matter—in the late '80s and early '90s. It doesn't hurt that Hackett's pushing for me, telling Ganzer's crew that I'm worth that and a whole lot more.

This girl named Mercy works at Jimmy'z. She's always nice to me, but when she sees me gathering clothes like one of the real housewives of Beverly Hills, she says, "Christian, I don't know if I can okay this." I say, "No, it's okay; call the big dog [Ganzer] and see what he says." She calls Ganzer to say that I'm taking massive stacks of clothes and he replies, "Give him anything he wants." I pull my convertible Mustang up and stuff the trunk, the backseat, the floor, and the passenger seat, stacking stuff higher than the roof. I have *everything* in that pile, including women's coral pink, light yellow, and powder blue items, and super tight girls' pants and spandex shorts that I'll wear everywhere. I'm wearing skinny jeans decades before it's a fad with skaters. There are so many clothes strewn everywhere that there's barely any room left for me to drive home. They say I'm taking like $8,000's worth of clothing home every month. Most of it I'll never even wear. But I'm the main guy for Jimmy'z and their line is selling insanely well, so I must be worth it.

Man, do I make Hackett earn his pay. He sets up demos at places like Dillard's department store. He calls me right as I'm supposed to be skating one morning, around eleven o'clock. He says, "Dude, there are five thousand people here, all waiting for you. Where *are* you?" I'm like, "Chill, bro. It's all good." My plan is to slip in at the last minute, which (granted) it is by now, so the crowd is frothing by the time I arrive. Apparently it works, cuz when I cruise up in my signature rented white Lincoln Town Car with the music blasting, every kid within blocks goes ballistic. It's like a rock concert where the fans are pumped up for their favorite band to play an encore.

I don't just jump out and start skating right away; my usual routine is to cruise slowly around the lot on my board, checking everything out, including the audience (especially the girls) and the ramp, and building the energy. The skating is the best part for onlookers and for me too, so I skate my heart out. After the crowd goes off, I stick around to meet everyone still there—people who came specifically to see me. I'm always the last to leave, sitting in the parking lot until the final kid has an autograph.

These demos are a huge success, but my last-minute timing makes some of the organizers nervous. Hackett starts trying to trick me, telling me a demo is at ten, say, instead of at twelve. He means well, but his method doesn't work, because I quickly catch on to it and adjust my schedule accordingly.

ALL GAIN, NO PAIN

The more popular I become, the better my boards sell. I'm having them manufactured by a company called Skull Skates, which is owned by Peter Ducommun and his brother, comedian/actor Rick Ducommun. Skull Skates is an old-school brand that I've seen in magazines since I was a kid. Hackett, Olson, Johnny Ray, and Skatemaster Tate all work at Skull Skates, basically running the place. Hackett, Olson, and Hosoi. Killer lineup!

My next deal is with Santa Cruz Skateboards' Rich Novak and Richard Metiver for wheels. Here I am, still a seventeen-year-old kid, proposing a business deal in an L.A. airport conference room to a pair of seasoned businessmen. I have a unique proposition: I'll exclusively ride Santa Cruz OJ II Wheels for a mere $1,000 a month and a small percentage of each wheel. They're shocked initially, because nobody has ever been paid for endorsing wheels before, let alone gotten a royalty off each one. I can tell by the look on their faces that they're wondering if I'm serious. I state my case, then boldly ask, "Okay, so do we have a deal?" What can they do but agree?

ROCKET WHEELS STICKER.
HOSOI FAMILY COLLECTION.

I propose a series of Santa Cruz ads for the inside cover of *Thrasher*. At the time *Thrasher* is new and still printed mostly in black-and-white newsprint. Only the covers, outside and inside, are glossy and in color. We buy the inside front cover, which makes us really stand out. The ads hint not only that these are the best wheels available, but that you'll travel the world and get hooked up everywhere you go just by riding them. Production skyrockets from like 12,000 wheels a month to somewhere around 65,000. We combine forces and I switch my board production from Skull Skates to Santa Cruz. Now Santa Cruz is a one-stop shop for me.

Next I launch my own Hosoi Rocket Wheels with Santa Cruz, and that enterprise takes off. When you add what I make at Santa Cruz to my Jimmy'z checks and my other sponsors—Converse Shoes, Independent Trucks, Swatch Watches—along with appearance fees and contest winnings, it all adds up to hundreds of thousands of dollars a year and puts me in a tax bracket beyond any other skateboarder ever.

I love the work and put in long hours every day, not just to stay on top but simply because I love skating so much—especially the feeling of doing big airs. That sensation of weightlessness when you're flying under your own power, that centrifugal force on a ramp or in a pool—no drug can ever compare to that feeling. (So why was I getting high?)

In spite of my crazy lifestyle I'm in great shape, physically. I never do any form of exercise other than just riding my board all day on the streets and in ramps and pools, something that's good for developing legs and abs. For upper-body strength I pull myself up on the ramp instead of climbing the ladder or the steps, grabbing the coping to do a pull-up as I approach from below. I play at work and work at play, enjoying endless

LOVE AND ROCKETS AD IN *THRASHER* MAGAZINE.
MONTE GIBO'S RAMP IN KANEOHE, HAWAII. CIRCA 1986.
HOSOI FAMILY COLLECTION.

skate sessions and parties with my best friends. My life is fast and furious every day of the week. There are no days off.

I'm not sure when or how it happened, but the competition has narrowed to just Tony and me, battling for first place most of the time. The hope for the rest of the field is basically for third place.

You might think that all the girls who line the stands at the contests are a distraction for me. Actually, though, they're an incentive to win. I'm putting on a show, performing for them, and having a blast. I love performing to songs that annoy most people, like Tone Lōc's "Wild Thing" or Madonna's "Like a Virgin"—not even the original version, but the slower remix. On the ramp, I raise my hands in the air and dance before my run. It drives some people nuts. Once in Ohio they boo and yell for me to start skating. But this is my way of communicating to the crowd that I'm in control, and my pelvic thrusts preview exactly what I'm about to do. I laugh and hoot and basically clown around, taunting the crowd at every contest.

That's before the heat starts. Once I drop in, however, everything changes; my focus on skating becomes laser sharp. Tony Hawk figures I'm showing off. Later, though, he concedes that it gets the crowd fired up. One thing's certain: Tony and I are pushing each other harder and harder until we're going places nobody has ever been on a skateboard. He ends up taking first more often than I do, but there are trophies to win other than the cup for the contest, if you know what I mean.

DEATH AND REBIRTH

The skatepark boom is already over by the early '80s, with some parks closing only a few years after they open. One problem is that the parks aren't always well designed, and many of them aren't friendly to the first-time skater. Kids watching experienced skaters often attempt tricks that are beyond them, and some get badly injured. Then, of course, there are lawsuits. Though Marina was booming in its heyday—the late '70s—by 1981, it's among those struggling to keep their doors open. Only the hard-core locals skate there, and it's about to go under.

I've spent more time at Marina than anywhere else, including my own house. I've grown up skating there: I went from being a little kid in the shallow end to being the top amateur in the world, breaking altitude records, all in less than three years. The final battle at Marina is close as always, but by blasting my hardest and flying my furthest I ended up beating everyone, even Tony Hawk. If the park has to close, that's a good way to end things.

Marina was demolished after only three years in existence, leaving Pipeline Skatepark in Upland, Skate City in Whittier, and Del Mar Skate Ranch just north of San Diego as the last big parks standing in Southern California. They say that Yankee Stadium is the house that Babe Ruth built. If that's so, then Del Mar is the house that Tony Hawk built. Del Mar is a legendary part of skateboarding history, and it wouldn't be that way without Tony. What most people don't realize, though, is that the place has a jacked-up pool. One wall is mellow, one is kinked, and one you can barely skate at all. One wall, however, rises to over vert, and that's where you can *really* blast.

Beating Hawk is always challenge number one, but beating him in his home park in Del Mar would be huge. Yet that's my goal in the spring of 1984. To make things even tougher, the organizers of this particular contest are using a double-elimination format, meaning you have to lose twice to be out. I've already lost once and Tony is still undefeated. As if beating him once wouldn't be difficult enough, now I have to take him out twice in a row. I doubt even my friends are betting on me. Tony's tricks are coming so quickly that nobody can learn them in time to compete against him, but I don't let that stop me; I just stick to my own method—fly higher and further with as much style as possible. I end up winning that day—one of my all-time highs. Skating against each other brings out the best in both of us, and his success as a skater helps open a door for everyone who has chosen skateboarding as a career, including me.

Tony's like me in that he does the most radical tricks he can but thinks through the risk factors before dropping in. There's nothing impromptu about it for either of us. Probably because of that, neither of us ever gets injured very badly until years later, when he ends up in the ER after trying to complete a 360 death loop.

Though I always work through individual moves carefully at each park, generally speaking I don't plan my routines out as much as Tony does.

HOLIDAY HAVOC AT ANAHEIM CONVENTION CENTER. HIGH-AIR
CONTEST. © *MORIZEN FOCHE COURTESY OF* THRASHER *MAGAZINE.*

That's certainly how he sees it:

MY SKATING WAS MORE METHODICAL AND PLANNED OUT, AND CHRIS-
TIAN'S WAS MORE GO-WITH-THE-FLOW. WHEN I SKATED A PARK, I
KNEW EVERY WALL—I KNEW WHAT TRICK I WAS GOING TO DO AND HAD
A BACKUP PLAN IF THAT DIDN'T WORK OUT. I HAD THINGS SO DIALED,

IT WAS ALMOST BORING. THEN I'D SEE CHRISTIAN, AND HE SEEMED TO BE JUST THE OPPOSITE. HE'D LAND SOME-THING PERFECTLY THAT HE HADN'T EVEN DONE IN PRAC-TICE. THAT WAS SUPER EXCITING TO WATCH, AND WHEN HE WAS ON FIRE, HE WAS UNBEATABLE. BUT I WOULD SAY HE WAS MORE FREE-FORM, LIKE, I'M GONNA DROP IN AND SEE WHAT HAPPENS.

Tony's the most successful skater of all time, and whenever someone reaches that sort of pinnacle, there will be those who try to knock him down. When I catch people putting Tony down as a skater, I realize they're jealous, or they don't know what they're talking about, or they think that's what I want to hear. It's wrong, though: just because they don't like his style or where he's from doesn't mean they should take anything away from him.

Anyway, comparing my skating to Tony's is almost like comparing vert (as skating on vertical ramps and in pools has come to be known) to street skating; they're basically two different aspects of skateboarding, since we don't do our tricks the same way. In the end, it's all about what the judges *prefer:* my style or his. How do you score it when one guy busts out five tricks that nobody has ever seen before and the other guy blasts the highest 540 you've ever seen? I know that I have to bring something extraordinary to the table each time, in order to stand out.

It's probably no coincidence that the two skaters whose dads are always there for them are the ones at the top. The big difference is that while Tony's father, Frank, is out watching Tony warm up before the event, my dad's sharing bong loads with me in the car before my runs.

With most of the skateparks gone by the mid-1980s, skating leaves a commercialized phase and returns to

SEQUENCE: FLATLAND OLLIE OVER A STACK OF BOARDS AT A SKATE DEMO. *HOSOI FAMILY COLLECTION.*

its soulful, underground roots. That's where it started, and that's just the way many of us like it. Not every skater connects with that idea, of course, and some guys quit skating or just fade away as the times change. The whole Pepsi Team and Rad Ramp glitz is instantly ancient history, giving way to something far more hard-core. It's the same way that music has gone from '70s glam rock to underground, revolutionary, aggressive, and artistic. *Organic* might be a good word for it. "Skateboarding is not a crime" is the sticker on everybody's car, and while we aren't all total criminals, nobody is gonna tell us what to do, or organize us with colored jerseys and team jackets. That's why punk-rock music, backyard ramps, and the rad articles in *Thrasher* magazine fit so well together. That's why skateboarding even today has an edge to it.

Street skating is making a comeback. Fine with me; I love street skating. In Venice we set up jump ramps on the boardwalk, put quarter-pipes up against the walls, or just skate straight up walls. Nobody ever stops us from setting up our own little stage on the Venice boardwalk. Why should they? We're not really bothering anybody; in fact, we're entertaining them in droves, with thousands of people standing around to watch. Hey, the local businesses aren't complaining. Wall rides that seemed impossible a few years earlier are now everyday occurrences, and we're regularly topping seven feet, straight up.

The first big street event is in San Francisco's Golden Gate Park. I drive up there with Jay Adams. He doesn't enter the contest but I do, and I get second behind Tommy Guerrero. Since Tommy has signed up as an amateur, I—as a pro—get the first-place money. Doesn't seem quite fair, but that's the way it is. Tommy's the new street kid, the new big sensation, and he'll go on to make a huge name for himself. (Do I have to say that Jay and I smoked weed all the way there, *while* there, and all the way home? Oh, and we might have done a little coke too.)

Skaters like Natas Kaupas, Tommy Guerrero, Eric Dressen, and Mark Gonzales are big on the street scene, while backyard pools and ramps make the sport accessible to everyone. As street skating ramps up, we discover places to skate hiding in plain sight. Handrails, curbs, freeway on-ramps, bridges, and handicap ramps all present an open invitation to skate. Without a legal facility, we ride anything we're told *not* to—the less legal the better. We invade every available inch of corporate property, and nonskaters can't stand us. Every bench, every curb, every wall, and every backyard pool is fair game for us. Public facilities all have skateboard paint smeared all over them, and none of the handrails have any paint left on them at all. ✸

360 AIR OFF JUMP RAMP. EARLY RELEASE. © IVAN HOSOI.

HIGH ABOVE
THE CLOUDS

W. C. FIELDS MUST HAVE HAD GREAT TASTE.

—CHRISTIAN HOSOI

CHAPTER09

As I said before, I don't want to be tied down to one house any more than I do to one girl. So, instead of buying a home, I rent a classic estate that once belonged to legendary film comic W. C. Fields. It's nestled in the trees of Echo Park, right off Sunset Boulevard. First order of business, of course, is to have a state-of-the-art ramp built in the backyard. I have thirty-five-foot posts cemented into the ground to hold the ramp. As the last step, I have the crew hang camouflage on the backside of the ramp, because skaters would jump the fence and be all over it if they knew it was there. Days at that house are a blur of shooting pool with friends and skating hard. My friends and I live a wild, joyful existence. Not much is out of bounds on that property.

B ut I've reined myself in, and I'm living a pretty clean life by my standards. I've even begun training a little: Eddie and I ride mountain bikes each morning through Elysian Park. All of L.A. is visible from the Hollywood Hills before the city wakes up and the town is blanketed in smog. We skate the rest of the day, then party all night. It's a pretty rare evening that any of us skaters stay home. When we do, it's usually because the party is at my house. My life is like that Sade song: "Every day is Christmas, and every night is New Year's Eve."

W. C. Fields must have had great taste, because the place is awesome. It has an octagonal breakfast room overlooking the property, which features a rad, gin-bottle-shaped pool with a lush garden surrounding it; the pool drops off down behind some adjacent bungalows occupied by my neighbors. Cactus the size of Dodge vans border the property. Sunset Boulevard is on one side and Echo Park on the other. If people happen to glance up from Sunset Boulevard toward my house, they see nothing but trees and camouflage. But if they keep looking, they might spot one of the world's top skaters flying through the air. The sight of a skateboarder at altitude isn't a common one for nonskaters, especially away from a skatepark, and people must think they're seein' a space alien invading L.A. Hey, that's kind of true, in a way.

My bedroom has a typical-size closet, but there isn't enough room for all my clothes. I convert the master bedroom into a walk-in closet: problem solved. I have two racks and two poles set up in there, top and bottom from wall to wall. There are four shelves with nothing but T-shirts on them. The floor is about three feet deep in clothes I've worn only once. I never do laundry cuz I rarely wear the same thing twice. My staple for the clubs is one of the many vests I buy from a Hollywood boutique store called Aardvark. I don't wear a shirt under it, but complete the outfit with jeans and cowboy boots. If I'm skating, I wear something from Jimmy'z, always customized in my own style. If it's boys' night out on the town, we hit the club, shift to an after-hours party, and then eat at Canter's or Damiano's on Fairfax. Then it's off to Hollywood Billiards until like five in the morning.

A large part of the pleasure for me in making money and living on the estate is being able to share with friends. The guys and I have been hanging out together for years. The only difference is that now we can do it in more style.

Robert Rusler, who is one of the regulars at my new place, recalls that time:

CHRISTIAN WAS MAKING MORE THAN ANY SKATEBOARDER HAD EVER MADE, LIKE $20,000 TO $30,000 A MONTH. I WAS DOING ALL RIGHT AS AN ACTOR ALSO, STARRING IN A SHOW CALLED *THE OUTSIDERS* AND BRINGING DOWN $28,000 A WEEK, WHICH WAS A LOT OF MONEY IN THE '80S. THAT HOUSE MUST HAVE COST A LOT TO KEEP, BUT CHRISTIAN NEVER ONCE ASKED ME FOR RENT.

We had an amazing time at the W. C. Fields house—all of us—and I was totally relaxed living and skating there. Rusler remembers one particular morning when I went out skating alone:

I HAD JUST WOKEN UP AND I LOOK OUT MY WINDOW TO SEE CHRISTIAN WEARING NOTHING BUT A TOWEL. HE'S STROLLING IN THE BACKYARD, SMOKING A J, AND HE KIND OF MOSEYS ON OVER TO THE RAMP. HE GETS ONTO THE RAMP AND STARTS DOING FAKIES WHILE HE'S SMOKIN' THIS J. HE JUST KEEPS GOING AND GOING, SLOWLY AT FIRST, LOOKING UP AT THE BIRDS AND THE SUN. AFTER A WHILE HE'S RIDING HIGHER AND HIGHER, AND ALL OF A SUDDEN HE DOES A SMITH GRIND.

NOW HE'S DOING 50-50S. THEN ALL OF A SUDDEN HE'S DOING TAIL TAPS AND THEN—*BOOM!*—HE LANDS A FRONTSIDE AIR, BACKSIDE AIR, FRONTSIDE AIR. ALL WITH A JOINT IN HIS HAND AND NOTHING BUT A TOWEL ON!

SOON HE'S BUSTIN' OUT LIKE SIX- OR SEVEN-FOOT AIRS, ONE RIGHT AFTER ANOTHER. HE PULLS HIS LAST AIR AND WINDS IT ALL BACK DOWN, IN REVERSE OF WHAT HE HAD BEEN DOING. NOW HE'S GRINDING, THEN SLIDING, BACK TO FAKIES, SLOWER AND SLOWER, UNTIL HE'S STOPPED AND STEPS OFF THE BOARD. BY THE TIME HE DOES THAT, THE JOINT IS DOWN TO A ROACH.

I HAD SEEN ONE OF THE MOST INCREDIBLE EXHIBITIONS OF SKATEBOARDING EVER, AND CHRISTIAN DIDN'T EVEN KNOW ANYBODY WAS WATCHING. IT WAS LIKE HE HAD REACHED SOME SORT OF MAGICAL PEAK, AND I REMEMBER LOOKING AT HIM AND THINKING, MAN, YOU'VE GOT IT—SKATEBOARDING, STYLE, CONFIDENCE, PRESENCE.

BREAKING MY OWN RULES

I don't remember when Louanna first came around, but she stood out, even among all the hot girls at Venice Beach. Louanna Rawls is the daughter of famed soul singer Lou Rawls, and because of her I break my rule about not having one single girlfriend. She's nineteen and I'm twenty when we become a

"SACTO" STREET CONTEST. SACRAMENTO, CA. © IVAN HOSOI.

couple. My memory is that we met in the club scene, but she says it was on the Venice boardwalk. Either way, she becomes my first full-time girlfriend. We notice each other right away, but she's not just another girl to me; and pretty soon it's just the two of us, going out seven days a week, three clubs a night.

It's a high-wire act since I'm in this boys' club, and our deal is to rage together, go out and pick up chicks. Because of that long-standing connection, some of my friends, including Rusler, don't get along with Louanna at first. Rusler remembers:

THE FIRST TIME LOUANNA AND I MET WAS AT CLUB LINGO, WHERE NOTHING BUT GIRLS HUNG OUT. CHRISTIAN NEVER REALLY HAD A MAJOR GIRLFRIEND BEFORE THAT, AND NOW WE HEAR HE'S GOT THIS NEW CHICK, AND WE CAN'T WAIT TO CHECK HER OUT. I MEET THIS HOT-LOOKING GIRL AT THE CLUB, AND I'VE GOT HER SIZED UP AS A CROSS BETWEEN A VALLEY GIRL AND THE PRINCESS OF MONACO. FOR SOME REASON WE AREN'T GETTING ALONG VERY WELL, THOUGH, AND ARE KIND OF TRADING INSULTS, WHICH IS SOMETHING I ALWAYS ENJOY DOING WITH HOT GIRLS. JUST THEN CHRISTIAN APPEARS AND PUTS HIS ARM AROUND HER. THAT'S WHEN I REALIZE THAT THIS IS THE NEW GIRLFRIEND I'VE BEEN HEARING ABOUT. OOPS! SHE LOOKS AT ME AND THEN BACK AT CHRISTIAN AND SAYS, "DO YOU KNOW HIM?" CHRISTIAN'S LIKE, "YEAH, THAT'S RUSTY DOG." NO MATTER HOW WE BATTLED, LOUANNA AND I REALLY DID LOVE EACH OTHER, BUT THAT WAS A ROUGH RELATIONSHIP AT FIRST. NEITHER OF US WAS GOING ANYWHERE.

While some of my friends don't understand Louanna's attitude, that's part of what intrigues me about her. She has her own opinions, challenges me, and always speaks her mind. We have a lot in common—an interest in fashion and loving to dance and go out. People love us each separately, but they love us even more when we're together.

We're continuing my rock-star sort of existence—a life filled with excess. Most of the people I know from the party scene need "bait" to lure somebody in. They need the best clothes, the best cars, the best pickup

lines, along with lines of cocaine or XTC for insurance—but Louanna and I have each other.

At first Louanna and I are on-again, off-again as a couple. I mean, what could I expect since I told her that I wanted an open relationship? Of *course* someone like her isn't going to stand for that situation long, and she breaks up with me. With me out of the picture, it's just a matter of time before someone else moves in. That someone proves to be none other than actor Eddie Murphy. I think it's my friend Scott Oster who tells me that Eddie has sent Louanna a bouquet of flowers the size of a Volkswagen. On top of that, he gave her a $20,000 Rolex. Louanna still has some of her things at my house, and when she comes to get them, I say, "Okay, what's it gonna be?"

She chooses to get back with me, and after that we're solid for quite a while; she even moves in with me full-time. Having Louanna at my side gives me a sense of structure that I've never had before. I don't spend all my time trying to hustle girls any longer, and I'm faithful, at least for a while. We work days: I skate and she does modeling or acts in various music videos, where she always seems to get the lead, as she does in a classic video with Howlin' Wolf and Bonnie Raitt. When she returns home, it's time to hit the town.

Here's Louanna's take on our relationship:

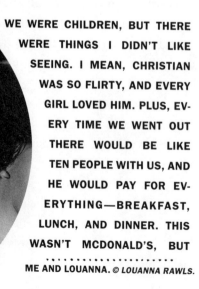

WE WERE CHILDREN, BUT THERE WERE THINGS I DIDN'T LIKE SEEING. I MEAN, CHRISTIAN WAS SO FLIRTY, AND EVERY GIRL LOVED HIM. PLUS, EVERY TIME WE WENT OUT THERE WOULD BE LIKE TEN PEOPLE WITH US, AND HE WOULD PAY FOR EVERYTHING—BREAKFAST, LUNCH, AND DINNER. THIS WASN'T MCDONALD'S, BUT

ME AND LOUANNA. © *LOUANNA RAWLS.*

PLACES LIKE PACIFIC DINING CAR, WHERE A SALAD IS FIFTEEN BUCKS AND AN ENTRÉE IS LIKE THIRTY. HE WAS ALSO SPENDING ABOUT SEVENTY-FIVE BUCKS A DAY ON WEED FOR HIM AND HIS FRIENDS. THEN OF COURSE THERE WERE THOSE TRIPS TO HAWAII WITH THE ENTIRE CREW. HE'S ALWAYS BEEN SUCH A GENEROUS, GIVING PERSON, AND HE ALWAYS PAID FOR EVERYTHING. I THINK I WAS THE ONLY ONE TRYING TO CONVINCE HIM TO SAVE SOME OF HIS MONEY.

I WASN'T ATTRACTED TO HIM BECAUSE HE WAS A FAMOUS SKATEBOARDER. IN FACT, I DIDN'T KNOW THAT ABOUT HIM WHEN I WAS FIRST ATTRACTED TO HIM. I HAD SKATEBOARDED WHEN I WAS ABOUT SEVEN, BUT BY THE TIME WE WERE GOING OUT, I THOUGHT SKATEBOARDING WAS A JUVENILE THING. BACK THEN IT WASN'T WHAT IT IS NOW, AND I THOUGHT HE HAD SO MANY MORE TALENTS THAN JUST SKATEBOARDING. I DIDN'T LIKE THE CONTESTS, THE GROUPIES, AND EVERYTHING THAT CAME ALONG WITH THAT, EVEN THOUGH I WAS KIND OF USED TO ALL THAT BECAUSE OF MY FATHER.

LAS VEGAS WITH (LEFT TO RIGHT) PETER BILL, RODNEY HARVEY, DAVID ARQUETTE, RICHMOND ARQUETTE, ME, LOUANNA RAWLS, AMANDA ANKA, AND ROBERT RUSLER. *HOSOI FAMILY COLLECTION.*

We're always on the move, flying or driving wherever we feel like going. One of our journeys takes Louanna and me to Vegas along with actor David Arquette, Amanda Anka, and some other friends. We're sitting with Amanda when her dad, the famed singer Paul Anka, visits our table and sings his big hit "Put Your Head on My Shoulder," along with other songs that made him famous. His driver takes us all to play baccarat at one of Anka's favorite hotels. We head back to our room at the Riviera, where we enjoy our two-story penthouse suite. We're up at least twenty stories, but I still decide to open a window and tiptoe out onto the ledge. With the window open there's something to hold on to, so I turn and tell someone in the room to close the window behind me. I'm standing there looking down, and I feel what everybody says you feel in that situation—that you're being pulled over the edge. Once I experienced that feeling, I say, "Okay, you can open the window now."

Waiting in line at the clubs must be a drag. We wouldn't know; we don't wait for anything. Actors and various local celebrities wait in the VIP line, and others queue along the sidewalk or cluster around, hoping they can get inside at all. Whenever we arrive, the velvet ropes are magically lifted and we float right in, every time. The doormen approach us and say, "Hey, come on in." Both Louanna and I are famous in our own right, and everybody knows us everywhere we go.

Sometimes we hit crazy underground clubs downtown like Water the Bush, where only the owners, the bouncers, and the bartenders recognize us and know what we're about. These places are filled with nothing but gangsters and other hard-core types lining the walls, staring us down, checking us out, and sizing us up as we enter. There's a feeling of danger that we find attractive somehow. I park just outside, at the red no-parking curb, far less worried about the ticket I'll get than about having my car jacked. I'm confident, despite the neighborhood and clientele, because I'm strapped with my nine-millimeter Walther PPK. It's a James Bond–type gun—small, but powerful enough to stop whatever it hits. It's a nice friend to have along, just in case. Here we are—a little guy with three months' salary on his wrists and fingers, and a hot-looking girl who's wearing hardly anything at all. Oh, and she can have an attitude! Carrying a weapon offers the illusion that I'm invincible, which I basically feel I am anyway.

Friends say I'm skating better than ever, and that's probably because I'm not doing hard drugs like I once did. I'm considered a nondrinker these days: at the clubs I nurse my usual two or three Coronas and slam a shot of Cuervo Gold tequila. That's it. Well, that and chain-smoking weed, with a little XTC here and there, but not every night. Louanna and I have fun while we last, just living that Hollywood dream, until like most dreamers in that town, we break up, break down, and wake up alone again. But we hang in there for three and a half years, which might be some kind of a record for anybody raging in the Hollywood party scene.

AT HOME IN HAWAII

I feel like I have two homelands, one in L.A. and the other in Hawaii. In Hawaii I'm not just another *haole* tourist, but I'm treated like royalty, or at least a respected local. David Nuuhiwa Sr. is considered a Hawaiian *kahuna*. One of the top martial artists in the world, he's respected by everyone. Whenever I see "Uncle" David, which is usually at the tradeshows, he

SANDY BEACH, OAHU. SCOTT AND MARK OBLOW, JOHN MANILDI, ME, AND GRANT FAKUDA. © CESARIO "BLOCK" MONTANO.

always goes out of his way to talk to me and my father and to catch up on what's going on in our life (and catch us up on his). My parents are from the Islands and I'm part Hawaiian myself, so I'm family.

Once my contracts are in place and money's rolling in, I fly to Oahu as often as I can, which is maybe three or four times a year, paying for as many as ten of my friends to travel with me. Once there, I rent my usual—you guessed it, a white Lincoln Town Car—before we all head out. Our adventure always starts the same, but we never know how it will end up.

As soon as we get off the plane we drive straight to the Rainbow Drive Inn in Honolulu, order and scarf down plate lunches, and drive to the Local Motion Surf Shop, where they loan me anything I want. I have surf racks and a stack of surfboards to use while we're in town. My friends all rip at surfing, but I can't surf for nothin'. But I'm not in Hawaii to ride waves. I'm here to hang out, party all night in Waikiki, and skate these sick ditches—underground places with names like Wallos, Off the Walls, Pipeline Bowls, Uluwatus, A'ala Park, and Stoker Hill. These drainage ditches are perfect for skating—and they're illegal, which only adds to the fun.

As many times as I trespass in order to skate, I never get a ticket for skateboarding. But I do get chased by cops fairly often. I say *chased*, but I never bother running. Everyone else hits it right away, cuz they all have criminal histories or bench warrants. The cops come up to me

GRANT FAKUDA'S RAMP IN KANEOHE, HAWAII.
© IVAN HOSOI.

and I welcome them and say, "How you guys doin'?" as I position myself to continue skating. When they ask why I don't run with everyone else, I say, "Why, I'm just skateboarding. What's the big deal?" I tell them I'm a pro skateboarder, and they say something like, "Let's see what you got." Once I'm done skating, they say, "Okay, great—now get out of here."

Hawaii is basically just an extension of home, especially because I bring the party with me. Block has really been around, but when I first met him he had never been on a plane before. Block surfed and skated and basically had my philosophy of doing what you want, when you want. We were really close and eventually traveled a lot together. He remembers the first time I took him to Hawaii.

WE'RE DOING A DEMO, AND CHRISTIAN ASKS ME WHERE THE HOT CHICKS ARE. I TELL HIM THAT THERE ARE SOME IN THE BLEACHERS BUT THAT THE HOTTEST ONE IS THE HAWAIIAN TROPIC GIRL WHO IS A MODEL FOR THE COMPANY. HE GOES, "OH, I'VE GOT THAT." HE SKATES AROUND HER, WHICH IS HOW HE FLIRTS WITH ALL THE GIRLS. IN NO TIME SHE AGREES TO GO OUT WITH HIM. SHE'S BEEN GOING OUT WITH SOME MODEL GUY, AND HE SAYS, "OH, THIS SKATER COMES TO TOWN AND NOW YOU'RE HANGIN' OUT WITH HIM?" SHE'S LIKE SIX FEET TALL ALREADY, AND THEN SHE WEARS THESE FOUR-INCH HEELS. CHRISTIAN LOOKS LIKE A MIDGET NEXT TO HER. HE HAS THIS LEATHER BOMBER JACKET ON, DRIVING AROUND IN THAT LINCOLN TOWN CAR, JUST RUBBING IT INTO EVERYONE'S FACES.

I never have any trouble in Hawaii, but things *can* get rough there, even for someone who grew up on the streets of L.A. There was an event at the University of Hawaii that Ice-T came out for. This big fight breaks out, and Ice looks at me and says, "Later, Hosoi. I'm out—these Hawaiians won't quit fighting." They just keep fighting: it's brawl after brawl after brawl. I love watching a good fight or two, so I stick around till the cops finally break things up.

WAIKIKI BEACH. SCOTT OSTER, ME, AND SERGIE VENTURA.
© CESARIO "BLOCK" MONTANO.

Aaron Murray, my skateboard buddy from childhood days, usually travels with us, but he's often on the injured list after doing one radical thing or another. The first time he lost a finger he was in a junior high woodshop class and routed the tip of his middle finger off. We thought that was pretty gnarly. This time he rips his little finger off, reinjuring the same hand. He's wearing a pinky ring that catches between the coping and the ramp. The finger just plain rips off below the first joint. That's how he gets the nickname Fingers.

One of my Rocket Wheel team riders, Scott Oster, is just fifteen years old when I take him to Hawaii for his first time. I'm only three years older than he is, but I'm "responsible" for him and the nine other skaters that accompany me. I visit Scott's dad before our departure and tell him all the wonderful things we're going to do in Hawaii, emphasizing what good care I'm going to take of his son. Scott is an amazingly talented skater, and I tell his father that his son has a big future in skateboarding. In the end Scott is allowed to miss school and travel with me.

In Hawaii, we cruise through town, stopping to rage at various clubs, when for some strange reason the girl with Oster steals a NO SMOKING sign from a hotel. Back at our hotel afterward, all of us are crammed into two rooms. With that many people in each room, with five surfboards and all our bags stacked to the ceiling, it's usually a disaster area. Needless to say, we're not exactly on good terms with housekeeping. The maids are at the point where they don't want to clean our rooms anymore, so when they *do* clean and find that sign, they use it as an excuse to call the cops.

The cops come to the door and say, "You've got stolen property in your room." I say, "Stolen property? I'm no thief." I'm convinced that they have

BURNIN'. © IVAN HOSOI.

the wrong room. I'm a little uneasy, though, because I know that one of my friends has an ounce of weed stashed in the room safe. The cops are persistent: one says he can arrest me for that stupid sign, and I'm like, "*Really,* you're kidding? You're gonna take me in for a NO SMOKING sign?" I keep talking to the cops, acting nice and being apologetic, trying to distract them while my buddy, right behind them, is getting his buds out of the safe.

As soon as he removes his weed, I say, "Okay, we'll go; we're outta here." Because of that sign we're kicked out of the hotel—it's an Outrigger, which most of the hotels in Hawaii are—and we're barred from staying in any other Outrigger for a year. Now we have to find somewhere else to stay, all because Scott Oster's girlfriend wants a NO SMOKING sign. Ridiculous! ✺

HOSOI

SKTBRDS

DR, SOQUEL, CA. 95073 8) 475-9434 TELEX 172476   Send $1.00 for decal

FOTO: C. KATZ

HOSOI SKATEBOARDS AD AT PATTY SELLER'S "PERFECT RAMP." *HOSOI FAMILY COLLECTION.*

540 MCTWIST AT GRANT FAKUDA'S RAMP IN KANEOHE, HAWAII. © IVAN HOSOI.

ALOHA
TO REALITY

We're just climbing up wet volcanic rock to who knows where, still frying our brains out on 'shrooms . . .

CHAPTER 10

MOUNTAINS OF PINK JELL-O

On our next trip to Hawaii, we again have a big entourage, including Oster and a recovered Aaron Murray. We're just off the plane, and the first thing we do after eating plate lunches at Rainbow Drive Inn is head to Kaneohe to pick mushrooms. We have to commando over a fence into the mushroom-rich field, lying low and crawling around as we seek the biggest cow patties, which contain the most mushrooms. We need to avoid the field's owners, cuz they're making money from selling the 'shrooms, and we hear they have shotguns loaded with salt pellets that they don't hesitate to use on intruders. As always, we like that element of danger. We eat some 'shrooms, pick some more, and throw some in a bag to eat later.

I'm driving and we're all starting to 'shroom as we head back to town. But to get back to our hotel we have to drive through the Wilson Tunnel. Everyone's laughing hysterically—even me, though I'm tryin' to maintain and make it through without ending up as part of the wall.

· ·

WAIKIKI HOTEL ROOM BALCONY. ME, SCOTT OSTER, ERIC DRESSEN, AND SERGIE VENTURA.
© CESARIO "BLOCK" MONTANO.

Somehow we get up to our room in Waikiki, way up on the seventeenth floor. Someone's like, "Let's make paper airplanes." First we tear pages out of various magazines in the room and fold them for flight. Then we launch our planes off the balcony. We quickly finish up all the magazines and look around for something else to use, settling on the phonebook. We're all making the best paper airplanes we know how; we're churning them out like pros. We make all different kinds of them, throwing them off the balcony, until we've torn through the whole phonebook. We're looking for more paper when someone glances down and discovers that there are paper airplanes *everywhere*—on every car, every rooftop, all over the street. Not wanting to get thrown out of yet another hotel, we close the balcony door and race down to the garage. We split, heading for this place near town, Manoa Falls.

Manoa Falls is just inland from Waikiki. It's a beautiful place, and you can hike right up to the falls. Beyond that, though, there's a big fence with a KEEP OUT sign. We jump right over the fence, of course, and head up the trail. It gets steeper and steeper until it's pretty much vertical. Then there's no more trail, just ropes. After a while even the ropes quit and go to vines. Then there are no vines—nothing to hang on to—and we're just climbing up wet volcanic rock to who knows where, still frying our brains out on 'shrooms and totally ignoring the fact that we've gotta come back down at some point.

There are like ten of us, all really competitive friends and skateboarders, and so of course we have to have a race for the top. After a while we're hanging on to this vertical wall by our fingertips and our toes, really high up. When we look down it feels like we're a mile up, and we're trying not to fall. When somebody says that we should puff a fatty, everyone agrees that it's a good idea. We have weed on us at all times: there are some joints stashed in our hats.

Problem is we're not in a position to smoke anything. We're trapped there, balancing against the side of the wall, our hands in use for safety. We can see a pool with a flat area just a little ways away from us and conclude that we can smoke there. But we have to get there first, which means stepping over to one rock, letting go of any support, and leaping off in hopes of landing in or near the pool. The rock's really slippery, and

IN RIO DE JANEIRO WITH BLOCK. ON THE WAY UP TO CRISTO.
© *CESARIO "BLOCK" MONTANO.*

the water's rushing off the cliff right beyond it. It would be easy to lose our footing or mistime our jump. If anyone does, he's gonna die for sure. But we're all just laughing, clinging to the rock, ready to take this leap of faith by pushing off the rock to get to the pool.

Aaron makes it first, and one by one so does everybody else. Finally it's Oster's turn. As he kicks off the rock, his foot slips. Everyone holds their breath as he does the running man in midair over the rock before trying to push off with his other foot. That foot also slips, and now he's scratchin', desperately trying not to go over the falls and down the cliff. If he doesn't make it, I'm gonna have some real explaining to do to the authorities and especially to his dad. He barely makes it into the pool. Then we're all laughing, rewarding our accomplishment of not dying by smoking a joint or two.

Someone hikes a little further up and we all follow him to the top. We're just trippin', standing on what Aaron would later describe as pink Jell-O. Way down below we can see trees growing out from the side of the cliff and a jungle all the way to the bottom. If you've ever seen this area you know it's pretty much vertical, but for some reason we decide

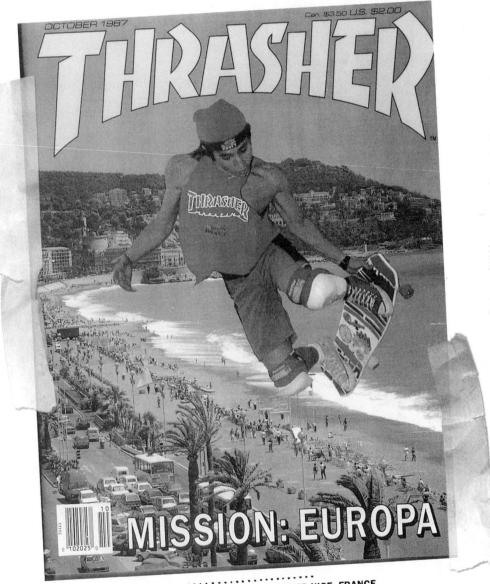

THRASHER MAGAZINE COVER. AIR OVER NICE, FRANCE.
© THRASHER MAGAZINE.

not to take the trail back to the bottom. Instead, we venture where there's *no* trail, facing down the mountain, backs to the wall, just kind of crab-crawling at first, then grabbing branches and vines, swinging on anything on our way down, jumping from tree to tree, hooting and screaming insanely.

Once we're back to the bottom pool, we see our friend Eric Dressen, who was too fried to climb. He's there alone with two models—Block swears they're mermaids—swimming in the pond. The girls end up hanging out with us for the night.

As the sun sets we head down the mountain, and simultaneously we come down from the 'shrooms. Back in our hotel rooms, it's time to get ready for a night of partying on the town. The day's over; the night's just beginning.

THE ONE AND ONLY AARON MURRAY

Aaron and I have never lost that feeling of freedom we got when we climbed trees to the top as little kids. It's fun when you're young, but it doesn't always work so well when you're grown up.

We're on Speedway in Venice, and this guy is there with sheets of acid. Aaron buys some, eats some, and gives some to anyone who wants a hit at the party we're attending. Suddenly we see Aaron on the roof—and then he jumps. Where usually there might be a soft landing or a pool below, now it's nothing but concrete. Somehow he manages to grab a power wire with one hand, holding a beer in the other. "Anybody want a beer?" he says, laughing hysterically. I don't remember how he finally gets down, but I know that he's like the rest of us in a way; none of us ever seem to think things all the way through.

AARON MURRAY. © IVAN HOSOI.

Maybe Aaron and I are just born that way. As a child he once fills a trashcan with water and jumps into it from his roof, having gotten that idea from seeing someone jump into a teacup from a diving board in a cartoon. After he lands in the trashcan, he has to wiggle around to tip it over just to get free. I'm just glad he didn't have a teacup around, or he probably would have used that.

HANDLIN' MY BUSINESS. POP'S ART IN THE BACKGROUND.
© IVAN HOSOI.

This one time, we're staying at a hotel in Waikiki. We're all hanging out at the pool, chillin', when he tells us he's gonna jump into the pool from the fifth floor. Now, the pool is only five feet deep. Still, he takes off, running up the stairs in his trunks and Chuck Taylors. We're like, "Cool, let's video it." We knew he was crazy, but we didn't think that even he would actually jump from there. Suddenly we see him way up there. He vaults over a little wall on the stairwell and stands on the ledge for a moment. He's just a speck, so far up—there's no way he's gonna do it. Next thing we know he's just flying toward the water! Suddenly there's water everywhere, and he jumps up out of the pool like he's shot from a cannon. Five floors up into five feet of water, and no injuries. Not a scratch. The hotel workers hear the commotion and bolt out as we slink away, acting like nothing has happened. If they'd seen what happened, we would have been kicked out of yet another hotel.

I guess Aaron's got this thing about jumping into water. Rusler remembers one time at my house when Murray was looking at the pool and mumbling, "I can make that." Before we can try to talk him out of it, we hear his feet on the roof. He's up like twenty-seven feet, which is bad enough, but the pool is a long ways out from the roof. Next thing you know he's in the air Butch Cassidy style; he's this flying squirrel in trunks and sneakers. He lands on his feet with a huge splash, stands up, smiles, and says, "I told you I could do it." I ask, "Don't your ankles hurt?" He replies, "Yeah, a little bit." *That* pool was only *four* feet deep.

WHY I LOVE SURFERS BUT HATE SURFING

Hawaii, as everyone knows, is a surfer's paradise. On one occasion when we're on Oahu there are great waves, so I borrow some boards and invite everyone I'm with to surf. I've never been a surfer except as a little kid, riding the shore break with Pops at Kailua Beach. Never one to back down from a challenge, I decide to surf with the guys. Aaron, Dressen, Block, and all my other friends who surf take me to this spot they know. The waves are breaking way outside.

I have a little five-foot-ten Thruster, and I start paddling out, following far behind them. Turns out the break is about a quarter-mile from shore. I finally get out there, exhausted, and find that the waves that looked so small from shore are really massive. It's getting dark, and the tide's getting low. The guys all catch waves and look at me and yell, "Catch the next wave in!"

I'm out alone as the biggest set of the day pours in. I spin around and start paddling for the moon, scratching for the horizon. Everything's turning black as the waves shade the water beneath them. Somehow I barely make it over each wave, five or six of them in each set, hoping that none of them will break too far in front of me. When the set finally subsides and I finish paddling, I look back to see that I'm so far out that the hotels on shore are just dots. Everyone's already halfway in, and now I've got to paddle in alone, without ever catching a wave, and thinking how much this sucks. I'm stoked to get back on solid ground, but I can barely hold my arms up for the next three days.

A few days later the guys take me to a place called V-Land, in the area known as North Shore. They tell me to paddle out with them, saying, "Look, it's mellow. Come on!" I'm thinking about paddling out when all of a sudden Oster, who's first out, comes back in. He's bleeding from his chest after getting dragged over the coral reef. What am I thinkin'? Aaron and Oster are full surfers, and they want me to go out there? Those guys are nuts. Finally our friend Johnee Kop, another skate legend, says, "Okay, let's go to Diamond Head."

Although Kop assures me Diamond Head will be mellow, I get out there and can see sharp coral reef and sea urchins directly below me. A wave breaks just beyond me. I white-knuckle my board and get dragged over the reef, at this point not caring that the board I'm riding isn't mine. Finally I lose my board in the whitewater and start swimming in. This is not mellow at all and I am *not* stoked—in fact, I almost drown swimming in. I'm really glad to see shore, but when I arrive there's this big local guy who wants to kill me because my rogue board nearly hit him.

Riding the waves in California with Jay and Shogo is even worse. Those guys head for the surf at four thirty in the morning. I don't know why, but I sometimes go with them and watch as they ride waves, playing it close to a bunch of big rocks. The whole time I'm thinking how crazy they are and how I could have slept in, cruised to the skatepark at noon, and skated with a bunch of hot girls watching, instead of freezing alone on some wet rocks. And my friends wonder why I rarely surf!

DEATH OF THE PARTY

I celebrated my twentieth birthday at Chateau Marmont, the hotel in Hollywood where comedian John Belushi died from a speedball. That's the name given to an often deadly combination of heroin and cocaine: it takes you up and down at the same time, until your heart has had enough and finally gives out. But that's not on my mind this night. I'm here to celebrate.

We go out to a club for those twenty-one and up, but I have the door open, letting thirty of my friends in, all under age, some as young as fifteen, and all them rowdy skate punks. The place is packed with these gnarly dudes, and it's just insane. A fight breaks out in one corner, and everyone watches until another fight breaks out somewhere else. I've never been in a fight in my life and work at breaking them up whenever I can.

We spend the night and the next day at Chateau Marmont. I look out at the pool and at the big trees surrounding it. It crosses my mind that you couldn't just jump out of one of *those* trees into the pool, cuz it's way too far a jump for anyone. Well, *almost* anyone. Aaron is still intoxicated from the night before when he climbs high into one of the trees, swaying back and forth so he can use it as a springboard. He's got the branch flexed back as far as it will go, and when it starts to spring forward he jumps. He barely makes it into the pool that time.

Most of my time is spent in Hollywood or Venice Beach. These are exciting and strange places to be a skater, and I love the artist, movie star, and rock-band energy that vibrates through the streets. As a kid I had a friend named Jamie Slovak. Jamie is the younger brother of Chili Peppers' guitarist Hillel Slovak. I'm friends with Hillel and the rest of the band, but I'm closer with Jamie because he's my age. We hang out on Melrose in front of Fairfax High almost every day, skating and terrorizing the tourists.

Years later Hillel will make headlines when he dies from a heroin overdose. I attend the funeral. This is a really sad day and a wakeup call for the Chili Peppers and all those who are in our scene and the music world.

But I don't feel a need to change any more than I already have. After all, in my mind I'm no longer using anything that could kill me. ✺

THE FIRST MANEUVER I INVENTED, THE TWEAK AIR. © *CESARIO "BLOCK" MONTANO.*

ANDRECHT HAND PLANT AT MY HOUSE IN HOLLYWOOD, CA.
© CESARIO "BLOCK" MONTANO.

VERT IS DEAD;
LONG LIVE VERT

The way I lived, I never thought
I would live to see twenty-one.
—CHRISTIAN HOSOI

CHAPTER 11

When you're all about raging like I am, you look forward to one day more than all others. That's right, your twenty-first birthday. My twenty-first arrives right on schedule, October 5, 1988. There's a lot more to celebrate than just staying alive for over two decades, though that in itself has been quite a trick.

Life is about as close to perfect for me as it gets in this world. I'm at the top of my game in both vert and street skating, battling it out for first on vert ramps with Hawk and with guys like Tommy Guerrero in street skating. I appear on TV and in countless videos, and I'm moving into a popularity that soars past the world of skateboarding. I'm featured on a Converse poster where I have nothing on but my Converses. The caption reads, "All you need!"

I continue to push my skating, my image, and my partying. Everywhere I go people recognize me, and while I don't know all of them, I know everybody I care to. I have the respect of my peers, and since I'm generous with my friends, I have more of those than I can count. Everyone is healthy and happy, and most are prosperous. What better time to celebrate with an insane party?

I have some T-shirts made up for my twenty-first with graphics of a dog biting a skateboard on them. I give them out to all my friends at the party, but it turns out I don't have one for everyone since over three thousand people attend. I'll spend over $15,000 on that bash by the time it's finished! That's a lot of money in 1988, but to me it's worth every cent, since a person turns twenty-one only once.

I want to mark that occasion in my own style and yet in typical Hollywood fashion, so I rent an entire floor of the Park Plaza Hotel, including the ballroom and the restaurant. Max Perlich is the DJ, and Skatemaster Tate is the MC. Hot local bands Schoolly D and Charlie Chan get the crowd pumped as they rip a few sets to warm things up for reggae star Eek-a-Mouse.

The place is booming when Eek-a-Mouse takes the stage dressed like a skater, with a borrowed Pro-Tec helmet perched on his head. He's a big act back then, and the crowd just goes off when he rolls out. The helmet doesn't fit him. Besides being a big act, he's a big guy—huge, like six-foot-six. Most skaters are about half his size. He's squeezed

FIRST EVER PUBLISHED PHOTO OF ME, IN *SKATEBOARDER* MAGAZINE. TAKEN IN 1979. PUBLISHED IN JUNE 1980. © *TED TERREBONNE.*

RIDING FOR THE BONES BRIGADE. MARINA DEL REY SKATEPARK.
GOLD CUP SERIES. 1980. © GLEN E. FRIEDMAN.

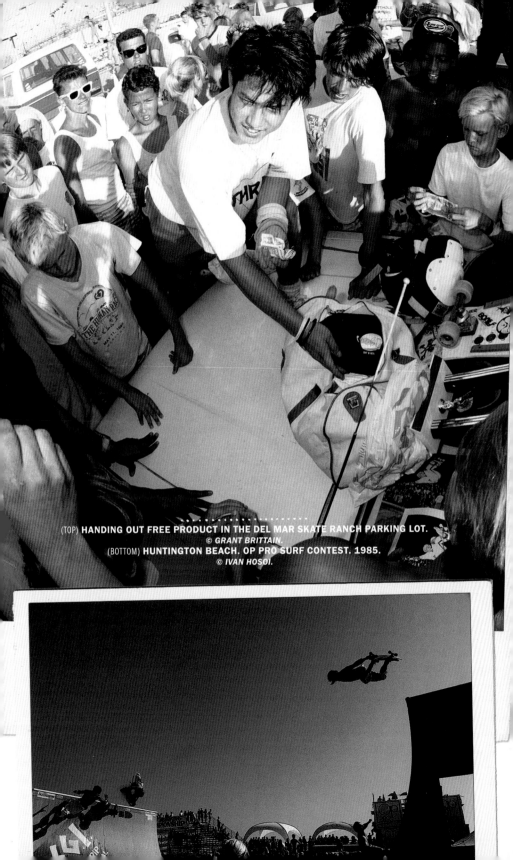

(TOP) **HANDING OUT FREE PRODUCT IN THE DEL MAR SKATE RANCH PARKING LOT.**
© *GRANT BRITTAIN.*
(BOTTOM) **HUNTINGTON BEACH. OP PRO SURF CONTEST. 1985.**
© *IVAN HOSOI.*

ROCKET AIR AT WESTMINSTER RAMP. JEFF GROSSO ON DECK. CIRCA MID-'80S.
© GRANT BRITTAIN.

NOVEMBER 1985 $1.50

THRASHER

TM

CAPITOLA CORRUPTED

EUROPE EXHAUSTED

BANNED IN BOSTON

DEL MAR DAMAGE

11
0 17112
102025

HOLIDAY HAVOC AT ANAHEIM CONVENTION CENTER. HIGH AIR CONTEST. 1985.
COURTESY OF HOSOI FAMILY COLLECTION AND SANTA CRUZ.

(TOP) **MASTER BEDROOM WALK-IN CLOSET. CIRCA 1989.** © *GRANT BRITTAIN.*
(MIDDLE) **VENICE BEACH VSA RAMP. MID-'80S.** © *IVAN HOSOI.*
(BOTTOM) **KNEE-ON AIR. 1987.** © *IVAN HOSOI.*

FIRST PUBLISHED IN *HIGH TIMES* MAGAZINE. EAGLE ROCK RAMP. 1984.
© *GLEN E. FRIEDMAN/STRAIGHT EDGE.*

TEAM HOSOI

49ERS SUPER BOWL HOSOI SKATEBOARDS AD. 1989. *HOSOI FAMILY COLLECTION.*

LAX FULL PIPES. EARLY '90S. © CESARIO "BLOCK" MONTANO.

RAMP RIOT IN BELLS BEACH, AUSTRALIA. HAND-DRAWN MARK "GONZ" GONZALES ART.
HOSOI FAMILY COLLECTION.

AT KELLY BELMAR'S POOL.
(TOP) **FRONTSIDE INVERT. 1991.**
© *GRANT BRITTAIN.*
(BOTTOM) **INDY AIR.**
© *GRANT BRITTAIN.*

PHOTO SHOOT WITH RHYTHM AND CLASSIC IN FRONT OF THE SANCTUARY CHURCH. 2008.
HOSOI FAMILY COLLECTION.

....
(TOP) **ALO OHANA FAMILY REUNION: JENNIFER, ME, MOM, AND RHYTHM.** 2005.
(BOTTOM) **POPS AND ME.** 2009. *HOSOI FAMILY COLLECTION.*

....
(TOP) **MOTHER'S MEMORIAL SERVICE AND SCATTERING OF
ASHES AT LANIKAI BEACH, OAHU. 2010.**
(BOTTOM) **TRUE LOVE.** *HOSOI FAMILY COLLECTION.*

HURLEY PRO. COASTAL CARNAGE IN HUNTINGTON BEACH. 2011.
HOSOI FAMILY COLLECTION.

into a pair of elbow pads that look the size of dimes on him. He's not wearing shoes as he rides out on Tate's longboard. He stops, grabs the mic, smiles broadly, and says, "It's my friend's birthday-y-y-y." When he starts singing "Happy Birthday," everybody joins in. Having a few thousand of your best friends sing "Happy Birthday" to you is one insane rush.

A twenty-first birthday is the closest thing we have in the United States to an occasion that symbolizes a kid becoming an adult. It's also the first time a kid can buy alcohol legally. Of course, you *need* alcohol for such an occasion, and we are well supplied. Just as at my twentieth birthday bash last year, not everyone is old enough to drink legally—not by a long shot. But some of my younger skater buddies are pushing to get into the bar, and who's gonna stop them? There aren't any graduates from finishing school here, but street kids and a gnarly mixture of artists, actors, musicians, models, dealers, and gangsters, all colliding with a wall of crazy skaters. Everyone's surging with energy, and they're all easily set off. Fights break out here and there, but the music just keeps bumping. As I said before, I'm no fighter, but I don't mind seeing a good brawl from time to time. These guys don't disappoint.

DOMINICAN REPUBLIC STADIUM DEMO WITH SERGIE VENTURA.
© CESARIO "BLOCK" MONTANO.

So . . . those are some of the highlights of an amazing night and what looks to me, when I get up the next day, like the perfect launch pad for the next phase of my career.

RISING SON

My friend Ice-T has just finished a rap song called "Body Count," and he wants to run a skate video over it. He has Duncan and me gather all the skate videos we can find, and he edits them to the music, showing all these skaters slamming down hard. Smashing your face into concrete fits perfectly with "Body Count," and I'm paid $4,000 for my trouble. With some of that money I buy an immaculate all-white 1977 Eldorado Biarritz Caddy with gold trim, white-leather interior, and hydraulics, letting me lift it or drop it at will. It's the perfect ride for the club scene. Thanks, Ice!

Ice invites us up to his place in the Hollywood Hills. From the balcony he points and says, "Madonna lives down there." He's a cool and smart businessman, especially considering where he's from: the streets and the L.A. gang scene. I admire him and what he's done, but I'm thinking that one day I'm gonna move up here and I'll be telling someone else what he told me. For now, though, I'm content living right where I do. Echo Park is beyond halfway there.

You don't usually think of stoners as being career-driven, but I sure am, and it's paying off. Everything I put my hand to works out, and I continue to break new ground in skating, business, and the publicity I get for it all. I never save any money, though, because it flows like water and I don't anticipate a drought anytime soon.

There are no more than fifty pro skateboarders in the world, and only a few of them seek to make an actual living at it. And yet at a time when the average NBA player is taking down maybe $300,000 a year, my estimated annual income stands at nearly $350,000. I appreciate the success, but to me money is nothing more than fuel to keep the party raging.

Even with all the distractions at the business end of things, skateboarding is still the most important thing in my life. Most skateboarders are specialists, good at either vert or street. Having grown up at Marina

Skatepark and on the Venice boardwalk, I've learned from the best in both, and I win or place in every street or vert event I enter.

ABOUT TO GO UNDERGROUND. *HOSOI FAMILY COLLECTION.*

I'm on a roll all the way to Japan, where my name is huge. People tend to be much more reserved in that country than they are in California, and their style is basically the polar opposite of Brazilians'. But I really love Japan and the Japanese people. In addition, I enjoy helping break down the cultural barriers between us. From the first I've been received there like a full-blown celebrity, and I feel totally at home.

It's 1990 and the Lotte gum company has flown a bunch of us to Japan for a big skate contest. Jay Adams, David Hackett, Dave Duncan, and Mofo are the judges. In all we travel there with an entourage of about thirty-five skateboarders. We're all on the same plane, partying hard. As

例えば、駅のトイレをどんどんキレイにする　JR

· · · · · · · · · · · · · · · · ·
(TOP) JAPAN. BLOCK, SERGIE, POPS, AND ME.
(BOTTOM) WITH MISTER KAZAKI,
THE SANTA CRUZ
SKATEBOARDS DISTRIBUTOR IN JAPAN.
© CESARIO "BLOCK" MONTANO.

I move up and down the aisle with my ghetto blaster at full volume, I see guys chopping lines of coke on the armrests. When we drink our section of the plane dry, one of our friends demands that the flight attendants hit up first class for their alcohol. She refuses, telling us to keep quiet and try to get some sleep. No chance *that's* gonna happen. Craig Johnson yells right in her face at the top of his lungs, "Bring me more beer now!" She bursts into tears and runs away, but she returns with a bunch of beers to keep him quiet. It's a full party in the air, lasting for hours, until everybody else is sick of us.

As we're landing, Jay plays an Andrew Dice Clay cassette at top volume. He cues up the tape where the comedian says, "What do you use to blindfold a Japanese man?" Answer: "Dental floss." We're laughing hysterically as our fellow passengers, many of them Japanese people heading home, look on in disbelief. I can tell they're really irritated with us, but true to their polite and reserved style, they don't say anything. When we get off the plane, the cops are there to meet us. They don't detain or arrest anybody, but they escort us to the personal bus that they have waiting for us.

First prize in the Lotte event is $7,500 for vert and $7,500 for street. All expenses are paid for everyone, and even the judges make out, each earning $5,000 for the week. We're treated to the best of everything. While the kids all go crazy for us, their parents don't know what has hit them. (I'm bummed now, in retrospect, that we were so rude and served as such bad examples, but we never thought of that then; it was all about *us*. Pedal down, join us, or get out of the way.)

Jay is on the judges' stand, but he looks bad; something is clearly wrong. I find out later that he took a full bottle of NoDoz the night before. Suddenly he freaks out, thinking he's having a heart attack, and he gets rushed to the hospital. Turns out instead to be a full-blown anxiety attack.

I take out both the street and the ramp events, get a huge trophy, and return home with the equivalent of $15,000, the biggest cash prize in skateboarding history to that point. The money is paid in Japanese yen, which translates to a lot of paper. I shove it into every article of clothing, in my luggage and carry-on, to transport it out of the country. We celebrate in Japan and all the way home, on the plane. When Pops picks us up at the airport, we carry the celebration on in the car. I'm laughing and shouting as he drives, throwing handfuls of money into the air as if it were confetti. I have so much cash coming in that this seems like Monopoly money. I never contemplate not being able to get more. I'm so cavalier about cash that I carelessly stash a big wad of yen behind the TV at my house, and I forget about it until I find it by accident about a year later.

CH-CH-CH-CHANGES

According to the skate media, vert is basically dead. To some this is a slap in the face they will never recover from. As much as I hate admitting it, vert really *is* over, at least competitively. But I'm not stuck in any one gear; I'll need to adapt (or die with it), expanding my already strong street-skating roots. According to Stacy Peralta, "When skateboarding changed, Christian was right there to change with it."

Not all vert specialists cope with this very well. Just as they did when the parks closed down, some skaters quit skating, and others seem to quit on life altogether. Some of my friends who have dabbled in alcohol or hard drugs before now retreat deeply into them. For many it's a one-way trip.

Many of my early skate heroes abandon the scene completely, and I hear rumors that TA isn't skating much and is getting out of control. I realize that's possible, but I know not to believe everything I hear. Everyone in the skate world talks about TA the way people in the music world talk about Bob Marley. Something's up with TA, but I'm not sure what. Maybe a girl, maybe a drug. Actually, the way we're all living, it could be just about anything.

It doesn't take long for Jay to completely drop out of the skate scene. Like TA, Jay still rips, but he doesn't like how commercialism has puffed up so many egos. He no longer wants the identity of Jay Adams, professional skateboarder, opting instead for Jay Adams, guy who surfs and skates for fun.

Jay is fully locked into his punk-rock thing and plugs right into the rage, chaos, and pandemonium which that scene often inspires. "For me to have a good night," he says, "someone else is gonna have a really bad night." A good example: Jay and Polar Bear attend a Suicidal Tendencies party, where Jay steals a six-foot-long sandwich that he stashes in the trunk of his car. The two of them drive to this place called Oki Dog on Santa

LIEN JUDO AIR. APRADO SKATEPARK
ON THE BEACH IN RIO DE JANEIRO.
© CESARIO "BLOCK" MONTANO.

AIR OVER A RAMP IN ITALY. © *MORIZEN FOCHE COURTESY OF* THRASHER *MAGAZINE.*

Monica Boulevard. Once at Oki Dog, they spread the sandwich out on the table and invite everyone to join in eating it. Of course, that's bad for business, and the Oki Dog's owner tells them to leave. Jay nearly starts a fight with the owner, but he and Polar Bear eventually do split. Out on the street again, they're pumped full of adrenaline and rage. When they see two guys walking arm in arm toward them, Jay shouts something derogatory. One guy responds with a heartfelt "F--k you!" Jay returns the words, and it's on.

Jay's taking off his shirt to fight when the guy runs over, socks him, and knocks him down. Polar Bear swings immediately and knocks the guy out. Jay struggles up and charges at the other guy, knocking him over a row of newspaper machines. When the guy that Jay knocked down finally gets partway up, Jay runs over and kicks him in the face. Both guys are unconscious when Jay and Polar Bear split.

After they leave, five or six guys who'd been watching come up and one of them finishes the job, kicking the guy to death with a steel-toe boot. Jay and Polar Bear are arrested for their role, and Jay ends up doing four months in jail for manslaughter. The guys who actually committed the murder go free after falsely testifying against Jay and Polar Bear. That's the way Jay tells it, and I have no reason not to believe him.

Life continues down a dark path for Jay when his brother is killed and his mother dies, both within a few months' time. According to Jay, "I was so angry I wanted to shoot everybody; instead, I shot myself," meaning that he put needles into his arms. Soon he'll face other charges and other problems, all stemming from his being strung out on heroin.

I can't imagine that even worse news is coming, but there it is, announced on TV. It's February 1991, and Louanna and I—still together at that point—are spending a rare quiet night at home, cuddled together watching *A Current Affair* or some other TV news show. We're shocked by a big story about pro skater Mark "Gator" Rogowski, who has allegedly killed Jessica Bergsten. What? Jessica is a friend that *I* introduced to Gator. The whole story is so brutal that we can't believe it.

We all know and love Gator, and we certainly had no idea he would ever do anything like this. Rusler remembers seeing him shortly before

he got arrested. According to him, "Gator was unique and funny and we all got along," he says, thinking of the old days. "Then one day we saw him at a tradeshow, carrying a Bible. We called to him, and he ignored us like the plague. Christian and I didn't say anything; we just looked at each other and wondered what was up. We had no idea of the complexity of his problem, but we knew that something weird was going on."

Not long after Gator's arrest for murder, he calls me from jail to say that Jessica accidentally suffocated. I was short with him: "Gator, Jessica's dead; you have to tell me the truth." He repeats that it was an accident and then says he hasn't been to court yet and that his calls are being recorded.

That's the last time I speak to Gator, but he sent me a letter recently apologizing for not being truthful with me at the time. He's now serving thirty-five years to life, and I hear that someone stabbed him in the throat, as prison justice for what he'd done. Now I realize that he was crying out for something back then. I only wish I'd had some words of wisdom to offer him at the time. ✳

HOSOI FAMILY COLLECTION.

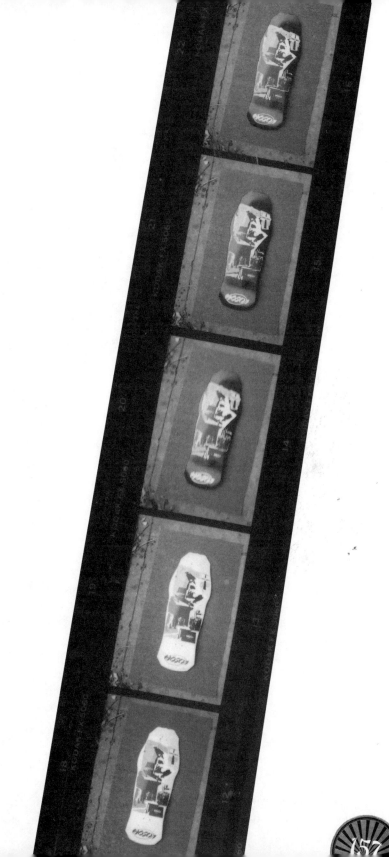

VENICE BEACH PAVILION. QUARTER PIPE TO WALL. *HOSOI FAMILY COLLECTION,*

CRACKS
IN THE FOUNDATION

There's ringing in my ears,
and a little blood trickling from my
head and down my neck.
—CHRISTIAN HOSOI

CHAPTER 12

Ever since its birth in the 1960s, skateboarding has risen and fallen in popularity. Many companies start up in the good times, make money for a while, and fold in the next downturn. Since styles in skating evolve so quickly, it's a tough business; very few companies survive for more than a decade.

In the early '90s the entire skate industry hits one of those walls and chases the rest of the economy into the black hole of recession. Nearly everybody in the industry gets smacked down. Prior to 1992 I've made hundreds of thousands of dollars each year just for skating. I'd make $1,000 an hour for a skate demo, for example. That's more than my attorneys squeeze from me. It seems as if there's no end in sight to the empire I'm building. Then the hangman pulls the lever and the floor falls out. It's not fatal for me, but it about kills the skateboarding market and I'm left standing alone.

I'm forced to put Hosoi Skateboards on hold, which is okay, but now one of my major sources of income—the sponsorship with Santa Cruz Skateboards—is being cut. They've gone up to paying me $8,000 a month by this time, but with the economy in the tank, they're gonna cut me back to $1,500. Only $1,500? I'm insulted. That's what I made when I was fourteen. I spend more than that on weed! I'm so pissed that now my main motivation in competition is to demolish every Santa Cruz rider. They're all my friends, but I can't wait to smoke every one of those dudes when we face off at an event. Nothing personal, mind you. One by one I take 'em all down, and it feels good. But I can't savor the victory because my other big sponsor, Jimmy'z, has just been sold to Ocean Pacific. Without Ganzer's creativity and leadership, the company fades until it's nothing but a memory. That's about it for my income. Now what?

CORPORATE TO CORE

Brad Dorfman is the owner of a skate-clothing company called Vision Street Wear. Vision is coming on strong, thanks to Dorfman being a smart businessman, so I call him to set up a meeting. At the meeting, I tell him straight out that his clothing brand sucks.

"You mean my stuff's not cool?" he asked, startled by my response.

"Not cool with my crew," I reply, knowing that he knows that my crew are the tastemakers in the skate industry. If they don't like it, nobody's gonna get near it.

Brad and I settle down to talk things out, and I convince him of the value of sponsoring me. I agree to endorse Vision's line and have them do board production in exchange for $60,000 the first year. Things go well until Dorfman begins focusing on the burgeoning snowboard industry. Orders for my skateboards pour in to Vision, but the wood needed for them is tied up by the snowboarding department. My boards simply aren't getting made.

When Vision doesn't work out, I'm left with nothing except what trickles in from demos and contests. Now I'm making even less than I did at fourteen. A lot less. Basically a few dollars more than nothing.

Even at my peak, the expenses from my high-rolling lifestyle nearly equal my income. I need tons of cash to keep the machine burning clean. I somehow continue hanging on to the W. C. Fields house and Louanna. That relationship, once fueled by nothing but fun, is now strained by the realities of life. We begin arguing all the time, and the tension snaps the cord that kept us together. Soon it's over and Louanna moves out, this time for good.

No sooner is Louanna gone than some of my hard-core skater buddies move in. Ray Bones, Peter Bill, and Robert Rusler are now there full-time. Eddie Reategui already has a room there, and Pops has been there since the beginning, living downstairs. True to form, we continue to rage while our world crumbles, spending down to the last penny. There's nothing and nobody to hold us back.

The best nightlife in the world is happening either in my bedroom or up the street on the Strip, even though I can no longer afford any of this. Oh well—since the match is lit, might as well burn it all to the ground.

Eric "Lil Man" Garber is a regular guest at the house; he hangs out and skates there a lot. The driveway's made of brick and stones. It's super steep and slippery. I'm out of town when trouble happens, but I'm told by those on hand that this is how it went down: Lil Man has parked the new Mustang 5.0 that his dad gave him at the top of the driveway. Some say he forgot to set the parking brake; others say someone—I won't say

who—loosens the parking brake and pops it out of gear. Anyway, the car rolls down the driveway, picks up speed, hits a rock ledge that acts like a jump ramp, and gets launched high into the air before landing on the roof of one of the bungalows below. Apparently the car stands up on end for a moment before it comes crashing down: boom! It's on the

RAY "BONES" RODRIGUEZ, ME, AND CESARIO "BLOCK" MONTANO.
© *CESARIO "BLOCK" MONTANO.*

news that night, talking about how they have to remove the vehicle with a giant crane. If you need a better visual, think *Blues Brothers* meets *Animal House* on steroids and weed with skateboards blasting through the air, along with the best friends and the hottest girls.

Besides skating, getting high, and hustling chicks, we love playing pool. We play for hours on end, days on end. Oster and Rusler are my main pool partners, and we basically own every table we ever hit. Here's what Rusler has to say about our pool-playing days:

IF YOU SAW CHRISTIAN'S DOCUMENTARY *RISING SON*, YOU KNOW THERE'S A PART IN THERE WHERE I SAY, "BRUCE LEE'S A LEGEND; CHRISTIAN HOSOI'S A LEGEND—GUYS LIKE SCOTT BAIO? I'M SORRY, BUT CHARLES IN CHARGE ISN'T A LEGEND." I SAID THAT BECAUSE OF ONE PARTICULAR NIGHT WHEN WE WENT OUT TO PLAY POOL. IT STARTED AFTER WE ROLLED INTO HOLLYWOOD BILLIARDS TO FIND A GAME. ONE NIGHT THERE'S SCOTT BAIO WITH THIS GUY JUSTIN MUR-DOCK. THEY'VE BEATEN EVERYBODY IN THE PLACE, SO THEY THINK THEY'RE PRETTY HOT.

WE STROLL IN. THEY KNOW WHO WE ARE, AND OUR REPUTATION AS POOL PLAYERS, SO THEY ASK US IF WE WANT TO PLAY FOR MONEY. WE DECIDE TO START WITH TWENTY BUCKS A GAME. BAIO BREAKS AND SINKS A FEW BALLS. IT'S CHRISTIAN'S TURN NEXT, AND HE RUNS THE TABLE. BY THE TIME CHRISTIAN FINISHES CLEARING THE TABLE, BAIO'S SO PISSED THAT HE SAYS, "I'M NOT GONNA PAY YOU." I STEP IN AND REPLY, "FINE, HOW 'BOUT I WRAP MY POOL CUE AROUND YOUR HEAD INSTEAD?" IT WASN'T THE MONEY—NONE OF US AT THAT TABLE WOULD HAVE MISSED TWENTY BUCKS—BUT HE WAS BEING SUCH A JERK. FINALLY WE AGREE ON DOUBLE OR NOTHING.

THEY RACK, AND CHRISTIAN BREAKS AND RUNS THE TABLE AGAIN. HE'S DOING THESE ICONIC BANK SHOTS, LOOKING STRAIGHT INTO JUSTIN'S EYES WHILE CALLING THE POCKET BEFORE SINKING IT. NOW I'M FEELING LIKE PAUL NEWMAN IN *THE COLOR OF MONEY*, AND I'M SAYING, "OKAY, PAY UP, BRO." IN THE END SCOTT AND JUSTIN PAY US AND ARE COOL ABOUT IT. FINALLY SCOTT COMES UP, SHAKES HANDS,

AND SAYS, "THAT WAS A GOOD GAME." LATER JUSTIN AND I BECOME GOOD FRIENDS.

ANOTHER TIME WE'RE PLAYING AND IN WALK L.A. LAKERS OWNER JERRY BUSS AND THE LEGENDARY NBA STAR WILT CHAMBERLAIN. CHAMBERLAIN SAYS, "WE'LL PLAY YOU GUYS." WELL, WE SMOKE 'EM, WIN EVERY GAME.

NOW WE'RE BACK AT THE HOUSE AT THE POOL TABLE, AND CHRISTIAN LOOKS AT ME AND SAYS, "RACK 'EM." I'M LIKE, "I THOUGHT YOU'D NEVER ASK." HE'S SMOKIN' A FATTY WITH ONE HAND, SLAPPIN' THE CUE, AND SUCKIN' HIS TEETH THE WAY HE SOMETIMES DOES WHEN HE'S CONCENTRATING. HE'S WAITING FOR ME TO GET THIS TIGHT RACK. I TAKE THE RACK OFF AND I'M LIKE, "BREAK 'EM UP, PUNK." ALL OF A SUDDEN IT'S LIKE, *C-R-RACK!* I WOULDN'T HAVE BELIEVED IT IF I HADN'T SEEN IT WITH MY OWN EYES: HE BREAKS ONE-HANDED—THE FATTY IS STILL IN THE OTHER—AND SINKS THE EIGHT BALL, MEANING HE WINS THE GAME OFF THE BREAK! HE JUST LOOKS UP AND IS LIKE, "RACK 'EM AGAIN." SO I RACK 'EM AGAIN AND *WHACK!* AGAIN HE SINKS THE EIGHT BALL WITH ONE HAND. I WAS SO DEVASTATED I THREW A BALL ONTO THE FLOOR AND WALKED OFF TO BED.

My memory is that I sank the eight ball using two hands the first time, and with one hand on the second game. I like Rusler's version of the story better, though.

DOWNSIZING AND DOWNSLIDING

True to my long-standing practice of spending all my money as I earn it, I haven't saved a cent. With little or no income remaining, I'm forced to vacate the awesome Fields house and move back in with my mom around 1991. I can't move my ramp, so I leave it there, hoping beyond hope that the next tenant will skate it, even though I know there's no way any other skateboarder but me could afford to move in. What breaks my heart most is leaving my nine cats behind. I can't abandon them to the shelter, where their number might come up before adoption; they'll have better survival chances right on the grounds. The property is big and wild, and I figure they'll be better off finding their own dinners of squirrels and mice.

My mom lives only a few blocks away from the place I'm leaving. I drive there with some boxes of stuff, but the rest will have to go in storage. I'm broke, but my exodus is in style, in my McLaren sports car. That car was like $40,000 back in the late '80s, and I bought it with $12,000 down. After the move I gave it to my mom. I have to part with my classic '62 Harley-Davidson motorcycle too. Man, I've acquired a lot of stuff in a few years. I've got enough clothing to open a department store—including probably fifty leather jackets and hundreds of shoes—along with jewelry, artwork, furniture, all kinds of trophies and awards, stacks of skateboards, and various other fruits of the good life.

With hundreds of storage companies to choose from, I pick a unit owned by the exact wrong one. I have no idea, of course, that everything I store is going to be demolished by something I can't see coming, the 1994 Northridge earthquake, which we live near the epicenter of. The violent shaking seems to last forever at Mom's place. I later hear that some motorists have been buried beneath tons of concrete and steel when a portion of the Santa Monica Freeway collapsed on them, and I also learn that a chunk of I-10 landed right on my storage unit. While my loss is nothing compared to that of

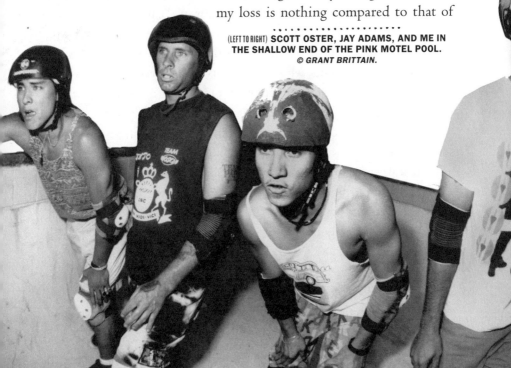

(LEFT TO RIGHT) SCOTT OSTER, JAY ADAMS, AND ME IN THE SHALLOW END OF THE PINK MOTEL POOL.
© GRANT BRITTAIN.

those who died, the earthquake has cost me most of my possessions and many of my mementos. Eventually everything gets dug out and moved to another storage area.

I don't even recognize my belongings when I see them again. All my trophies—everything I stored there—are smashed beyond repair, and I feel detached from my legacy. As much as I pretend otherwise, my life has taken an abrupt turn and is now far from perfect. I've pushed the envelope in every area, risked it all, and for the first time I haven't come out a winner. Something beyond my control seems to be taking over.

A calculated risk is different than a crapshoot, where you throw the dice with no idea of what number they're gonna land on. I'm a risk taker, but a calculated risk taker. In skating I won't do things unless I'm pretty confident they'll work. That's why I never really get hurt on the ramp. I won't just go for broke without knowing the outcome; that's do or die. I'm not a do-or-die type, although most people watching me probably figure that's how I operate. I rehearse the motions mentally before I attempt a trick, and consequently I've only broken one bone and never had any concussions. If I had gotten hurt, I would have been really badly hurt. I usually skate without a helmet or elbow pads, not even a shirt on. I should be all scraped up, but I rarely have cuts or bruises on my body.

The closest I ever get to disaster on a skateboard is when I'm doing a demo as a kid in St Louis, Missouri, at a Six Flags amusement park. The ramp there has a weird transition to it, and I pump at the wrong time and am soon flying through space. When you're upside down, flying twenty feet above the earth, lots can go wrong. When things spin out of control in vert skating, you slam back down to the bottom of the ramp, hard. I'm nearly at full height when I launch my board, and I land on the ramp before it does.

I hit hard, but I know how to fall and so I land without injury. Still, in the split second that I lie there, I hear the crowd sucking their breath in and realize that my board is following me back down. In fact, out of the corner of my eye I see it rocketing right at me. Before I can move aside it hits my helmet so hard I nearly pass out. There's ringing in my ears, and a little blood trickling from my head and down my neck. I pull off my helmet carefully and check myself out further: it turns out to be nothing more than a scratch on my ear. If I hadn't been wearing a helmet, I could have been killed. Instead, I brush myself off and wave to my fans to let them know I'm okay.

Others haven't gotten away so cleanly. I've seen injured legs, arms, teeth, chin, eyes, ankles, wrists—you name it. I can't tell you how many times I've watched skateboarders carted off in ambulances. The way I've lived, I should have a history of broken bones and stitches all over my body. Actually, I should be dead.

I'm never one to give up, and I figure I'll bounce back even if the rest of the skateboarding industry doesn't. I'm still at the top of what's left of the skateboarding world, winning contests, making appearances, signing autographs, and living a pretty good life, all things considered. Even though I'm making a fraction of the money I used to and I've had to move back home, the radical downslide doesn't begin until 1989, when I'm twenty-two.

The trouble starts on a typical night at a typical club, where not much is happening. Someone asks if I want to do some speed, something I haven't done since I was seventeen, back when I was snorting coke. I'm bored, so I'm like, "Yeah, whatever; let's do it." We snort it right there at the table and it burns like—well, I can't believe how badly it burns. Following the burn, though, I'm pumped with energy and feel really good and alert. That fix turns out to be meth, and I like it.

Meth doesn't make me feel anything other than up and ready to take on the world. I never experience any of the negative side effects my friends do: uncontrollable twitching, an inability to eat or sleep. They don't want anything but more and more meth, and they don't take very good care of themselves. They look sucked up and bugged out. I eat, sleep, and keep myself clean, cuz I still want to get with chicks.

Since I've smoked an ounce of weed a week since the age of fifteen, I understand how to do drugs and maintain my life. As I mentioned before, compared to most of my friends I'm basically a nondrinker, so I usually drive when we go out. That helps me think of myself as a responsible user, whatever that is. So now I snort meth from time to time, but it doesn't have its hooks in me. Not yet.

POINT OF NO RETURN. © CESARIO "BLOCK" MONTANO.

NO TURNING BACK. *HOSOI FAMILY COLLECTION.*

OUT OF FOCUS

You could die down here,
be just another accident statistic.

—BOB DYLAN

CHAPTER 13

As the skateboard recession drills deeper, everybody in the industry is either crashing and burning or scrambling to stay afloat. One of my top team riders, Sergie Ventura, works as a waiter, and Duncan has returned to carpentry, making ramps for all the companies and events that require them. I hear that Hawk's company, Birdhouse, is teetering on bankruptcy. Here he is, the most famous skater of all time, and he doesn't even have his own skateboard model any longer. Like me, he's fallen from being a highly paid pro to scraping to get by. Neither of us has ever really worked before, unless you count skateboarding as work, and we aren't about to start now.

We're scrambling to get other things going, but his temporary solution to the downturn is to perform skate demos at Six Flags, Dallas. He performs three demos a day for a total of a hundred bucks a day. Two years earlier we would have earned thousands for that sort of gig. But Tony and I love skating more than anything, and we're convinced it will soon make a comeback. We continue sharpening our skills for the next time we meet in competition. We're still skating hard, improving, and setting the pace for the sport.

While we concentrate on skateboarding, the rest of the country has more significant matters on its mind. There's an undercurrent of violence in the United States that could erupt at any time.

FATAL ATTRACTIONS

In 1992 I'm still living in L.A. when the city boils over into what's euphemistically called civil unrest or the Rodney King uprising. Call it what you want; this is a full-blown riot. As soon as the verdict is announced and King's arresting officers are proclaimed innocent, people take to the streets—some to protest, some to loot, some to unload years of pent-up frustration on the people and structures around them.

While people flee the city in droves, I head the other way, toward the heart of the action. A friend of mine who owns a bookstore on Beverly, right near Melrose, has asked if I can watch his store for him so he can get home. I've never experienced a major riot before, so I snap at the opportunity. The city is blanketed in smoke and violence, and I'm casually cruising toward this war zone in my Mustang with Pops, trying to avoid all the military-type stops.

Martial law has been declared. Cops are out on patrol, and you can be arrested just for being out after 6:00 P.M. Still, I'm a master at deceiving the law, and I'm sure the cops will believe me if I say it's an emergency and I need to get somewhere. Maybe I'll tell them I'm rushing Pops to the hospital. But the cops more than have their hands full that night, and nobody ever stops us. We arrive at my friend's store near dark to see walls of flames devouring shops up and down the street.

To one side is a camera store with its doors blasted open, fully on fire. The neighboring shop is smoldering after being burned to the ground. Windows and doors are smashed in stores as far as we can see, and there's nobody around to stop the anarchy. For looters, this is the ultimate shopping spree. Everything is up for grabs: people race up and down the streets carrying purloined TVs, furniture, cases of liquor, stereos, and other big-ticket items. The entire world looks like some Jim Morrison nightmare—and I love it!

My friend sees us coming and rushes toward us. "Hey Christian, thanks for agreeing to hang around and make sure nobody breaks in," he says, grabbing a few things to take with him. "I'm glad to help keep your place safe," I say, relishing the thought of blasting off a few rounds with my nine-millimeter gun if some fool walks through that door with bad intentions. Then the owner races away from the riot zone. While that's the smart thing to do and most people wouldn't blame him, I'm perfectly happy to stay put, thinking about all the fun Pops and I are gonna have.

We hang out at the store all night, cuz once people are in the area, the cops won't let them leave. The streets are haunted by the distant sounds of people shouting, the sirens of cop cars and fire trucks, and occasional gunshots. We just kick back, smoking joints all night, and I stay armed and ready. We have front row seats for the best show ever and are disappointed that nobody tries entering the shop.

Looking back on that night now, I see my reaction as bizarre. While I didn't enjoy the prospect of other people being hurt and harmed, I *did* enjoy the scent of danger. I got the same sort of rush from tempting fate that I get from skating big ramps.

BRAIN-FRYERS, BELL-RINGERS, AND OTHER DELIGHTS

I'm regularly buying quarter-pounds of weed now, not to make money but so I can get my stash for free. My friends want to get high nearly as much as I do, so when I sell them a little something, they often break me off an eighth of an ounce. Now and then I score a bunch of mescaline pills and move them for twenty bucks each. The pills are so tiny that some skeptics comment, "That little thing won't get me high." Then they take it and get obliterated and run back to me for more. Sometimes we burn weed soaked in PCP. That's a brain-fryer. Once in a while we'll freebase cocaine or take big crack hits, which people call bell-ringers cuz you get a ringing in your head. But that buzz comes in and goes out quickly; it's a short, intense high. That's why crackheads keep hitting the pipe again and again.

By the mid-'90s I'm still okay, but anyone who looks closely can see that my life is beginning to fray around the edges. It doesn't help that Pops moves to Hawaii to take care of his father, who's dying of cancer. Shortly after that, my mom tells me she's moving to the East Coast to get remarried. I ask her, "Does he love you?" When she replies yes, I give the marriage my blessing, which is kind of strange since I'm the child and she's the parent. My mother's marriage to her husband, Mitch Mitchell, turns out to be an excellent decision. And I'm left with a great stepfather. I call him Pop. There have never been many restrictions forced on me, but having my parents around has been at least somewhat stabilizing. If I needed to borrow twenty bucks, get encouragement, or sit down to a homemade meal, I could always drop by my mom's house, and she took me back in when I lost my place in Echo Park. If I needed sage philosophical advice on life, I could drop by to visit my dad. That's no longer the case. One chapter in my life is ending and another is about to begin.

Suddenly, none of the anchors in my life is in place. Because I'm using more and more meth, I don't like being around my friends and family that much anymore. Nobody I grew up with is using drugs as heavily as I am, so I avoid the very people who could help me. Pops is probably the least strict dad in history, but even he's concerned, asking what I'm up to. When I answer that I'm raging, he says, "Okay, just be careful while you're raging." But even he will give in to the power of meth when I visit him years later on Oahu. In the mid-'90s, though, when I offer him meth for the first time, it's no big deal. After all, we've done acid and coke together since I was fifteen and once smoked heroin together when I was seventeen. He doesn't get strung out; he just does a little bit once in a while.

As for me, I'm well past that point. Drugs are no longer just part of life; they are life itself. My friends and I have all tried everything there is to try, and one by one we've settled on our drug of choice. For some it's coke; for others heroin; for me it's crystal methamphetamine. You know, *meth, speed, tweak, ice*—whatever you want to call it. I can handle it, I tell myself; but not everyone else can. Like Rusler, for example. I'm not exactly sure what drugs he's using, but whatever they are, he's not handling them well at all. He's no longer a fun, outgoing guy, and we don't see him around much. When we do he looks terrible. Turns out he came to think pretty much the same thing about me. His recollection of those days:

I WAS GETTING HEAVILY INTO THE DARK DAYS OF ADDICTION, AND I STARTED ISOLATING. CHRISTIAN AND MY BROTHER GARY CAME BY AND TALKED TO ME. I REMEMBER CHRISTIAN SAYING THAT HE LOVED ME, THAT A LOT OF PEOPLE CARED ABOUT ME, AND THAT I STILL HAD A LOT LEFT TO DO. I'LL NEVER FORGET THAT. HE BROUGHT TRUTH TO ME, AND HE STAYED WITH ME DURING ONE VERY DARK NIGHT. OF COURSE HE WAS PARTYING THAT WHOLE TIME. THAT MADE ME KIND OF JEALOUS THAT I COULDN'T HANDLE IT, WHILE HE AND MY BROTHER COULD. CHRISTIAN TOLD ME THAT I NEEDED TO BALANCE THINGS BY QUITTING HARD DRUGS, JUST SMOKING WEED AND TAKING CARE OF MY RESPONSIBILITIES. HE SAID THAT IF I DID THAT, I'D BE FINE. THAT WAS ALL COOL, BUT IT WOULDN'T WORK FOR ME. WHAT STUCK WITH ME WAS CHRISTIAN TELLING ME THAT HE LOVED ME.

NOT LONG AFTER THAT TALK I WENT TO REHAB AND GOT CLEAN. CHRISTIAN HAD MOVED OUT OF TOWN BY THEN, AND I STARTED HEARING HORROR STORIES ABOUT HIM. BUT I WAS THINKING, THERE'S NO WAY HE CAN'T BEAT WHATEVER CHALLENGE LIFE THROWS AT HIM. I NEARLY WENT TO AN INTERVENTION WHERE EVERYONE WAS TRYING TO GET HIM TO QUIT. BLOCK WANTED TO KIDNAP HIM AND BRING HIM BACK HERE TO L.A. I WAS WORKING THE TWELVE-STEP PROGRAM BY

THEN AND KNEW THAT I WAS POWERLESS TO HELP HIM IF HE DIDN'T WANT TO QUIT. I WENT TO VISIT HIS MOTHER AND SHE TOO WAS WORRIED ABOUT HIM. PEOPLE WERE SAYING BAD THINGS ABOUT CHRISTIAN, AND I WOULD TELL THEM, "SHUT UP; YOU DON'T KNOW HIM."

NAVIGATING THE NO ZONE

It's late in 1993, and I'm in what I call the "no zone." With no direction home, I'm drifting through a sea of drugs and empty promises. Micke Alba rescues me for a time by inviting me to check out a new skate scene, especially this one pool he's skating in Huntington Beach. Sounds intriguing, so I agree to go. Together with Micke and Eddie, I speed down to Orange County. The pool is everything Micke claimed it would be, and we skate it for hours on end, not just that one day but often. In Huntington Beach I meet some friends for life, including the guy who owns the pool, Barrett "Chicken" Deck. Chicken and I share the same birthdate and have lots of other things in common.

Prior to this time, I rarely ventured beyond L.A. unless I was traveling to a demo or a contest. At the time Huntington Beach was nothing more than a freeway sign I passed on my way to someplace else. Now, though, it quickly begins to feel like home, and the Orange County vibe there is new and appealing.

Chicken has a successful screen-printing business, knows business generally, and has a lot of good ideas. We get along great and I've been contemplating a new venture anyway, so I mention, "Hey, why don't we start a company together?" He agrees enthusiastically.

We knock around some ideas for a skateboarding company and fix on the name Milk Skateboard Goods (MSG). The name, which has no relation to anything in skateboarding, is intentionally bland, and that's exactly why we like it. All the artists and hard-core skaters think it's sick, but the public probably thinks it's kind of weird. Anyway, we run with it. Problem is that the pie is shrinking in the skate industry and the economy in general has fallen on increasingly hard times.

We have a silent partner in Milk who received a big settlement after his parents died in a plane crash in Orange County. He seems cool for a while, but he doesn't want to follow our direction. After a while, he splits from us to do his own thing. Another company down the drain.

Starting a skateboarding company is tough, even in the best of times. Now we have two strikes against us—the country is in bad shape financially, and skating has a bad name. Skaters are wearing baggy pants that few parents like, and with street skating blowing up, skaters are out all night carving up the streets, grinding handrails, curbs, and any other pieces of private property worth skating. Being an underground sport makes it popular with the rebels we gravitate toward, but it also makes it challenging to sell products to the people with the money, the parents.

While the skate industry is dying, the party scene seems to get bigger. By the time I move to Huntington Beach the place is one big raging party. Eddie is living at Chicken's too, and he's started his own company, called Public Skates. He's working hard, and his boards are starting to sell well. Chicken and I decide to start another venture, a skate company called Focus Skateboards, and we encourage him to join forces. Eddie wants to keep Public Skates going, but I say, "No, you've gotta get rid of it and concentrate 100 percent on Focus with us." He's uncertain of what to do when the phone rings for Public Skates and I answer it saying, "Focus Skateboards." I look at Eddie and start laughing. He's in and we're doing Focus! I thought I was doing him a favor, but it didn't turn out that way.

I move into Chicken's house in October of '93. At first it's Chicken, Eddie, and me living there and running the company. When our friend Dave Duncan shows up a bit later, he joins the company and sleeps on the couch. We all know the cliché about not doing business with your friends, and that's one of the reasons we *want* to do it: to prove everyone wrong. We also know there's a great opportunity to do something different and grow a major company from nothing.

I'm the company's biggest asset, with my name and record of wins, but I'm also about to become the biggest obstacle to our success. We all want to run a serious business while having fun and keeping a foot in our fantasy rock-star world. Soon, though, everyone is butting heads. Duncan and Eddie, who are best friends, threaten to fight each other nearly every day. They've never even argued before, and now they can't be in the same room together. Every time Duncan tells Eddie to do something, Eddie, being one of the partners, feels that he's being disrespected.

The word *focus* is popular with skaters and can be interpreted a number of ways. Of course, there's the original meaning of the word ("the center of interest or activity"). While that word as our company name works on its own, to us the meaning goes deeper than that. When skaters get bummed on tricks they don't make, they sometimes stomp a foot through the center of the deck. That's called "focusing" your board. Then there are the initials of the company, FSU, which means "Focus Skateboards Unlimited" and, well, you know.

Where it was once crowds of screaming fans in bleachers, now it's hard-core skaters in somebody's backyard. Street is really coming on strong, as I explained in an earlier chapter, and that's what we focus Focus Skateboards on. We sponsor tons of hot street skaters and hire one of the best, the legendary Mark "Gonz" Gonzales, to draw our graphics. If you don't know about Gonz, he's basically responsible for morphing freestyle into street skating. His ollie at the Embarcadero in San Francisco was so amazing that the site of his accomplishment is forever known as Gonz Gap. In December 2011, *TransWorld Skateboarding* magazine voted him the most influential skateboarder of all time. With all we have going for us at Focus, we're prepared to launch something huge, relevant, and cool. And I've got just the thing to fuel this next phase of creativity.

In Hollywood not everyone uses meth, mostly because they can afford coke. Meth is cheap—"the poor man's coke," they call it. Since not everyone in Orange County is wealthy, a lot of people there do meth. Meth makes me more amped than ever to skate pools and ramps for hours on end. I've skated on PCP, on acid, and once on mushrooms in the dark. Skating on crystal meth is just a step up from normal skating, like comparing smoking a joint to smoking a cigarette. No big deal, at least not at first. Like all drugs, though, this one eats you slowly from the inside. Then, when you're feeling comfortable, it lets you have it.

I never really get into meth until I move to Orange County. Eddie is into it early on, though. He went on a tour with MTV and he's gathered three thousand names and addresses from kids who have signed their release forms. He sees an opportunity to use that list to help our business.

This is before e-mail, so he begins the task of hand-writing all these kids about the new company, Focus Skateboards. The way he tells it, a friend comes by and says, "Here, you need some of this to help you." At first Eddie's like, "No, I don't do that stuff." Then the guy says, "Look, it'll speed you up so you can finish your work in no time." Eddie finally tries it, and he's suddenly in a good mood while he writes all these letters and mails 'em without breaking a sweat.

Eddie calls me one day to say he has some octane that he wants me to try. I'm always up for a new rush, so I ask, "What's octane?" even though I kinda know he means meth. Meth is taking over the streets of Huntington Beach, and skaters are right in the crosshairs of the epidemic. I buy some of it, try it, and do just a few lines here and there, maybe once or twice a day. It's really no big deal. Soon, though, I start wanting it all the time.

A guy we know makes bongs from ornate cognac bottles and uses them to smoke meth from. While meth is highly addictive, the drug itself is only part of the problem. The ritual is the other main component that hooks you. It doesn't matter if you're cutting holes in bottles or blowing glass pipes with propane torches, using Pyrex glass tubing or incense tubes from the liquor store—it's all part of the ritual that fuels you to want more and more. I

like smoking from cognac bottles and ornate pipes, but at this early stage I can skip the ritual; it doesn't make that much difference to me how I do it.

I stay up for days at a time now, and once I even attempted staying up for a week. I go and go and go and then just pass out for an hour or two, then sleep for maybe eight to ten hours after crashing. First thing I do when I wake up is take another hit of meth, and it's go time again. I'll be at some girl's place where I have a comfy, cozy little den. There I can eat, smoke, get it on, shower, and begin another two-day experience.

Pretty soon I'm doing Focus part-time and crystal meth full-time. My days are spent partying and my nights cruising the clubs for chicks. We're up all night, every night. But work goes on. When the guys drag in to Focus at ten or eleven, I complain that they need to be at work by eight thirty or nine at the latest. (I'm so amped that I'm always the early bird.) I explain that they have to be there early because the East Coast is three hours ahead of us and we're starting to get some accounts there.

I try and they try, but nothing really changes. It's difficult to see your own hypocrisy when you're in the middle of it. Imagine, *me* telling *them* to be responsible! Worse than that is what's happening to our friendship. When we began Focus Skateboards it was one big happy family and we had a blast. We skated together and partied together and the business ran pretty smoothly. Those days are gone.

There are some big investors and buyers looking at our company, and that puts a lot of pressure on me from my partners to clean up. But who are they to tell me how to live? As far as I'm concerned, they need a little straightening up themselves. It seems that once the first profits roll into the company, the fun rolls out, and we begin arguing a lot. When we speak to each other now, it's mostly loudly and aggressively, and mostly about business.

Eddie's met a girl that he's really into. I don't remember this, but he tells me that one night I take his car without telling him. Now he's stranded with this girl he likes, and when I return he says, "That wasn't too cool to take my car; you should've asked me." Apparently I reply by saying, "F--k you, Eddie." That's something I never said to him or any of my close friends in anger before. He's pissed, of course, and he says, "F--k you," back to me. Finally I throw him his keys.

Eddie drives me home and is so disgusted that he walks away from the business for a few days, to cool off. When he returns, I'm living at the warehouse with a bunch of whacked-out guys and chicks, and the place is just a mess. Everything we've worked to build at Focus has disappeared, but all I'm thinking about is where to score more dope and what new chick I can hook up with.

Chicken remains the cool one, always listening, never yelling or saying much at all. He must be frustrated, though, with our dysfunctional ways. He owns a third of the company before Duncan invests. After that Chicken says he'll settle for 10 percent, so Eddie, Duncan, and I can basically split the company three ways. Chicken's screen-printing business is doing well and he doesn't need the headaches. The rest of us continue arguing over anything and everything.

With nobody able to slow me down, my drug use does nothing but escalate. Occasionally I think about getting clean, but I enjoy the party lifestyle, the drugs, and the girls too much to give them up. Other than attracting new investment money, there isn't much incentive to clean up. There aren't many big contests to train for, and the whole skateboard industry is pretty much in the tank. I have no sponsors left, but I never quit believing that I'll soon be back.

I'm what you might call a functioning addict—in other words, I'm holding it together pretty well, considering. I don't impress the venture capitalists, though. Apparently there really are some money people serious about buying our company, but they all want more involvement on my part, which isn't going to happen in my condition. When I don't respond to my partners' pleas for rehabilitation, they try an intervention. What a well-intended joke!

Max Perlich drives down to Chicken's from L.A. and joins Chicken, Eddie, and Duncan, who are all waiting for me at the Focus office when I walk in. I suspect what it's about as soon as I sense their mood. They sit me down nicely and start lecturing me on my problem. I don't take it well. "Who are you guys to tell me what to do?" I demand. "Just because *you* aren't doing meth every day . . . Look, I don't have sores all over my body; I can still skate. I'm okay. Leave me alone and take care of your own problems!"

The intervention is a complete failure, isolating me further from my friends. If I'm a functioning addict, apparently I'm not functioning all that well. ✸

BARCELONA, SPAIN. © MORIZEN FOCHE.

A JUNKIE
LIKE ME

As skateboarding's rock star in the
'80s, Christian was everywhere. It's like
we turned around and he was gone.
—GRANT BRITTAIN

CHAPTER14

Ironically, one of the things that holds me together when I'm on meth is one of my original vices, girls. Because I want to be with them all the time, I keep myself well groomed. Sex and drugs are all I think about. I'm out nightly at every club, still riding on my past reputation and remaining on every VIP list. I'm still the life of the party and remain goal-oriented in that regard. My primary goal has shifted, though, from being the best skater I can be, to figuring out what girl to connect with. That works well on speed because a meth user's senses are on high alert, almost like in the movie The Matrix.

artying is now my main occupation, and I often bring the party to the office. We have an upstairs room for smoking weed, but I don't limit it to just that.

ARTISTIC REBEL OR LOST CAUSE?

The intervention attempt confirms that I'm a nightmare to my partners. How can they operate a company with me always MIA? Still, if they want me, this is who I am. Take it or leave it. Besides, my outlaw image has sold in the past and probably will again. Maybe things aren't perfect, but these guys should be stoked owning a company with such vast potential. If we can hang on, we'll become the next Quiksilver.

I direct them to do their jobs and leave me alone, so I can get out in front of the public and do *my* job, which is to represent Focus by skating. But they know and I know that I'm not making many public appearances anymore, and I'm not skating nearly as much as I used to. My Bruce Lee ambitions have evaporated in a drug delusion. I'm still young, but where's my drive to be the best and to break old records? If I set any record now, it's for getting the least amount of sleep in history.

I barely sleep at all, moving from one high to another in the hope that the *next* hit will be the one that gets me there, and things will be like they were at first. I keep chasing the sensation of that first high—doing it, doing it, doing it—while pushing the limits of life. Yet nothing I try or accomplish has any lasting satisfaction to it.

Meth delivers its strongest effect when smoked, but I'm not totally into that yet. I love the way a big hit makes me feel, but the people I see smoking meth do *nothing* but that. No matter how high I get, I still want to go out and do something fun. Most of my friends who smoke can't leave the house because they know they'll get busted if they try to smoke meth in the open. But I can *snort* meth anywhere, even right in my car, and I've learned to love the feeling it brings. Oddly enough, I'm even kind of addicted to the burn. Little by little, though, I'm starting to crave the better high that smoking it offers and to appreciate the ritual that I described earlier.

I cast a blind eye at guys who smoke, though a part of me still thinks, Man, you never even look outside, and you haven't taken a shower in *how* many days? I ask one of them if he ever thinks of chicks. He halfheartedly replies, "Yeah, bring 'em here." I say, "Okay, but they're not gonna want to hang out with you, the way you're looking."

It's like anything else, though: eventually you become who you hang out with. Despite my friends' precautionary example, I start smoking meth more and more until that's the *only* way I use that drug. I mean, if you're going to do something, do it right, right? I've always hung out with *everybody*, from skaters to street thugs to movie stars to businesspeople. Once I start smoking meth full-on, my associates are limited to convicts and drug addicts. Everyone else is pushed aside, traded in like a used car for my next high.

Life remains manageable, barely, until I begin getting busted. The first bust is for possession of a pipe with about ten bucks' worth of meth in it. The next time, I'm caught with some pills somebody gave me. These are both mere misdemeanors and can be dealt with by attending a few classes. Once I finish those I should be done with my legal hassles. Turns out to be wishful thinking, because I'm busted a third time. Now I find myself in water above my head.

I call Block and a few other friends to see if I can scavenge some money for a lawyer. I'm hoping I can get everything dismissed outright. Block and Scott Oster both put up some cash, but Block is pissed at me for my drug addict ways and insists I pay him back. I promise I will.

The lawyer I line up is a character with a big cowboy hat. He seems to know everybody in the Westminster Police Station, where he takes up my case with the authorities. He comes back and says, "Look, you're going to have to do a little jail time. What you've done would normally get you six to nine months, but I got you fifty days. The good news is you'll only have to do thirty of them."

CHICKEN'S POOL IN HUNTINGTON BEACH, CA. BACKSIDE OLLIE. MID-'90S.
© GRANT BRITTAIN.

Somehow I can't share his enthusiasm. Jail time? I don't think so. But with my dad in Hawaii and my mom on the East Coast, for the first time in my life I feel truly alone. With nowhere else to go I head totally underground, ignoring a scheduled court appearance and causing the issuance of a bench warrant for my arrest.

The word on the streets—my new hangout now that I'm moving from place to place, couch surfing around—is that David Hackett is looking for me. He's a great friend, but I know what he wants: he's found sobriety and hopes to get me to one of his meetings. I guess that's good for him, but me, go to meetings? Yeah, right! I'd love to see Hackett, but please, spare me the sermon. Getting used to being on the run, I learn how to slip through the cracks. Although David tries to find me seven or eight times, I'm always gone before he arrives.

Where I once loved being the center of attention, now I avoid the public eye entirely. I really don't want to get locked up. Some of my other friends are more successful at finding me than Hackett was. My friend and team rider Sergie Ventura was on crack for a while. When he cleans up, he finds me at this house where I'm staying. Sergie's an amazing skater and a nice kid who was always at the top of his class in school. He comes from a good family. But drugs don't care about your accomplishments, where you're from, or your family background.

When Sergie finally finds me, he realizes that all the stories he's heard about me being emaciated and out of my mind are untrue. (He told me recently that he'd heard that someone saw me under the Huntington pier with a toy gun at six o'clock one morning, talking to myself and apparently out of my head. That never happened.) He can see that I'm not my old self, but I'm nowhere near as bad as he'd heard. He hints at the idea that I should get clean, and we talk for a while. To get him off my case I lead him to believe I'm on the road to recovery, which I'm definitely not.

Other close friends like Scott Oster also locate me and try talking sense into me. To Scott I look faded and gray, not the same guy I was when he saw me last. As well-intentioned as he is, his words of encouragement don't penetrate. He and my other friends mean well, though—and God bless them for trying.

Block is more direct:

I HAD GIVEN [CHRISTIAN] SOME MONEY FOR A LAWYER AND HE DIDN'T SHOW UP FOR COURT; AND OF COURSE HE HAD NO PLANS OF PAYING

ME BACK. I WAS SO MAD THAT I LEFT A RECORDING ON MY PHONE MA-
CHINE: "ANYBODY CALLING, LEAVE YOUR NAME AND NUMBER. IF THIS
IS CHRISTIAN HOSOI, F--K YOU; YOU'RE GOING TO PRISON." I PROBABLY
WOULD HAVE SLAPPED HIM IF I SAW HIM. AROUND HERE, YOU DO WHAT-
EVER'S NECESSARY TO GET YOUR FRIENDS TO LISTEN. ONCE THAT'S
OVER, YOU GIVE THEM A HUG. WE WERE A LONG WAYS FROM THE HUG.
WHEN EDDIE OR DUNCAN CALLED TO SAY THAT CHRISTIAN WAS IN PRIS-
ON, I SAID, "I DON'T GIVE A S--T. THAT'S WHERE HE NEEDS TO BE."

Where others see me as a drug addict throwing my life away, in *my* mind
I'm an artistic rebel on the run from the law. This is something new for
me, and kind of a fun rush at first. I'm afraid to drive around in my car
for fear I'll get picked up, so I skate around town, sometimes carrying a
dartboard, looking for a place to find a game of darts and hunker down
with a little meth. I sometimes carry a file with me and use it to carve
notches on my skateboard. Years earlier I had invented the Hammerhead
by altering the traditional deck of a skateboard. That was a huge success,
so I figure maybe I can do something radical in board design again. Of
course, most people just think I'm whacked out and neurotically filing
away on my skateboard. That's how rumors begin, right?

I'm always on the go, driving here and there (as long as it's out of our
local police jurisdiction). Occasionally I'll hustle enough cash to fly between
California, Hawaii, and Japan, where my name still carries considerable
weight. Like many other places, Hawaii has fallen to the crystal meth epidemic. There's lots of "ice" in Hawaii, so I'm more at home there than ever.

IDENTITY CRISIS

Meanwhile, Eddie and Duncan are still trying to hang on to Focus
Skateboards. They get a booth at the San Diego Action Sports Retailer
Trade Expo. I love the party atmosphere at that annual tradeshow, so I
fly in from Hawaii and drop straight into the show. What I didn't know
but soon discover is that two bail bondsmen, twin brothers (with identical
moustaches), are there searching for me. The picture they have of me is an
old one, though, with long hair, necklaces, and earrings. I show up with

short hair and a clean-cut look—a recent effort to convince the world, and myself, that I'm not an addict—so they don't recognize me. Focus is taking its last gasp and could certainly use my help, but I stay clear of our booth so I won't get busted.

A rising young skater named Choppy who's being called the new Christian Hosoi is apparently hanging out at our booth. The bail bondsmen roll up and say, "We've got some free passes for Christian Hosoi." Choppy says, "Yeah, that's me." They handcuff him and say, "Okay, Christian—you're busted."

Choppy tries to set things straight, saying, "No, I'm *not* Hosoi; I'm Choppy Omega. There's been a mistake here. Look—that's me on the cover of that *Thrasher* magazine over there." From what I hear he was crying. They were making it pretty rough on him, I guess, since they really had it in for me. They say drug use is a victimless crime. Try telling Choppy that. Later Choppy says that was the only time in his life he didn't want to be me. (It would get worse, of course. But if he knew how my guts were churning all the time and how frustrated I had become even then, he wouldn't have wanted to be me at all.)

There's a ramp set up at the show, and my partners in Focus want me to skate a demo. I say, "No, they'll find out I'm here and I'll get busted." Duncan's the announcer of the event, and he claims he won't call me Christian when I'm on the ramp; he'll call me Holmes, which is one of my nicknames. I really do want to skate for the crowd. It would be a rush riding right there in front of the guys who are out to capture me. Finally I agree.

As I skate, Duncan's saying, "Holmes is up, blasting a big method air." It's fun hiding in plain sight, and the bail bondsmen pay no attention to some skater named Holmes on the ramp. Unfortunately, when I finish skating the demo some kid gushes, "Dude, did you see Christian? He *ripped* that ramp." One of the bail bondsmen overhears him and says, "What, Christian Hosoi's here? Where?"

I get wind that they're on to me, so I head for the door. An old friend of mine, wanting to talk, catches my arm as I move past. He doesn't realize what's up—I haven't seen him in a long time, so he probably isn't aware of my troubles—and he obviously wants to hang out. I feel bad about it, but I throw him off and jog for the exit.

Just as I hit the sidewalk, luck comes to my aid: there's my friend Big Daddy Larry, driving by in a cab. I signal him to pull over, and I climb in the cab. When I explain my situation to Larry, he offers a suggestion. He says he's leaving town but still has a few days left on his room, and I'm welcome to use it. Slipping me his room key, he drops me off at the hotel. I stay there a few days, enjoying the adventure of hiding out, before moving on. I've always lived on high doses of adrenaline, and being on the run and dodging cops all the time supplies its share of that natural drug. ✸

NOSE GRIND TAIL GRAB ON A HANDRAIL. LOS ANGELES, CA.
© CESARIO "BLOCK" MONTANO.

FRONTSIDE TAIL GRAB. BACKYARD POOL. © GRANT BRITTAIN.

ALL IS
VANITY

I SAID IN MY HEART,
"COME NOW, I WILL TEST YOU WITH
MIRTH; THEREFORE ENJOY PLEASURE"; BUT
SURELY, THIS ALSO *WAS* VANITY. . . .
"VANITY OF VANITIES, ALL *IS* VANITY."
—KING SOLOMON, ECCLESIASTES 2:1, 1:2

I WON EVERYTHING I SET OUT TO WIN,
HAD EVERY GIRL I EVER WANTED, HAD
FRIENDS AND BUSINESSES AND GREAT PARTIES
AND ALL THE MONEY I COULD SPEND,
AND I STILL WASN'T SATISFIED.

—CHRISTIAN HOSOI

CHAPTER15

I'd probably be a millionaire right now if I had skated in the first Extreme Games (an extravaganza that would become the X Games). Then again, I would have had to be clean and in shape to have a shot at gold, and I was neither.

hen the first X Games is launched in Rhode Island in 1995, skateboard competition finally hits the world stage. With his stellar showing, including first place in vert, Tony Hawk becomes the first skater to be a household name and a truly major sports figure. I hear that someone in the sports world is calling him the Michael Jordan of skateboarding. They're not calling me at all—but hey, Tony deserves the title.

The media needs someone to challenge Tony. Guys like Chris Miller, Lance, Cab, and me are capable of beating him on their best days, but I'm in no condition to challenge Tony. Besides, I'm thousands of miles away from the event. I'm living in Japan, where I'm skating a little and partying a lot. I celebrate the news of his victory by lifting my pipe and taking a hit.

FROM HIGH AIR TO THIN AIR

A few months earlier I flew to Japan to do a demo with skate stars Omar Hassan, Tony Hawk, Wade Speyer, and some other guys. We skate various demos and I show up for the last few minutes each time, when I have to. Unlike the days when I deliberately made everyone wait and it got fans stoked, now I'm just being slack, and I can tell that people are getting irritated with me. When it comes time to return home to L.A., I tell Tony and Omar that I'm gonna stay. Not only am I trying to dodge incarceration with this decision, but the entire X Games concept seems lame to me at the time. I figure it's just another corporate method of making money off something that's traditionally been soulful and underground.

Here's what Tony Hawk has to say about those days:

IN 1995 CHRISTIAN, OMAR HASSAN, AND I, ALONG WITH SOME OTHER PRO SKATERS, GOT INVITED TO JAPAN. OMAR HAD MENTIONED TO ME THAT CHRISTIAN WAS IN BAD SHAPE, BUT I WAS EXCITED TO SEE HIM

AGAIN. I DIDN'T KNOW IT THEN, BUT THIS WOULD BE THE LAST TIME I WOULD SEE CHRISTIAN FOR NEARLY A DECADE.

ESPN CAME TO JAPAN TO INTERVIEW ME AND CHRISTIAN FOR WHAT WERE THEN CALLED THE EXTREME GAMES. THE GUYS FROM ESPN WERE ACTING LIKE THE X GAMES WERE SAVING SKATING, AND IN A WAY I THOUGHT THEY WERE RIGHT. WE WERE STILL SKATING AND DOING WHAT WE'D ALWAYS DONE, BUT NOBODY FROM OUTSIDE OUR LITTLE CIRCLE REALLY CARED.

I NEVER SAW CHRISTIAN SLEEP ON THAT TRIP IN JAPAN. I KNEW SOMETHING WAS UP BUT DIDN'T KNOW WHAT, SPECIFICALLY. THERE WASN'T MUCH HAPPENING IN SKATING, AND NOW WE WERE GETTING PAID LIKE $300 A MONTH FROM THIS COMPANY IN JAPAN, AND THEY EXPECTED US TO SHOW UP ON TIME AND SKATE. I WAS LIKE, "YEAH, SIGN ME UP." THAT'S WHAT WE HAD TO DO TO MAKE A LIVING AT THE TIME, AND IT WAS TOTALLY WORTH IT.

WE HAD DONE OUR DEMOS AND THIS GUY ASKED US TO STAY AND DO MORE SHOWS. THEY SAID THEY'D PAY US MORE. OMAR AND I SAID, "SORRY, WE CAN'T; WE'RE GOING TO THE EXTREME GAMES; WE HAVE TO GO TO THAT." WE KNEW IT WAS GOING TO BE THE BIGGEST THING WE'D EVER SEEN. I REMEMBER CHRISTIAN SAYING, "I'M HERE; WHAT-EVER YOU NEED." CHRISTIAN WAS SLATED AS ONE OF THE MAIN GUYS TO WATCH AT THE X GAMES. TO ME, IT WAS CRAZY, HIS STAYING IN JAPAN. OMAR LATER TOLD ME THAT HE THOUGHT CHRISTIAN WAS "TWEAKING."

OMAR AND I WERE TALKING AFTER THE X GAMES, SAYING, "CHRIS-TIAN WOULD HAVE LOVED THIS—HE'D HAVE BEEN THE MAN HERE." IT WAS SAD FOR SKATING, CUZ THERE WASN'T A LOT OF PERSONALITY SHINING THROUGH AT THAT TIME, AND CHRISTIAN COULD HAVE OF-FERED THAT AND MORE. I DIDN'T SEE HIM AGAIN UNTIL THE X GAMES IN 2004.

Grant Brittain, who was *TransWorld Skateboarding*'s photo editor at the time, recalls it this way:

THE FIRST X GAMES WAS NOTHING LIKE ANYTHING WE'D EVER SEEN IN SKATEBOARDING BEFORE. THEY DIDN'T EVEN WANT THE SKATERS TO WEAR THEIR SPONSORS' LOGOS, EVEN THOUGH THAT'S HOW ALL THE SKATERS MADE THEIR LIVING. THERE WERE THESE BIG-SCREEN TVS, AND THE ORGANIZERS KEPT PLAYING TONY'S AND CHRISTIAN'S INTERVIEWS ON THEM. THEY WERE THE ONLY TWO GUYS FEATURED ON THE SCREEN, AND EVERYBODY NATURALLY THOUGHT CHRISTIAN WAS COMING. THERE WERE ALL THESE RUMORS THAT HE WAS HIDING OUT IN HAWAII, BUT HE NEVER DID SHOW UP. I KEPT HEARING HIS VOICE, AND I'D LOOK UP AT THE SCREEN AND DISCOVER THAT IT WAS OLDER VIDEO CLIPS OF HIM TALKING.

Since there's now a bench warrant out for my arrest, I've gotta keep air travel to a minimum. After I'm told I have to leave the hotel in Japan, I stay at the house of a rich kid I met through the skating community. He skates and does ice, so we have a lot in common. He even has a ramp in his garage!

Meth is a heavy-duty epidemic in Japan; lots of people out there do it. Living in Japan is expensive, even without the drug costs, but my friend is funding it all. We're having a great time: every night, all night, we skate and party—different girls all the time. It's almost like we're re-creating the scene I had going in Orange County.

One thing that's different about Japan is that major businesspeople smoke meth somewhat openly there. I visit big publishing houses, for example, and suit-and-tie businessmen pull out crazy-looking glass pipes with water in them and smoke meth with me.

My problem with the X Games is similar to the one I have with our current company, Focus. These people want me to conform so that they can market me as something I'm not. I can't see it, but by then it hardly matters; I'm not marketable to anyone but other speed freaks, and they don't have a lot of expendable income. Who's gonna pay a drug addict (even one who functions reasonably well) to do anything other than act or play rock 'n' roll? Fans who had seen me skate against Hawk in the past might have missed seeing me at the X Games, but the general public is basically unaware of my existence. As big as *I* think I am, the show goes on without me. I'm yesterday's news.

A few years prior to the X Games, big skate companies had paid ESPN to get our events aired. Now, bigger companies than we've ever associated with are paying skateboarders for the right to record and market them. That sounds good, but if they're *paying* us, that means they *own* us, right? We've lost control of the direction of skateboarding.

To be fair, the X Games eventually develops into an awesome event and becomes something healthy for skateboarding. At the time, however, I think I'm above it all. I'm not, of course; I've become nothing more than a partying fool, hanging on to a thread of pride while believing I'm nobody's puppet. It's great making your own choices and being free, but that doesn't describe *me*—not anymore. I'm being held by a set of strings more powerful than any corporation could dangle me from. And these strings are strangling me and everything I've worked so hard to build. Meth is ruining it all—my company, my cash, my friends, my family, and my health.

On the rare occasions when I do enter some obscure contest, I no longer threaten the top spot but am lucky to get eighth place after guys I could have destroyed any day of the week, if I were in good skating shape. Though I don't look like those before-and-after pictures you see of withered meth skeletons with no teeth and with scabs all over their faces, I can feel something eating at me, down in my soul. I showed more sense than this at seventeen when I quit coke after realizing it was taking me down. What helped me quit coke was the fire within, motivating me to be a winner. That's no more than an ember now.

Without that fire, I don't have a hope of skating clean or skating well. I'm falling behind quickly. Skateboarding is changing again, and the new tricks are becoming increasingly difficult. Of course the companies all want to hire the *new* pros to promote their stuff. I have no illusions about trying to dominate the new crew of seventeen-year-old kids doing back flips on vert ramps, and I'm *sure* not gonna risk breaking my neck doing 720s against some freckle-faced kid half my age. I'm not jumping through hoops for anybody.

FATHERHOOD

Let's back up a little. While I'm living in Huntington Beach I get to know a woman named Kim Baird. We see a lot of each other, and I stay with her off and on during my at-large days. She gets pregnant in 1997.

BIRTH OF RHYTHM. 1997. *HOSOI FAMILY COLLECTION.*

I continue smoking meth all the way through Kim's pregnancy, but she quits doing drugs before she even realizes there's a child growing inside of her. I'm determined to be there for the birth: when my son is born, I'm in the delivery room, telling Kim to breathe and push. At the crucial moment the doctor says to me, "Get over here; you're going to deliver your baby. You're going to catch him like a football." He shows me where to sit and how to hold out my hands. I yell for Kim to push one final time, and she gives it all she's got. Suddenly . . . there's my boy, and I catch him! He's blue and his head is shaped like a cone. I think, Oh no, something's terribly wrong, or he's dead. But it turns out all right.

I've never lost my desire to do things differently, so we give our son an original name, Rhythm. He's lived up to that, being right in sync with the beat of life every minute. We both love him from the moment he emerges, but I'm not ready to settle down in a normal relationship and be there to raise a child. As amazing as my son's birth is—as amazing as *he* is—I feel little direct connection with him; in fact, I have no connection whatsoever to anybody.

As soon as we're all home from the hospital I resume my drug ritual, smoking meth morning, noon, and night. The months go by and Rhythm begins to grow up, but I remain stuck in my childish drug world. I continue doing drugs and take my son with me everywhere, even to the bars and drug houses when I'm out to score.

I often flash on all the fun times I enjoyed as a child with my family. I want Rhythm to experience that too, but I don't see it happening. It would be nice to be at his side as he moves out into the world—to skate with him at the parks and show him how to ollie and trespass, how to carve ditches and drain pools. I dream of family vacations and Sunday night dinners with Grandma and Grandpa. For the first time I'm aware that my actions have far-reaching consequences. Maybe I really *can't* have it all. I've chosen one way of life over another, and my choice carries a high price tag. I'm searching for something that will bring me lasting satisfaction; and family life, as great as it is and as much as I want it for Rhythm, just isn't it.

How can I have any sort of family life anyway, when I'm surrounded by dealers and drug addicts? When I'm not staying at Kim's apartment or with a friend, I'm out on the street skating around with the homies looking for some dope. Kim's place provides a pretty cool home when I need it or want to get away—my own little meth/love den in her garage. I have a sleeping bag back there, along with all my clothes and a few skateboards.

I'm cool with sticking around for a while, but Kim and I are always fighting. I'm committed to her in my own uncommitted way. She repeatedly accuses me of going out on her, and I use that accusation as the excuse to do whatever I want—which is to do drugs and find chicks to do drugs with. I need to get away from Kim, and initially that's easy. I hang out in the garage where I can blow glass pipes from propane torches to get high and play darts with the guys. After one particularly brutal argument with her, I roll back to the streets for an extended time, moving from house to house, party to party, high to higher. Still, the door isn't completely closed at Kim's, and I keep relations open with her so that I can see her and my son.

At this point I figure that I'll do drugs for the rest of my life. I'll eventually quit meth, I tell myself, but there's no question I'll smoke weed, which I've never really considered a drug anyway. I have a vague long-range plan of being an artist and following in the footsteps of my father, passing on my thoughts and ways to my son. There's no doubt that he and I will get high together and party together, and that he'll inherit the ashes of the world I've burned down.

Here's how Kim remembers things:

CHRISTIAN WAS REALLY OUT OF IT MUCH OF THE TIME, AND HE WAS ALWAYS GOING OUT ON ME. I WAS GETTING OUT OF THE SHOWER ONCE WHEN THIS GIRL KNOCKS ON MY FRONT DOOR, SAYING SHE'S LOOKING FOR CHRISTIAN. I ASK, "WHO ARE YOU?" AND SHE REPLIES, "I'M SO-AND-SO, THE GIRL CHRISTIAN'S BEEN LIVING WITH FOR THE PAST TWO WEEKS." I TURN AWAY AND SAY, "CHRISTIAN, IT'S FOR YOU." THEN I FADE INTO THE OTHER ROOM AS THEY HAVE A BIG FIGHT. AFTER THAT, I RETURN AND CHRISTIAN AND I HAVE A BLOWOUT OF OUR OWN.

IT WASN'T JUST THAT ONE TIME, EITHER. WHILE HE WAS LIVING WITH ME, ONE TIME I CALLED A GIRL'S NUMBER TRYING TO REACH HIM, AND HER VOICE MAIL SAID, "HI, CHRISTIAN AND I AREN'T AVAILABLE RIGHT NOW."

I'D GIVE HIM MONEY TO EAT AT TACO BELL OR WHEREVER, AND HE WOULDN'T COME HOME FOR A WEEK. HE WAS WITH A DIFFERENT GIRL

EVERY NIGHT—WELL, MAYBE NOT EVERY NIGHT, BUT CLOSE. HE WAS RUNNING THE STREETS, RUNNING FROM THE LAW, BUT MOST OF ALL HE WAS RUNNING FROM HIMSELF. I DIDN'T REALIZE THAT UNTIL I GOT INTO RECOVERY. WE WERE TOGETHER TWO AND A HALF YEARS, BUT IT WAS RARELY GOOD.

LAX FULL PIPES. 1990.
© CESARIO "BLOCK" MONTANO.

CHRISTIAN
IN NAME ONLY

OKAY, WAKE UP, WAKE UP.

—CHRISTIAN HOSOI

CHAPTER16

I have no money and no income, but I still have a mouth and can talk my way into or out of just about anything. I've always been a good hustler.

Soon after my son's birth I hustle two brand-new vans from a major car dealer in Orange County. Not only do I show up at the dealership without a cent or any proof of income, I don't even have a driver's license! Apparently one of the salesmen wants to meet me, and I turn that to my advantage. I guess I make a good impression, because he says he can lease me a van. When he asks about my income, I inform him of my partial ownership in the now barely alive Focus Skateboards. That seems to satisfy him.

Of course I myself am never satisfied, so I push things: I tell him I want *two* vans, one for business and one for pleasure. "No problem," he says. He gives me the business van, a stock Grand Caravan, along with an awesome Grand Caravan with Pirelli rims, painted a sick shade of dark gray. I sign like seventy papers, and when he asks for my driver's license, I explain that I left it in my storage unit. In reality, my license has long since expired, and I can't apply for a new one because of my outstanding warrants. I show him my passport instead and he seems content, copying the information down. He sends me off in the first van, which I tell him that I'm driving back to the Focus office. A week later, I return to the dealership and drive off in the other van.

I immediately install one of those bouncy baby seats in the back of the van, not for Rhythm to ride in, but so that any cop looking inside won't become suspicious. It's a decoy: anyone checking the van out will see that seat and assume they're looking into a nice family vehicle owned by people who live behind a white-picket fence with two cats in the yard. I wash the van every few days and keep the dealer plates on so it looks like I've just driven it off the lot. I keep myself clean-cut too and wear a collared shirt and a nice watch whenever I drive anywhere. I styled a pair of glasses that look like something a lawyer might wear. They're just part of the facade too, frames without glass in them. In this disguise I cruise around without any worry of getting stopped. If cops stare at me while I'm driving, I stare back at them, nod, and drive on. I don't fit the profile of a strung-out junkie, so there's no reason to pull me over. You never see people who look like me being questioned by the cops.

I never make one payment on either car, and I never get pulled over. Those vans aren't just transportation, but often home—one of the best purchases I never made. The dealership would love to collect, I'm sure, but they can't locate me. I'm now a renegade, a drive-till-the-wheels-fall-off kind of guy. But I never see the wreckage I'm leaving on the road.

Focus Skateboards still exists, but I think the only things floating the company now are Duncan's credit cards and whatever scraps of goodwill remain from the relationships we've established with dealers over the years. Our orders don't always ship on time, and morale is at an all-time low. What finally sinks us are snowboards. Snowboarding is huge now, and Duncan and Eddie have ordered some for us to put the Focus name on. We have quite a few preorders, so it seems like a good idea. They placed their initial order with the best manufacturer in the industry, but when that company gets backed up on production and can't deliver, they order the boards from one of the worst manufacturers. Meanwhile, a Japanese client sends us a $50,000 deposit—good news!—but we quickly blow through it.

Finally the boards come in and we label and ship them. They're soon returned, one by one and by the dozen, after they delaminate or fall apart completely. We have to make good on them and pay off another $45,000 in credit-card debt. A few years ago that amount wouldn't have been insurmountable, but nobody in our crew has that kind of money anymore. Things are pretty slow anyway, so Focus finally shuts its doors.

When Focus dies, our friendship nearly dies with it. As with each of my earlier ventures, we'd been warned about getting into business with friends. And just as we always had, we were determined to prove everyone wrong and go our own way, against the grain. It looks like this time everyone was right, though.

I don't fret over things for long. After all, business and friendship aren't everything. There's still partying to be done, and I know just the guy to party with. Just like me, he has no limits.

The guy seems to be burning rocket fuel in his veins; he's willing to push things absolutely as far as possible. There's no way he and I could

push them any further without falling off the edge we're standing on. One time we're doing meth somewhere, and a UPS driver comes by and sees us in action. He says, "Hey, I'll take a bong hit." He takes one, looks up, and begins freaking. "Whoa, what is this?" he asks, stumbling a bit. "What *is* it?" he repeats. We'd like to help him out, but right now we've got places of our own to go. We send him off and hope he doesn't crash. Just afterward, we're driving north to do a skate demo, and we're sharing PCP-soaked bong loads. PCP, or angel dust, is a gnarly hallucinogenic drug that can lead to out-of-body experiences. That doesn't happen to me, but the drug definitely has an effect that doesn't make skateboarding any easier.

When we get to the demo we're just flying, and he's like, "Are you still gonna skate?" I'm like, "Yeah, watch me!" He's down below, looking up with psycho eyes, as I climb up the ramp. I feel like I'm floating on hot pillows. The air is thick and hot; electricity surges through my body. Everything happens in slow motion, and I feel as if everyone is watching to see if I'll survive dropping in. The other skaters have stopped skating as I step up to the lip of the ramp, put my board in a tail-drop position, and tell myself, "Okay, you've got this." My hope is just to make it to the other side. I do better than that: I survive the drop, move into rock 'n' rolls, then do grinds, and finally blast air. At those moments when I'm suspended in midair, I feel that I can do anything.

Together, my friend and I are such gnarly partiers that we attract the attention of the punk-rock underground. Soon we're hanging with all sorts of rockers, artists, and musicians, including some guys from the popular ska/punk-rock band Sublime who live in Long Beach. We're hanging out, smoking meth, and just chillin' with Bradley Nowell, the front man for Sublime. Bradley is a heroin addict who will soon join countless rockers who've sadly died before thirty from an overdose. But even if we could have seen the future, it wouldn't have stopped us. In fact, it would have made doing drugs even more worthwhile. I know that sounds nuts, but that's who we were at the time.

One time the guy rolls up his sleeve and says he wants to try shooting heroin. Bradley's like, "Yeah, okay cool. Try it out, killer." I mean, we're all druggies, so none of us has the good sense to tell him not to do it. Me, I've tried smoking heroin before, and for me it sucked. That stuff made me go to sleep when all I ever want to do is jam in sixth gear. I decided back then that I'd never use it again.

So Bradley is fixing a shot for himself, filling the whole needle with black heroin, and the guy's like, "Come on, give it all to me!" Bradley's like, "Dude, you can't take this much," and he replies, "I do all kinds of drugs all the time. If you can handle it, I can handle it." We're just sittin' there and Bradley's like, "All right. You sure you wanna do this? It's gonna hit you really hard."

Against whatever judgment a junkie has, Bradley shoots him up and my friend slumps over; he's out before the needle's even out of his arm. As I gently lay him down, Bradley says, "Make sure he's breathing." He is, and his heart is beating, so we leave him there and continue partying. I look over and check on him from time to time, saying, "Wake up, wake up." He doesn't wake up at my check-ins but he's breathing, so we leave him there and I keep smoking meth for hours. Late that night I finally head out and tell Bradley, "Okay, see you later." I slump the guy over my shoulder, walk him to the car, place him in the passenger seat, and drive him to Kim's apartment.

If you add it up, I'm getting only a few months' worth of sleep each year. Now it's kind of like he's sleeping for me, all night long. I'm still hitting the pipe when he opens his eyes and smiles, and I say, "Hey, buddy; how you doin'?" He replies, "Man, that was the best high I've ever had in my life!" I'm like, "Dude, you had a shot and went straight out. You're gonna say that's great?" This is what happens when the dragon bites you. I'm like, "Okay—whatever, bro." Where it used to be us doin' meth and PCP or whatever together, now the only drug he wants to do is heroin. Our highs don't mesh anymore: we pass each other while he's on his way down and I'm on my way up. We still hang out, just not as often anymore.

I'm so deep into addiction that I actually *shoot* meth for a couple months. The hot-looking girl I'm spending time with these days would rather shoot meth than smoke it. In fact, shooting meth is *all* she does or wants to do. She's not as fun as she used to be. We just sit in bed for days doing nothing but shooting meth. When I say, "Let's go do something"—meaning something *else*—she answers, "No, I just wanna slam more."

She has to wear long sleeves whenever we do go out, cuz there are gnarly marks all over her arms. I tell her, "You've got to stop; you're too good for this." All of a sudden I notice a gnarly mark on my own arm, and I realize that I need to wear long sleeves too.

I try pulling her back from the ledge, encouraging her to go back to smoking or even just snorting her meth. She says, "No way. I have to shoot it." The crazy look in her eyes lets me know that that's it for her. "Are you in, or are you out?" she asks. I hesitate a moment before answering, "I'm out." She's like, "Okay, I gotta go," and then walks away. I'm bummed, cuz she really was hot. Ironically, I can see what meth is doing to *her*, but not what it's doing to *me*. The beast blinds and controls you; it's so hungry that it devours every part of you.

Not that I feel I'm better than anyone else, but I don't want to do drugs and just hang around inside all day with the curtains drawn. Even as a drug addict I know there's more to life than that. That's why I turned away from heroin earlier. It's a sit-around drug. I hate it, but my buddy Jeff Grosso loves it. Grosso skated for me for a while. He's still a hot pro skateboarder in the late '90s, but dabbling in drugs has left him straight up addicted.

We spend some time together, both of us fighting our own demons. I don't remember much about those days, but Grosso does:

IT WAS 1997, AND I HAD BEEN IN JAIL FOR A COUPLE DAYS. WHEN I GOT OUT I DID THE THREE BEARS THING, TRYING TO FIND A PLACE TO STAY. FINALLY CHRISTIAN TOOK ME IN [AT HIS GIRLFRIEND'S PLACE]. WE WENT TO MY DEALER'S HOUSE, LITTLE RAY, AND THERE WAS A SHRINE FOR HIM ON THE DOOR. HE HAD DIED OF AN OVERDOSE.

AFTER THAT, CHRISTIAN TOOK ME TO COSTA MESA WITH ALL THESE SPEED-FREAK FRIENDS OF HIS. I SCORED, WENT INTO THE BATHROOM, SHOT HEROIN, AND FELL OVER. I HADN'T DONE ANYTHING FOR A FEW DAYS, AND THE HIT WAS JUST TOO STRONG. THE ONLY THING THAT SAVED ME WAS THAT I FELL INTO A BASIN OF RUNNING WATER, AND IT KEPT ME CONSCIOUS. THE PEOPLE IN THE HOUSE SAW ME AND TOLD CHRISTIAN, "YOU GOTTA GET HIM OUTTA HERE."

I SLEPT ON CHRISTIAN'S COUCH FOR LIKE A COUPLE DAYS WHILE HE DID SPEED AND PLAYED DARTS.

WHEN I FINALLY CAME TO, HE TOLD ME THAT I'D BEEN TURNING BLUE. THEN HE STARTED GIVING ME THIS LECTURE ABOUT DOING DRUGS AND HOW I NEEDED TO BE MORE CAREFUL. HE HAD A TORCH IN ONE HAND AND A PIPE IN THE OTHER, AND I SAID, "LOOK, YOU'RE A JUNKIE JUST LIKE ME, ONLY ON A DIFFERENT DRUG, AND BECAUSE YOU'VE HOOKED UP WITH THIS GIRL, YOU HAVE A PLACE TO GO." I TOLD HIM THE ONLY WAY HE GOT AWAY WITH IT WAS BECAUSE HIS GIRL WAS AT WORK SO MUCH. I ASKED HIM TO GIVE ME SOME MONEY, AND WHEN HE DID I LEFT.

THERE ARE A LOT OF THINGS THAT INTRIGUE ME ABOUT CHRISTIAN'S PERSONALITY. LIKE THE GIRLS HE CHOOSES. ALL THE GIRLS I'VE EVER SEEN HIM WITH HAVE BEEN SPITFIRES. I DIDN'T KNOW HIS MOM VERY WELL, BUT I'D BET SHE WAS CUT FROM SIMILAR CLOTH. AND THERE'S ALWAYS BEEN SOMETHING KIND AND GENEROUS ABOUT HIM. HE BROUGHT EVERYTHING GOOD FROM HIS PERSONA INTO THAT DARK WORLD, WHICH MADE HIM SUPER ATTRACTIVE TO ALL THESE JUNKIES. BUT THEY ALSO INFECTED HIM. BEFORE ALL THAT, HE WAS A LOT OF FUN. HE TOOK ME TO ENGLAND FOR THE FIRST TIME; HE TOOK ME TO JAPAN FOR THE FIRST TIME. HE TOLD ME I HADN'T SEEN ENOUGH OF THE WORLD. IT'S A STRANGE DICHOTOMY HE'S GOT GOING ON—HE'S AXL ROSE, EGO-GUY PRO SKATEBOARD DUDE; AND ON THE FLIP SIDE OF THAT, HE'S THE MOST LOYAL FRIEND EVER, AND YOU CAN COUNT ON HIM IN A PINCH.

I SUSPECT IT GOES BACK TO IVAN'S STRANGE PARENTING SKILLS. I'VE NEVER SEEN ANYONE MORE SECURE AND SELF-AWARE THAN CHRISTIAN. NO MATTER HOW BAD THINGS ARE, HE'LL ALWAYS SAY, "WE'VE GOT THIS—NO PROBLEM."

HE WAS MY FRIEND, BUT I THOUGHT THERE WERE STRINGS ATTACHED TO OUR FRIENDSHIP. HIM GIVING ME MONEY AND WANTING TO HELP ME THAT TIME I CRASHED SHOWED ME THAT HE REALLY DID CARE ABOUT ME. THIS WAS AT A TIME WHEN I DIDN'T THINK ANYONE ELSE DID, AND AFTER THAT IS WHEN I STARTED DOWN THE ROAD TO GETTING CLEAN.

**THERE'S SOMETHING ELSE—HE NEVER REALLY HAD ANY INSECU-
RITIES LIKE EVERY OTHER KID. HE ALWAYS SEEMED IN CONTROL AND
MADE IT SEEM LIKE EVERYTHING WAS OKAY. HE NEVER WAS THE TYPI-
CAL ADDICT, TRYING TO GET AWAY FROM EVERYTHING. MAYBE THAT'S
WHY HE LIKED SPEED, CUZ SPEED IS A CONTROL DRUG. YOU DON'T
CONTROL HEROIN; YOU'RE JUST ALONG FOR THE RIDE.**

Kim says that she was the one who found Grosso out in front of the
apartment and called me to come and help him inside. I remember something that Grosso said during that visit; it really penetrated and stayed
with me. "You're not Christian Hosoi anymore; you're a junkie just like
me, only on a different drug." He asks for some money, I give it to him,
and he splits. Of *course* I would do that for him: he's a good friend, and I
know that there's this awesome guy beneath his addictions. But if I'm not
Christian Hosoi anymore, who am I?

I know one thing: I'm smart, and I know how to handle drugs, just
like I handle everything else in life. Other people may fall off the edge,
but I'm not going to do anything but enjoy teetering on it and peering off into the darkness. I'm skating nearly as well as ever, or so I tell
myself—and when I clean up in a few months, I'll be better than ever,
and back on top. Everyone, including Tony Hawk, is gonna freak when
I make my comeback.

I'll put that on hold for a little while, though, I decide. Right now I
have to hustle and score. Maybe I can sell a few of my boards and get a
few bucks. I'll do anything short of robbery, unless you count keeping
vans I never paid for as robbery. ✸

ALAN "DJ ALCHEMIST" MAMAN, SCOTTY CAAN, AND ME.
HOSOI FAMILY COLLECTION.

THE ULTIMATE
HIGH

I asked someone, "Whatever
happened to Christian?" and he said,
"Oh, he's all methed out."
—JAY "ALABAMY" HAIZLIP

CHAPTER 17

I'm in an upscale hotel with this girl and we're cooking meth on the stove. Suddenly there's the sound of breaking glass—the beaker of meth exploded!—and smoke is pouring everywhere. I quickly shove everything we're cooking into the microwave in a futile attempt to confine the smoke. We can't open the door to air the place out cuz we're in a hotel. The smoke and smell would alert somebody to what we're up to, and we'd go to jail for sure.

We taped over all the sprinklers with plastic so that they won't turn on with the heat and smoke, and we disabled the smoke detectors. Despite my having put everything in the microwave, thick smoke gathers at the ceiling. We cover our faces with our shirts, wondering what to do next.

It's a sketchy situation, but we manage to escape without being caught. A fake ID and a stolen credit card is a great smoke screen to cover your tracks.

It's 1998, and I'm again visited by the thought of getting sober, making a big comeback, and blowing everyone's mind. I'll party a little more and *then* get serious, I tell myself. With that added "rest time," I'll be even better than before.

Same old song: drug addiction is all about *tomorrow*. The days blur one into another, and tomorrow never comes.

On speed you never actually *sleep;* you simply crash under the weight of being awake for so long. I'm basically perpetually running on empty, up for two full days (and nights) at a time, crashing one day, then awake for two more days in a row. I sometimes even go three or four days and nights at a time with no sleep. To me this is just another competitive challenge, a twisted contest to see who can be awake the longest, who can party the most, take the biggest hit of meth, blow the biggest cloud, or blow the best pipe. I show off by blowing perfect meth smoke rings and feel a perverse pride in always being the winner in this event.

Some say crystal meth is the devil, and if that's the case, the worship is done around the rituals that I've spoken of before: you score the drug, see how clean it is, examine it to see which of the different types it is, and then reverently begin the ceremony of snorting or smoking or shooting.

Among countless varieties of meth, there's lemon drop, peanut butter, and P2P (made from helicopter hydraulic fluid, if you can believe it—the best stuff you can get, from what I'm told).

I'm traveling further and further out there, toward oblivion and away from family, friends, and myself. No matter how far gone I am, however, I can still locate home base. Still, my story is starting to sound like that of a rock star who fell to earth, or like an episode of *Behind the Music*. I can't stand the thought that I've become just another Hollywood cliché, but there it is. Gone is the Hollywood mansion with beautiful people partying and skating all day and all night. The luxury cars have vanished as if blown away by an afternoon breeze. There are no world travels, champagne dinners, or sponsorship checks to cover expenses. The crowds chanting my name have been replaced by freaks screeching for me to blow pipes with them. I've torn it all down with my own hands, destroyed everything, and left the life I love in ruins. And now my habit is taking a jackhammer to whatever's left behind.

While I know too many people to actually be homeless, I'm still jumping from place to place. People still want (or are willing) to hang out and party with me, so I generally have decent places to stay when I need them. Mostly, though, I stay in my van. With no legal income, the only way I can get something beyond the necessities is to flip a little dope and turn a little profit. I'm a good customer and know lots of people who use lots of drugs—and I help connect those customers with suppliers—so when I go to a dealer's house he usually gives me without charge whatever I need for myself. However, if I want to hook some chick up, and I always do, I need twice as much. To get more means doing some sort of work beyond flipping dope—and that means transporting drugs. It's dangerous for sure, but in the end I'm rewarded with all the meth I can smoke, a girl for a night or two, a place to sleep for a while, and maybe a few extra bucks, which I eventually burn through to score more dope. You know, all the little things that make life worth living.

Before I was ever a drug junkie, I was an adrenaline junkie, risking it all on some ramp or pool. I love going to the edge and barely pulling it. That's where adrenaline lives. I now fire that adrenaline surge by avoiding

the cops, smoking pipes, and hooking up with crazy chicks. It's entertaining enough to keep me coming back for more, but it's starting to get old, and I know that my number could be coming up. Drugs are getting more and more risky, and the casualty rate around me is mounting.

What I love most about meth is what most people hate about it—any hit you take could be your last one. When you're as far into drugs as I am, the idea is to push the boundaries and stay just this side of death. You go as far as you can, until you're shoved right up against death's door. You can nearly *smell* death, but you survive—and you think, This is a good high; this is worth the money. If you don't brush up against death, it's not much of a thrill. That's like chasing the dragon, pushing the line further and further, until you've reached the ultimate high. You live on the thinnest line, balancing between life and death, approaching the line fast and backing off at the last second. You've been there before, so you recognize the signals. Cross that line and you're dead.

It may sound funny, but I'm particular about the tweakers I hang out with. I gravitate toward the ones who are talkative—not just babbling, but educated and wanting to discuss some of the important issues of life. I don't like the usual types of tweakers. They're always fidgety and are often "projing out," meaning tinkering with one ridiculous project or another. Those guys are always building meaningless contraptions, taking brand-new appliances apart, and never having all the screws to put them back together again. Then there's the addict who will snap on you for no reason.

Drug addicts are *definitely* not all the same. Some are kind of mellow and maintain decent lives. The saddest ones are the kindhearted, sensitive people that you think would never do drugs. You see them around for years, clean and sober, being responsible to their jobs and their families. When something rocks their world, the next thing you know they're using. Pretty soon they don't care about anything other than drugs. I've seen formerly good family men and women get so bad they'll smoke meth right in front of their babies and not seem to even notice.

As bad as I am, I always make sure the kid—whether it's my own or someone else's—is in another room, away from the secondhand meth smoke. If somebody is gonna use dope right in front of their baby, I'm out.

Drawing this line enhances the illusion that I'm both ethical and under control. But nothing about my life is under control. No matter where I go, there's meth and there are people who want it more than life itself.

People don't want to believe that meth has seeped beneath their white-picket fences, but it can get into any home. I've lived on the streets of Huntington Beach and up the road in some of America's richest ZIP codes. There's no shortage of dope in any area I've ever been.

Some of my homies from Venice, like Scott Oster and especially Block, get through to me more than most other people do. Block's a powerful person and a leader, and when he says to do something, it's a good idea to listen. He knows me as well as anyone, and he tries to help out:

I TOLD CHRISTIAN, "COME UP TO THE HOUSE OR I'M GONNA FIND YOU AND BEAT YOU UP." HE KNOWS ME, AND SO HE KNOWS THAT I'LL DO IT. HE DRIVES UP FROM ORANGE COUNTY AND IS BACK IN VENICE. HE CRASHES OUT UP HERE FOR A WHILE, AND HE'S TRYING TO GET CLEAN. OF COURSE I'LL HELP HIM. THE PLAN IS FOR HIM TO MOVE IN WITH ME. HE HAS HIS STUFF THERE, READY TO MOVE IN, BUT HE STICKS AROUND FOR ONLY A FEW DAYS. THEN HE'S BACK DOWN TO HUNTINGTON.

I'M NOT TOO WORRIED ABOUT HIM, THOUGH. I'VE SEEN FRIENDS A LOT WORSE OFF. I'VE HAD TO PULL THE NEEDLE OUT OF THEIR ARMS, BREAK DOWN THEIR DOORS, AND BRING THEM HERE, TO MY HOUSE. HE DIDN'T LOOK THAT BAD TO ME.

Block's right: I'm not "that bad." Not like those other speed freaks, imagining that my friends are conspiring against me or that they plan to turn me in. I never think that the guy nobody knows at the party is a narc. I've heard of other meth-heads running around the yard with a gun, pointing at people who aren't there. That's not me. Never even close. But I've seen people get that bad and worse. You have to be *smart* if you're going to do drugs. Of course, everyone thinks they're smarter than the guy who

doesn't make it. If anybody ever really expected they'd flip out, OD on someone's couch, become a street person, lose their teeth, or get all bugged out, they'd probably never do drugs. But nobody ever thinks that will happen to them. People don't know themselves as well as they think they do, and addicts are uniquely gifted in the art of self-deception. Because of my own self-deception, I've always believed I can quit whenever I want to.

So in what ways am I a "smart" user? My advice to other drug addicts is always, Don't carry drugs outside; you'll get arrested. I mean, I'm one to talk, right? I'm eventually caught carrying a large amount onto a plane and find myself busted big-time. Another way I try to be smart about my drug use is to put a line around how much I'm gonna do. Problem is I keep moving the line further and further back, using more all the time. I tell myself I'm not like those other drug addicts that use everything all at once; I use mine up a little (actually a lot) at a time. So many of my friends burn up their entire stash all at once.

And I play it smart by not becoming an actual dealer, although I have plenty of opportunities to do so. What I'm doing isn't dealing, I tell myself; it's simply carrying for someone else. It's funny how you can imagine you're okay when you're not. It's because of a game of comparison all drug users play. Jay Adams sums it up perfectly: "When you smoke pot you think, At least I'm not taking pills. When you take pills, you think, At least I'm not doing coke. When you do coke you think, At least I'm not doing heroin. When you do heroin, you think, At least I'm not shooting it. When you shoot it you think, At least I'm not as bad as that other guy." By the time you *are* as bad as that guy and there's nobody worse than you, it's game over.

But the chances of me turning up dead seem slim, especially living in Orange County. I mean, drugs can kill you anywhere, but I'm never going to OD—smart user, remember?—and there's little chance I'll get shot. As violent as things can get in O.C., with guys getting beat down pretty badly every so often, it's nothing like L.A. In Orange County there aren't that many people armed and ready to rob you at gunpoint or to gun you down for your dope. That's not to say it isn't gnarly in O.C., but it's never scary in the way it can be in L.A. *There* you walk the streets knowing that everyone's strapped and that someone might actually shoot you.

Even though I'm a mess, I'm still able to stick it to an old sponsor and the established guys in my own little way. It's my business partner Chicken's idea, actually. Powell-Peralta has done a skate movie called *The Search for Animal Chin*, staring the Bones Brigade: Lance Mountain, Tony Hawk, Cab, and those guys. The T-shirt naturally has the movie's name on it, *The Search for Animal Chin*. Rumors about my disappearance are always circulating throughout the skate world, so Chicken makes these shirts that say *The Search for Animal Christian*, and they pass them out to friends. I thought that was hilarious at the time.

The world is closing in, but in part because of the fun I still have with friends, I retain an optimistic feeling that things will somehow get better. They always have in the past, so even now I never get really stressed or depressed. Little things can ruin the moment, of course—like when I want to hang out with a girl and it doesn't happen, or I want to skate somewhere particular one day and I'm unable to. Usually if I want to skate a park, I just stealth it into the Huntington Beach Skatepark, take a few runs, and bail out quickly. I hear that people will later say, "Whoa, Christian Hosoi just cruised by and skated." That gives me a little rush, though I know I'm not in the same shape I used to be: I've lost some muscle tone and some people have told me my skin is taking on a gray tone, the color people turn after they die. I can only imagine what else they're saying. Who cares? I can live without all those hypocrites.

I've skated for so long on drugs that it's not difficult. It's an instinctive activity, like riding a bike once you know how, or maybe Keith Richards playing his guitar. You never forget how. I enjoy my newest role as a ghost that appears from time to time and quickly vanishes. And I still enjoy the rush of the cat-and-mouse hustle required to keep myself out of jail. My mojo's still working pretty well; I'm still able to pull a rabbit out of my hat when I need to, so in my mind I'm still the man.

THE 900

My life should be a warning to anyone who ever considers doing drugs—I'm on the run from the cops, living in my van, while Tony Hawk is reaching for the impossible as we approach the turn of the millennium. We've never seen a skateboarder stay on top beyond his midtwenties at that point, and

I sure don't expect to see anyone's career last double that—certainly not as long as Tony's has. Here's to clean living, right?

Tony is the first competitive skateboarder to reach middle age and still remain relevant. He's forever dazzling judges with new tricks; I think he has about a hundred of them to his credit. Still, I doubt he would be as big as he is now if he hadn't continued down the road he was on, reached deep into himself, and accomplished the unthinkable: the 900. (To make it more impressive, he's still ripping 900s at the age of forty-three, as this book goes to publication. Who knows how long he'll last?)

As we approach the 1999 Summer X Games, everyone is wondering what the skateboarders will do. Only a few years ago the 540 was considered nearly impossible; now someone has nearly doubled that—Danny Way nearly completed a full 900 a while back. The top young pros all try and fail, but Tony's like the Terminator; he won't ever quit. He's chased the 900 for thirteen years now, and has ended by slamming down hard many times. He finally pulls it off on camera at those 1999 X Games. It gets big press too: this isn't some tiny blurb in a skate magazine, but full features in publications like *USA Today*. They didn't get the press then, but it's like McGill when he did the 540 and Alva when he did the first frontside air; nobody else can claim those initial triumphs but them. Such accomplishments create a legacy for the individual and change the sport forever. Tony and I have always been stark contrasts to one another, but never as much as we are now. He's headed for superstardom; I'm headed for prison.

Tony helps put skateboarding further on the map with his *Tony Hawk Pro Skater* video game series. He's always been a computer whiz, so he can design all the games himself. They become the biggest-selling video games on the market, a feat that brings Tony a fortune and takes skateboarding into millions of kids' rooms around the world. (At the time all I can think is that I'll soon be getting my own gaming character.)

He's the right guy in the right place at the right time, a good image that no parents are afraid for their kid to imitate. It doesn't take long for kids, their parents, and their grandparents to realize that skateboarding isn't just some hula hoop or yo-yo fad that you fall into briefly before storing the board in the rafters forever. These days, you don't quit skating just because you turn sixteen. Skating has grown from a backyard, underground activity with several thousand hard-core participants to something every kid on every street is into. It's now a real sport and has a real future, paying real money for those who desire to be the best, fly the highest, break records, invent maneuvers, and win contests. Not everyone's willing to take it to the edge, however, cuz that's a price often paid in your own blood. ✹

ONE LOVE

We were living mainly in
Christian's van, completely methed
out. We didn't exactly keep a scrapbook
of that period of our lives.
—JENNIFER LEE HOSOI

CHAPTER 18

Life had been running downhill quickly until I meet Jennifer Lee Gilbert, a club dancer. Her roommate is a friend of mine, Amber, who has a picture of me in her photo album, one where I'm blowing a smoke ring of meth. Jen sees that photo and decides she wants to meet me. I'm couch-surfing when she calls the place I'm living, tells me her name, and asks if I want to come over. I'm like, "Yeah." What guy wouldn't be stoked on some hot-sounding chick on the line, saying she wants to get together? I cruise over to meet her at her apartment, and she's even hotter than she sounds. She and Amber are getting high on a drug known as GHB, so I join in. We get high, hang out, and I forget to leave.

A s the days go by, we move on to other drugs. Jen snorts meth regularly, but I quickly convert her to smoking it. Now we're smoking meth every day, and just hangin' out, always high. In time we fall in love, but neither of us will admit it initially, for fear of rejection. It's just us together late every night, and from that first day on I've never seriously gone out with another girl.

Because I don't hallucinate or have paranoid delusions, I think I'm in control, and I assume she is too. Jen's recollection paints a different picture:

IF YOU LOOK AT PICTURES OF CHRISTIAN ON DRUGS AND NOW, HE'S A TOTALLY DIFFERENT PERSON. HIS SKIN TONE WAS GRAY BACK THEN. BUT THANK GOD HE NEVER GOT VIOLENT OR TALKED TOTALLY CRAZY. I WAS THE ONE WHO THOUGHT THERE WERE PEOPLE FOLLOWING ME AND THAT THE COPS HAD SET UP IN THE EMPTY APARTMENT NEXT DOOR. MY BEST FRIEND, WHO WAS ALSO THE APARTMENT MANAGER AT THE TIME, WOULD HAVE TO ESCORT ME THROUGH THAT UNIT, TO SEE THAT NOBODY LIVED THERE.

EVENTUALLY WE WERE LIVING MAINLY IN CHRISTIAN'S VAN, COM-PLETELY METHED OUT. I WAS JUST AS BAD AS HE WAS. WE DIDN'T EXACTLY KEEP A SCRAPBOOK OF THAT PERIOD OF OUR LIVES.

Jen parties right alongside me, but I'm not there the day her girlfriend snaps from using too much speed:

THERE WAS THIS DANCER THAT WORKED WITH ME AT THE CLUB, [JEN REMEMBERS]. SHE WAS A HEROIN ADDICT AND SHE NEEDED NEEDLES. MY DEALER SLAMMED SPEED, SO I WAS ABLE TO GET HER NEEDLES. WE ENDED UP HANGING OUT. SHE GOT HER HEROIN; I GOT MY METH.

I WAS STAYING AT MY GRANDMOTHER'S PLACE RIGHT THEN, AND THIS GIRL MOVED IN WITH US AND STAYED IN THE SPARE ROOM. SHE WANTED TO GIVE UP HEROIN, SO SHE STARTED DOING METH. ONE DAY I WALKED INTO HER ROOM AND HER HAND WAS WRAPPED UP AND BLOODY. TURNS OUT SHE HAD BEEN SHOOTING UP IN HER HAND AND IN HER NECK AND WAS TRYING TO FIND A GOOD VEIN.

ANOTHER TIME SHE HADN'T DONE ANYTHING FOR A FEW DAYS SO THE DRUGS HIT HER HARD, AND CHRISTIAN AND I WERE BRINGING HER BACK TO MY GRANDMOTHER'S HOUSE. WE PULLED OVER IN FRONT OF A NEARBY EMPTY HOUSE FIRST, AND CHRISTIAN AND I SMOKED SOME METH. MY FRIEND THOUGHT PEOPLE WERE LOOKING OUT THE WINDOW OF THAT HOUSE AT HER, BUT NOBODY WAS IN THERE.

LATER ON, BACK AT MY GRANDMOTHER'S, SHE WAS SAYING THERE WERE ALL THESE LITTLE BABIES, AND THEIR HEADS WERE UNDER-NEATH THE BED. I WAS LIKE, OKAY, SHE'S DONE WAY TOO MUCH METH AND SHE'S TRIPPIN' OUT. THIS WENT ON FOR TWO DAYS.

AT ONE POINT I SAW HER LYING ON THE FLOOR IN THE HALLWAY, CA-RESSING THE FACE OF SOMEBODY WHO WASN'T THERE. WHEN I ASKED WHAT SHE WAS DOING, SHE SAID, "WELL, HEATHER'S HEAD FELL OFF AND I'M PUTTING IT BACK ON SO I CAN PUT HER MAKEUP ON." THAT REALLY SCARED ME. I DIDN'T WANT TO BE LIKE THAT. THAT'S WHEN I SAID, "I'M QUITTING DRUGS."

HIGH IN THE CHAPEL

I've seen people on drugs get close to death before, so I don't think much about Jen's story. But she's really shaken up, as I suppose most people would be. In fact, she's so freaked out she says she's quitting drugs and going to church with her grandmother. It's fine with me that she wants to go to church. I'm not invited, though, probably because her grandmother considers me a bad influence. I'm not hanging out at their house much anyway. I stay in my van up the street, hoping for Jen to join me. I've never once been to church before and don't know exactly what goes on there, but her grandmother and her uncle Chris, who's a pastor, seem to think it will help. I'm cool with that—whatever works is fine.

Jen may be going to church, but I'm certainly not getting any divine benefits. I get busted for the third time, this time in a raid. People are jumping from windows, hiding in closets and in bushes, but the cops nab most of them, including me. I don't have ID on me, and when they ask my name, I say Christian Hosoi. They miss a letter and record my last name as Hosi. Who am I to correct them?

They say it will take $2,000 for me to get out, which is 10 percent of a $20,000 bail. I know from experience, though, that it'll take a lot more than that if the cops learn my history. Because of the name mix-up, they don't yet know about my prior arrests. I've gotta move fast. If I can come up with $2,000 before I'm fingerprinted, I'll be free. Problem is I don't have that much on me or anywhere near me.

I call Jen and say, "You've gotta get me two grand. The cops picked me up, and if you can't come up with the money, they'll fingerprint me and figure out who I am, and I'll be going away for a while." Thinking she won't be able to come up with that much, I also call another girl I used to go out with.

Fairly quickly I'm told that bail has been paid and I can go. Jen and the other girl I called are standing outside the jail, both having chipped in on the bail. As my girlfriend, Jen is understandably angry about the other girl showing up. I tell the second girl, "Look, I'm going home with Jen." She's like, "I did all that for you and now you're going home with her?" I say, "She's my girlfriend now, and you know it." Unwilling to concede, she barks, "You'd better come over later," but I never do.

Apparently there's no record of that arrest—at least none connected with me—since the charging officer spelled my name wrong. I never hear about that charge again and never have to pay any additional fine for it.

Jen occasionally attends Calvary Chapel in Placentia. That's her grandmother's church, so she wants to attend there. On one particular day I'm supposed to pick her up and take her there. When I swing by late to get her, her grandfather is there alone, and he tells me that Jen has gone ahead to church with her grandmother. He tells me where the church is located and I head for it. I do what I always do: smoke meth all the way to my destination, and even in the parking lot.

I arrive just as the service is about to end, and I stand at the back. They're doing worship songs, and it all feels kind of nice and peaceful, but nothing I'm feeling emotional over. I walk up behind Jen when it's over and tap her on the shoulder. She turns around, gives me a big hug, and starts crying. Her grandmother knows the pastor, and she walks me forward to meet him. She says, "This is Christian Hosoi, my grand-daughter's boyfriend; he's a professional skateboarder." The pastor says, "Hey, my son's a skateboarder! It's really nice to meet you, Christian."

So now I've experienced church for the first time in my life. Church is cool, skating's cool, dope's cool, life's cool. And, if Jen's cool, I'm cool. Jen is my only friend who's *not* doing dope, but I figure we can still have a relationship since I've developed such deep feelings for her. The positive choices she's making to help herself live a better life further steal my heart.

Jen is saving her money now, and she's not about to waste any more of it on drugs. That's fine with me; I've always believed that if you want something bad enough, you'll find a way to get it. I'll score my own dope. Each day's the same—score drugs (doing whatever is necessary to "earn" them), do drugs morning till night, skateboard a little, and throw darts to break the monotony. The one thing that's changed in my routine is that I no longer look to hook up with anyone. I'm happy being with Jen. I'm out all day and meet her late at night, cuz that's when we get together in my van. You know that dumb bumper sticker, "If this van's rockin', don't bother knockin'"? That could have been written for us. Some days I'm almost surprised my van doesn't tip over or catch fire. We were like two puzzle pieces that fit together perfectly.

Over the months, we continue hanging out, and as always happens, bad company corrupts good morals. She eventually gives in, saying, "Okay, maybe I'll do just a *little* meth." I'm like, "Okay, here, do a little." I'm a horrible influence on her! Though she's doing just a little at first, in no time she's nearly back to where she left off. She remembers that process of getting clean and then falling back:

CHRISTIAN HAD GIVEN ME THESE TWO CANDLES WITH PICTURES OF JESUS ON THEM. I WAS PRAYING, LOOKING AT THEM, AND SAID, "JESUS, IF YOU'RE FOR REAL LIKE UNCLE CHRIS SAYS, PLEASE HELP ME; I CAN'T LIVE LIKE THIS."

LOTS OF THINGS HAPPENED AFTER THAT TO PROVE THE REALITY OF GOD TO ME—LIFE-AFFIRMING THINGS—AND THAT'S WHAT GOT ME SOBER. I WAS CLEAN FOR A MONTH, AND IT FELT GOOD.

CHRISTIAN KEPT SMOKING METH IN FRONT OF ME, THOUGH. ONE DAY I WAS WEAK AND JUST DID IT AGAIN. AFTER THAT I WAS INTO IT JUST LIKE I'D ALWAYS BEEN. I WAS AFRAID TO GO HOME AND COULDN'T FACE MY GRANDMOTHER. I JUST STAYED WITH CHRISTIAN PRETTY MUCH THE ENTIRE TIME AFTER THAT, UNTIL WE ENDED UP GOING TO HAWAII.

Despite Jen's backsliding, she's many steps ahead of me. At least she understands the concept of trying to quit and get her life together. One of her main motivations for trying to get clean is that she doesn't want her grandparents to see her high. She loves them and knows how much her using hurts them. According to Jen,

MY GRANDMOTHER LILLIAN AND GRANDFATHER TOM RAISED ME. WHEN THEY MET, GRANDMA LILLIAN HAD FIVE CHILDREN. SHE WAS THIRTY-THREE AND HE WAS TWENTY-ONE, SO MAYBE SHE WAS A "COUGAR" BEFORE COUGARS WERE POPULAR. EVEN THOUGH SHE WAS DONE RAISING HER OWN CHILDREN, SHE TOOK ME IN AS IF I WERE HER OWN CHILD. SHE TAUGHT ME WHAT LOVE IS. SHE TAUGHT ME ABOUT LIFE AND ABOUT RELATIONSHIPS.

With me it's different. I don't hide anything from anyone; I just come right out and tell people that I'm on meth.

Since Jen doesn't want to return home high, we stay in the van or, on occasion, get a hotel room or stay with a friend or one of her fellow dancers. That's getting old and I want to take better care of her, maybe get a place of our own. I say, "I'm gonna go to Hawaii to make some money; you wanna go?" She agrees to go with me. Babe and I are off to Hawaii.

We set off together and find a place near my dad. Once I get her situated in Hawaii, I leave her there temporarily and return to L.A. to score some meth. I've been offered a good deal to bring some over to the Islands.

Given that I've been on the run for five years and have been hanging out with dealers since I was a kid, you'd think I'd know (and appreciate the severity of) the penalties of interstate trafficking of narcotics. I certainly should know better than to jump at the possibility of $2,500 plus all the dope I'll never be able to smoke, in exchange for a large chunk of my life. It makes sense when I'm high, though.

And that brings me back to where my story started: busted.

JOYFUL TRIALS

You know that saying, "It's all good"? There's a book in the Bible called James, which made that same point nearly two thousand years ago. It says it like this: "My brethren, count it all joy when you fall into various trials" (1:2). I've been running so hard for so long that when someone approaches Eddie and asks, "Did you hear what happened to Christian?" he nearly collapses, thinking he's gonna hear that I've died. The body count for people involved in my lifestyle is mounting, not just among my friends but generally, and his reaction is kind of natural.

While my death might not have surprised many people, nobody could ever guess that I would become a Christian. Well, I have always been unpredictable.

Most people now, looking back, would list January 23, 2000—the day I was arrested at the Honolulu airport—as the lowest point in my life. I see it, with the benefit of hindsight, as the time when my real life began. Let's go back a decade, though, to see what happened *after* that event.

Those first few days after my arrest in Hawaii are the worst. I've got nothing and no one to lean on, especially since at first I can't reach Jen by phone. I'm looking at ten years and have been locked up for only three days; already I'm like a rat in a cage, looking for a way to escape. There isn't any.

As I said in the first chapter, when I finally get through to Jen on the

phone I express my despair, my fears that I won't be able to make it through ten years. She's crying, but she's strong. "I love you," she says, "and we'll get through this. We've just got to trust in God." She points out that it could have been a lot worse: I could have died, or it could have been *both* of us in jail that day, since she was originally going to carry dope with me on that plane.

I can't help wishing that I'd flown the dope somewhere within the state of California instead of all the way to Hawaii. If I'd been caught doing *that*, I probably would have received only a slap on the wrist and probation. Here, though, there's nobody I can pay off and nobody to help me. Several lawyers look into my case for me over the months, and they all conclude that there's nothing illegal in how I've been arrested. With no loopholes to squeeze through, I'm stuck wondering how to make the best of the next 120 months.

Even though I hate being stuck, stuck is right where I need to be. I'm finally still enough to hear what God has to say to me. I'm off all drugs, though by no choice of my own; and with no weed or speed in my system, I can think straight and start catching up on the years of sleep I've lost. Now, for the first time, the events of my life come into focus, and I begin to see the pattern of living that's brought me here.

It's not as if God's been silent over the years. Jen's uncle Chris, the pastor, has been reaching out to her forever, since long before we left California. Even after she started going to church with her grandmother she remained unconvinced, and *I'm* not even listening. Here we are, a stripper doing drugs and a strung-out pro skateboarder. In the world's eyes, and in hers and mine, that's about as far from God as it gets. In God's eyes, however, she and I are no different from some nice tea-drinking husband and wife who do good and productive work and coach their kid's soccer team on the weekends.

Just before I get busted that final time, we're cruising around Oahu when a woman at a gas station asks, "Have you guys ever gone to church? There's a good one not far from here." It's an apparently random comment, one I haven't heard from a stranger before, ever. God is tapping on our shoulders, but we simply tell the woman, "Yeah, we've been to church."

We have no time for that now; we're doing life our way, and our way is to score drugs.

Jen recalls the days prior to my arrest:

I WOKE UP AFTER SLEEPING FOR THE FIRST TIME IN DAYS WHEN CHRISTIAN FINALLY CALLED ME. I HAD BEEN CALLING, CALLING, CALLING. NOTHING. HE WAS SUPPOSED TO BE BACK IN HUNTINGTON BEACH FOR ONE DAY BEFORE FLYING BACK OVER TO HAWAII, BUT I HADN'T HEARD A WORD. WHEN HE FINALLY GETS THROUGH TO SAY HE'S BEEN ARRESTED, I ACTUALLY THINK HE'S JOKING. WHEN I REALIZE HE'S SERIOUS, I GET SCARED, THEN I'M RELIEVED THAT AT LEAST HE'S ALIVE. IT COULD HAVE BEEN A LOT WORSE. HE COULD HAVE BEEN DEAD OR IT COULD HAVE BEEN BOTH OF US IN JAIL THAT DAY. I WAS SUPPOSED TO CARRY DOPE WITH HIM ON THAT PLANE.

No matter what I do or who I talk to, it looks like I'm serving all ten years; that's actually the minimum mandatory sentence for my crime. Okay, now I've got to do what Jen says: "Trust God." That's the reality of life for all people every day, but it takes seeing it through prison bars for me to get a clear picture.

Jen tells me on that first phone call to get a Bible, so I begin asking around for one. A guy in another cell says I can use his. He hands it to me through the bars. Here's this great big book, all underlined and with notes in the margins, and I have no idea why it should be of any interest to me.

I open to the first book in the Bible, Genesis. To me that's an old *Star Trek* movie. I flip to the back of the Bible, Revelation. I've never had any sort of revelation before, not even drug-induced, so I can't relate. I go to the middle of the Bible and puzzle over how to pronounce the name of the book I've turned to. P-salms. What is P-salms? A nearby book, Proverbs, sounds like an old-school lecture, and John sounds really boring. I finally stop at the book called I Kings. Kings, now that sounds good.

The second chapter of I Kings begins with King David on his deathbed, charging his son Solomon to heed the voice of the Lord and follow that voice all the days of his life. God tells him that if he does that, everything will go right for him. But I then read the story of Solomon, and it doesn't end that well. Here's the wisest man in the world and even *he's* seduced by the temptations of lust, greed, and fame. The guy has a million times more of everything than I'll ever have, and he still blows it. I relate to him totally, and by seeing what *he* should have done, I begin to understand what *I* need to do.

JENNIFER AND ME HOLDING ON FOR DEAR LIFE. *HOSOI FAMILY COLLECTION.*

Jen could have said anything during my first phone call to her from jail. Instead of saying that she's going to leave me, that she wants to party with her friends and not worry about me, or that she wants to go straight and not be brought down by my mistakes, she tells me that we need to trust in God. Nobody has ever talked to me that way before, and it's got me thinking.

And I *keep* thinking, even as I'm flown from Hawaii to the mainland courtesy of the U.S. government. After landing in L.A.—this is about three weeks after my arrest—I'm transferred by van to a San Bernardino County jail. Driving through San Bernardino brings back a rush of memories. The last time I cruised these streets I was high on weed and laughing with a bunch of friends on my way to skate a contest. I'm sure our conversation was centered on what kind of weed we were smoking, the contest we were going to, and all of the girls we were about to hook up with. The world was ours. Now I'm clean and sober, cuffed and solemn, rolling down the road with a bunch of criminals I don't know. I look out to see the same world through different eyes, recalling all those memories: the skateparks, the epic battles, and the friends I made along the way. As we drive, it sinks in that I'll be over forty years old by the time I skate again.

I grew up thinking that I was an individualist and invincible and that I had life all figured out. Now I realize I don't even have my own identity, and I don't have a clue what life is about. I spend a lot of time reading the Bible—a copy of the Revised Standard Version—and Jesus's words in John 3:3 jump out at me: "Unless one is born again, he cannot see the kingdom of God." Or like that old hymn "Amazing Grace" says: "I once was blind and now I see." People sing these words all the time, but now I actually *live* them: I *was* blind and I now have twenty-twenty vision. It's awesome to realize there's a plan for my life, that I'm significant despite my failures, and that God loves me.

Soon I have a chance to take that realization to the next level. San Bernardino Jail gets so crowded that I'm transferred to the overflow jail, a place called Glen Helen Rehabilitation Center. Glen Helen is on bunk status much of the time, meaning that I can't walk around freely very often. This gives me even more time to think. While I'm in Glen Helen, Jen hooks up a three-way phone conversation between us and her uncle, Pastor Chris. He says, "Christian, do you know that God loves you?" I've experienced enough and read enough of the Bible by this time to know that that's true, so I simply answer, "Yeah."

Pastor Chris asks whether we want to give our lives to Jesus Christ. When we say yes, Pastor Chris shares the gospel with us—the good news of God's son, Jesus. He finishes by saying, "You have to invite Jesus in. If you do that—if you believe that Christ died for you and was raised from the dead, and you allow him to work in you—you too will be saved." At that moment we give our lives to the Lord, and our lives are changed forever. I feel a weight roll off my shoulders—a weight that I didn't even know I'd been carrying all those years. Jen and I are both crying tears of joy, even in the midst of the circumstances. For the first time in my life I feel a sense of belonging to something bigger than myself.

In my own tiny way, my life is like that of King Solomon in reverse. I go from having the best of the world but not knowing God, to losing everything and finding God. Solomon went from knowing God and walking with him, to letting the things of this world corrupt him, until he was left with everything but the peace of God. My commitment to God runs far deeper than my passion ever was for skateboarding, drugs, girls, or the rock-star life. It's as Jesus said in John 14:15: "If you love me, keep My commandments." I knew that before I ever read that passage in the New Testament. I understood it from my first reading of Kings, back in Hawaii. It's like the Bible says: I was adopted into God's kingdom and became his child. Now I have an assignment to carry out.

As my life continues to unfold, I realize I can make a real difference in the world—far more than I ever did as a skateboarder. I had never opened up a Bible in those days, and none of my friends had ever read one either. No wonder we all ended up with heartache and pain.

The apostle Paul says, "I count all things but loss for the excellency of the knowledge of Christ Jesus my Lord: for whom I have suffered the loss of all things, and do count them but dung, that I may win Christ" (Philippians 3:8, KJV). I so relate to that. Everything I've accomplished—the victories, the social status, the money, the sex, *all* of that—suddenly means nothing to me. It really *is* all dung, and I'm going to flush it. I would trade everything I've ever done for what I now have. I'm sitting here in prison on my triple-decker bunk bed, fulfilled in life for the first time ever. ✹

0010300158
LAST: HOSOI
FIRST: CHRISTIAN
MID: ROSHA
100567   33 WMA
507   150 BLK BRO

FED INMATE

LIGHT IN THE DARKNESS

In jail, problems get
dealt with one way or another.
—CHRISTIAN HOSOI

CHAPTER 19

It's difficult to say where one journey begins and another ends. I now see that God has been calling me all of my life. I'm named Christian and have worn crosses ever since I can remember. My nickname is Christ, and I invented a maneuver called the Christ Air, all without having a clue what the name Jesus Christ really means.

In one day I've gone from hooking up with nearly any girl I want to living in a cell block full of men. There are no women here, but I curtail my fantasy life and decide that I'm not even gonna masturbate anymore. I know that might make some of you uncomfortable, but if a guy is honest, he'll admit that sexual immorality is always knocking on our door. (It's now been over a decade since that commitment, and I still haven't masturbated—and don't intend to. Sexual purity with my wife is a wonderful blessing, but I realize that I've got to make a strong commitment to it. Now that I'm out of prison and living with my wife, sex has gone from an act of self-pleasure to something so much deeper. It's not just some performance to make me feel like I'm a wild stallion. It's now what it was meant to be, and it's awesome, even sacred.)

From prison I promise Jen that I'll save myself for her, no matter how long it takes to get released. That might sound insincere since there are no women around, but I want her to hear my commitment. I want her to know that I've found everything I've been searching for, including love and integrity, in one book and in one life, and that life includes her.

When I read the Bible passage about making your yes mean yes and your no mean no, found in James 5:12, I begin to understand true integrity for the first time. I mean, everybody's got his or her "good meter," but there comes a point when your value system breaks down and you compromise. Faith is based not on rules and regulations, but on a desire to please something, actually *someone*, greater than what we see with our own eyes. I've always valued honesty and truth; now I know the Truth.

ACCEPTING DIVINE WILL AND HUMAN LAW

It can be noisy in jail, so I often block everything out by pulling my blanket over my head when I pray. Once I get over the idea that God isn't going to open the cell door and set me free immediately, I begin praying for things other than my release. I still remember vividly one of the prayers I said: "Lord, I'll travel to the ends of the earth—to Africa, to the rain forests, to tribes that have never heard of you. I'll go anywhere and I'll do anything. I'll leave my family, I'll quit skateboarding—whatever you want, I'll do it." Ridiculous, right? I meant it too.

Immediately, though, I sense God whispering to me, "Christian, didn't I give you your loving family and bless you with your ability to ride a skateboard?" I thought for a moment and realized he was right. I was like, "Yes, Lord. Forgive me—I'll be the best husband, the best father, and the best skateboarder I can be, and I'll *still* go wherever you want me to go."

Pops sells his land in Hawaii and we hire a lawyer for $35,000, most of what he gets for the property. Jen feels from the first that the woman we hire isn't on the up-and-up, but it's like she would later say, "When you're as desperate as we were, you want to believe anything and will pay any amount."

The lawyer promises she can get me an early release, and that sounds good to me. She says she's about to become a judge and has connections; she can talk to the judge hearing my case, she says, and he will cut us a good deal. She says that with her help, I'll get five years instead of ten. We will later hear that she took our money and checked herself into a mental institution. A few years after that we will hear the tragic news that she has jumped to her death from a freeway bridge.

Next, a man we know in the Islands, a good friend of the family, gives us six grand for another lawyer. That lawyer looks into things and is at least honest enough to tell us the truth: that there is nothing he or anyone else can do to get my sentence reduced.

I finally, gradually make peace with the idea that I'll be here a long time. I'm okay with that reality, but my parents are really broken up over it. Here I am, their only child, facing ten years for drug trafficking. With time and distance on my side I can see the goodness of my parents and also their faults. It's kind of like opening the book of Genesis, the first book of the Bible, and seeing the way everything that was created was perfect before the fall. Even people with great intentions like my parents can't keep on track without God. I'm experiencing a freedom I've never known, and I tell people an ironic truth—that I didn't go from freedom to prison, but I went from prison to freedom.

INSIDE RULES

Life has its challenges for everyone, whether in jail or out, whether saved or not. Like jails and prisons everywhere, San Bernardino and Glen Helen are divided by race—now *there's* a challenge for you. There are the whites, the Mexicans, the Southsiders, the blacks, Chinos, and the Islanders—Samoans, Tongans, Asians, Hawaiians, Filipinos, Guamanians, and the like. That's where I fit in, with the Islanders. Things could be worse. For some guys, jail is much more isolating than it is for me. They're cut off from the world for their entire sentence, making no connections inside and getting no visitors from outside.

Other than fellowship with other inmates and visits from friends and family, I look forward to different types of food we order on commissary. My biggest treat is chili ramen. I like it best served with beef jerky, crackers, and Flamin' Hot Cheetos, all together in one soup. It's actually not bad. I have friends visiting me regularly, and from time to time they put money on my books. With that money I can buy a variety of food from the commissary.

Commissary equals currency on the inside, but there's no locking things up; you just leave your purchases right there, usually on the bed. I have about seventy-five bucks' worth of packaged soups, chips, crackers, candy bars, honey buns, and other things to eat.

Here's a story about when I first went to jail: Among my treats are four bags of popcorn. One day I return from the rec yard and find that one bag is missing. I don't really care, but I'm thinking, Man, I can't let someone get away with taking what's mine or I'm gonna get punked the whole time I'm here. We're in a tank of sixty inmates, and I stand up in front of them all and shout, "Hey, who took my popcorn?" When nobody admits to anything, I take further action and ask my shot-caller (a leader of a race) to investigate the situation.

Meanwhile, I take further action myself. I sharpen a pencil very publicly—something that sounds harmless but sends a message. See, the pencils they give you in jail are short so that you won't stab anybody with them. What people do is remove the blade from a disposable razor and use that blade to sharpen a pencil to a long, fine point. Then they take a playing card and roll it tightly around the sharpened pencil, along with another pencil for strength. Then they find something—say, the sticker from a deodorant stick—and wrap the two pencils tightly together. The result is a good shank.

So I'm standing there, sharpening the pencil, saying, "Look, somebody's gonna give up my popcorn." I'm shaking as I speak, but I look directly at this group of hard-core prisoners and think, It's me against them.

Each cell block typically has a shot-caller for each race, and every shot-caller basically oversees disputes between races. My shot-caller talks to the others after, and someone quickly gives the popcorn back and apologizes. I tell him it's okay; that it's all good.

A message has been sent—and received—not to take my popcorn or anything else of mine. I'd just arrived and didn't yet know how tough I was or what I'd do to survive. I also didn't yet know what consequences standing up for myself could have had. I had already seen a guy stabbed for being a snitch, bleeding everywhere. If you're a knucklehead and don't play by the rules in here, you're gonna get dealt with.

CONTRABAND: PERKS AND PUNISHMENTS

Cigarettes are allowed in the outside rec area in the federal prison, but they're not allowed at all in the county jail, intended for shorter-term holding, which is where I start out. Anticipating this, inmates carry cigarettes in with them, hiding them where the guards won't find them, usually up the poop shoot. When somebody new arrives with a pack of smokes, everybody waits eagerly in his cell while the guy goes to the bathroom and sits on the can. He's in there washing the bag off and comes out with two packs of cigarettes and, believe it or not, a jumbo lighter. Even knowing where those smokes have been, nobody can wait to light up. That really illustrates the sick power of addiction.

Inmates try to combat the smell of tobacco by blowing baby powder into the air as an air freshener. It's not terribly effective. Now, instead of the smell of cigarette smoke, there's a very noticeable combination of smoke and baby powder.

A lot of smart people are locked up, but not all of them use their intelligence for good. Some incarcerated genius figured out how to get a light from a power outlet in the corridor outside a cell, and that knowledge is now part of the lore that's passed on. Here's how it works: Someone takes the lead from a pencil. After buying an eraser for the pencil, he pokes two holes in that and inserts pieces of the lead. He then wraps toilet paper around the whole thing and attaches it to a rolled-up newspaper just long enough to reach the power outlet through the cell's bars. The lead sparks on contact, the paper catches fire, and you light up.

If an inmate wants to get a light the easy way, it costs him. Having a lighter in jail or prison is a good way to make some easy money, though. Somebody with a lighter can charge about a dollar just to light one smoke. People pay in soup or other commissary items. During my term, a soup equals eighty-five cents, for example. Since the currency often *is* food, the guy with cigarettes or a lighter ends up with a whole lot of commissary. You can always tell who has tobacco or a lighter in the house.

In lockup, people who work in the laundry can give out extra T-shirts and socks. They prepare regular rolls of clean T-shirts and socks for distribution, but every so often they roll up doubles of everything. When a guy in the laundry sees a friend coming, he reaches in and grabs one of the doubles. Recipients can get away with it until there's a shakedown. These are random inspections by the guards that are conducted in addition to the usual hourly cell checks. Illegal activities are always planned to go down between scheduled patrols, but shakedowns are designed to be unpredictable.

During a shakedown, the guards strip all the linen from the beds and tip the bunks over so that everything you have is strewn on the floor. The guards march us into the chow hall and line us up, twenty at a time. We're told to bend over and cough. If there are severe violations discovered, either on someone's person or in his cell, that person gets consequences—more on that in a minute. For everyone else, it's back to the cell, where everything is in shambles. Basically, that's what happens when the guards suspect tobacco, weed, a shank, or some other illegal contraband.

Despite the threat of shakedowns, people continue smuggling in cigarettes and intoxicating substances such as weed. With a minute of warning they can eat whatever weed they have and not get caught with it. Obviously, though, not even the most chronic smoker will eat an entire pack of smokes. Either substance, and many others, can earn you a trip to the hole, a cell not much bigger than eight feet by eight, with only one dim light burning. All you can have in the hole is a Bible, if you want one. You get one meal a day. It's called a brick, and it's all the food you normally get, thrown together in a pan, then baked and chopped up into square blocks. That and a drink is it.

That's the punishment when you're in jail. In prison, if you get caught breaking the rules, you might get tossed into the hole, but you'll also lose part of your "good time": the fifty-four days a year that get subtracted from your sentence if you don't have an incident. If you get a write-up or an incident report, your good time gets whittled away. In effect, you're just adding to your sentence when you break the rules.

No extra time for me, thank you. I choose to follow the rules, so I never get anywhere near the hole or lose any of my good time.

One of my favorite times in county jail or prison is mail call. All the inmates stand around quietly as someone calls out the names of people who have mail. Receiving mail makes an inmate feel loved and cared for. I'm one of the fortunate ones who has a loved one who sends a lot of mail. Much as I enjoy the letters, I sometimes wish I could give some of mine to guys who don't get any. That and phone calls are pretty much the only outside connections inmates have. Calls have to be collect, which can be very expensive: it's five bucks for me to hook up with Hawaii, for example, and a dollar a minute after that. I speak to Jen or my dad in the Islands from time to time, and I call my mom on the East Coast whenever I can.

My strongest personal link, both by mail and by phone, is with Jen; I send her love letters, she sends me love letters and notes, and I talk to her every night. Every month I send her a devotional called *The Daily Bread* and we read that together, over the phone. When we're about to get off the phone we sing "Amazing Grace"—every phone call till my release.

Knowing God offers me so much security that I'm no longer afraid of anybody or anything—not even of dying. But I never do get threatened or hassled in either jail or prison. I get along with everyone, and I'm vocal about my Christian faith. Like everything else in here, if you're gonna do something, you've got to push it to the limit. Nobody on the inside likes a poser, so prison tests your commitment and the authenticity of the stand you're taking. My commitment is to walk with God and not back down or compromise regardless of anything that might challenge my faith.

Everything's segregated here—I mentioned earlier how the races tend to group up together—but I hang out with people from all races and do Bible studies with them all. ❀

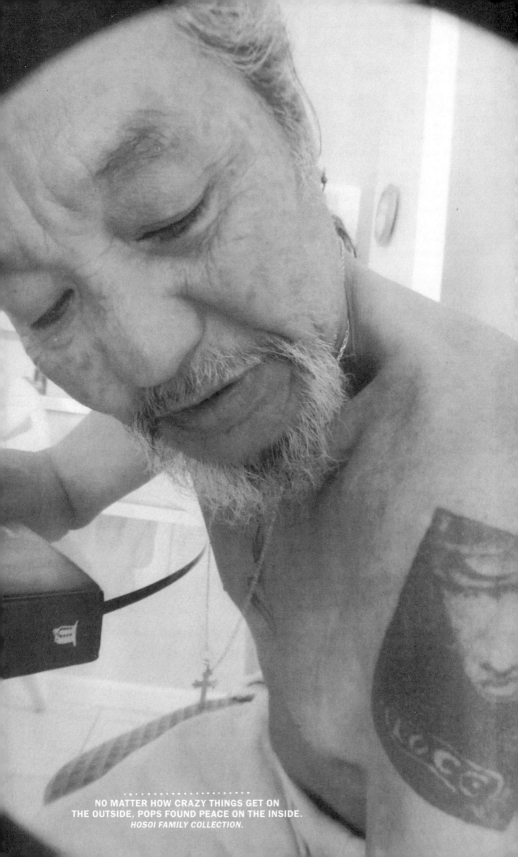

NO MATTER HOW CRAZY THINGS GET ON
THE OUTSIDE, POPS FOUND PEACE ON THE INSIDE.
HOSOI FAMILY COLLECTION.

WHO'S CALLING
THE SHOTS?

There's always a chance
that a race riot will kick off.
— CHRISTIAN HOSOI

CHAPTER 20

I learn that my old friend Jay Adams has been locked up for a parole violation. While Jay has some violence on his record, he'll tell you what almost every other violent offender will tell you: that every bad thing he ever did was related to drug use.

J ay's always been an awesome guy, but not so much when he's high. In the old days Jay and I set the trends, broke the rules, and challenged the records, but now, as we sit in prison and think about being free again someday, his letters express a desire to talk to kids about getting off drugs. I have some amazing letters from Jay. Like all of us, he's far from perfect. He's always been influential without trying to be. He never cared about his fame, but now he expresses a desire to use whatever notoriety we have to help at-risk kids.

Aside from Jay and me, there are quite a few other well-known skaters who are Christians. Three of them, Jay "Alabamy" Haizlip, Dennis Martinez, and Eddie Elguera, have actually become pastors. My old friends and competitors, Steve Caballero and Lance Mountain, have been Christians for a while now. Add Josh Harmony, Brian Sumner, Chad Tim Tim, and Richard Mulder to that list and that's quite a heavenly skate team.

The new millennium means a lot of different things to a lot of different people. To me, it marks the time when my whole world changed. Now that I'm saved, I'm thinking, Whoa! Where do my parents stand in all this?

As I mentioned earlier, Pops was an artist/philosopher everyone, including me, looked to for answers. He never followed anyone's rules but did everything his own way. While he made a lot of mistakes, mostly rooted in drugs, he really did have a lot of the right answers, and I've met few more naturally loving parents. Pops was a great father overall, the best he knew how to be. But there was a piece missing; and now—with my new relationship with Jesus—I know how to help fix the things that are broken in him.

I call Pops from jail one day and say, "I'm reading the Bible regularly, and I gave my life to Jesus. What do you think of that?" I'm genuinely curious. This is right up his alley, and I know he'll have an interesting take on it. I guess I've taken him off-guard, though, because for once he doesn't say much. He's just like, "Oh yeah? Cool." I recall one of the few times he ever talked to me about God when I was a kid. He said, "I believe in evolution and in God." That was good enough for me at the time, and I had no further questions back then. Now I remind him of saying that and ask if he still believes in God. He replies that he doesn't know. "Look, Pops," I say, "God is real and Jesus is real. I found that out for sure by reading God's Word." When I suggest that he read the Bible, he replies, "Oh, I've read it before." I tell him to read it again—especially to read about Jesus, starting in the book of John. I tell him that once he does that, I want to talk to him again. He agrees to look into it.

When Pops comes to visit in person, we begin where we left off. Again, he doesn't have a lot to say, so I start. I share with him how I came to believe that Jesus Christ really is alive, and I encourage him to come to his own decision about that and then figure out how he wants to respond.

Pops thinks back on his own history of religious matters. He tells me that he attended a Catholic church for a time when he was fourteen. He went on his own; nobody else in his family had ever been to church or had any interest, and he wanted to check it out. I say, "That's all cool, Pops, but what's your take on Jesus dying for your sins so that you can be saved?" He pauses, looking a bit uncomfortable with the direction of the conversation, and says, "That's a tough one." I tell him that if he doesn't put his whole trust in Jesus, he won't see heaven. I ask again if he believes that God is real, and this time he says that he does. I press him a bit: "Well, you need to open up your heart and ask God to forgive you and ask Jesus to reveal himself to you." Just like that, he says, "All right." I lead him in a prayer and tell him that he's got to read the Bible every day. He agrees to do that, and we wrap up our visit.

The next time he visits me, he's crying, broken up about our shared past and about the direction he helped me take in life. I've never seen him cry like that before, and it shows me that God is touching him deeply. He says, "Forgive me, son."

"I totally forgive you, Pops," I say, "and I love you. It's not your fault I'm here; this is the result of decisions *I* made. You need to forgive *yourself*, though." We've always been close before, but now we've forged an unbreakable bond that not even a prison wall can break. Now, I have to talk to my mom.

Phoning my mom is the next step, and it's a harder one. She hurts on my behalf, and she has tremendous guilt over her parenting, saying things like, "What did we do wrong? I don't know why we didn't raise you in the church. I don't know why we didn't read the Bible or pray." I say, "It doesn't matter what you did or didn't do; it only matters what you do from here out, Mom." I explain the idea of salvation to her and tell her basically the same things I told Pops—that I forgive her, that God forgives her, and that she now needs to forgive herself. I say, "Yeah, maybe my upbringing wasn't exactly right, but somewhere down the line in the family there was a disconnect. Your parents or your grandparents just hadn't made the decision to follow God."

It's the same with every family that falls away—you begin by missing church a little, and pretty soon you don't go at all. Finally there's no God in your life, or he's up there and you're way down here. By the time I was born, nothing was ever said about God in the Hosoi home.

I tell my mom that Jesus is real, and I talk about how I sense his presence in my life. As if wanting to give me something, she tells me that she can still recite Psalm 23. I say, "That's cool, Mom, but it won't save you." I say, "Do you want to spend eternity in heaven?" I tell her that there's only one way. As Jesus said, "I am the way, the truth, and the life. No one comes to the Father except through Me" (John 14:6). She's still struggling with her own guilt. "I can't believe it's happening this way," she says. "It should have been the other way around: I should have taught *you* about God."

I try to reassure her. "You've been a great mom," I say, "and you always did the best you knew how. Yeah, it should have been different, but as long as there's a way, that's all that matters. You still have time." She's crying now, saying yet again that she's a bad parent. I reply, "Whatever's done is done. That doesn't mean we can't start doing things right from this moment on." I tell her she needs to ask Jesus into her heart. We pray right then, and that's the start of a new life for her. That call happens about six months into my incarceration. Before we hang up, we're both crying on the phone together—this time tears of joy. She begins reading the Bible faithfully and sharing scriptures with me in letters and in phone calls. From then on we pray together during every call.

A couple years ago my mom had a bad stroke. I was blessed to spend time with her before she passed away. As difficult as it was seeing her after the stroke, the conversations we had then and during my days of imprisonment were the best times of our lives together. This has been an amazing journey, and I know I will see her again.

I've been locked up for a year and a half when Jen and I decide to get married after I'm transferred back to Hawaii. Hawaii's a lovely place for a wedding, even if it's held in district court. I tell her, "Look, you're beautiful and I love you. If you want to get married, I'll stay loyal and committed always, because of my love for you and our God." She knows

LOVE AND FREEDOM, BEHIND BARS. *HOSOI FAMILY COLLECTION.*

how unfaithful I was in the past, so she's naturally skeptical that once I get out I won't get sucked into my old womanizing ways again—not to mention the drugs. I tell her that I'm *never* returning to my old ways; that I'm done with that life for good. I say, "I'm ready to make a commitment for life, to be your husband, to love you, and to have children with you." I've rarely been so sure of any decision in my life, and this is certainly one of the most important ones ever.

It's obviously tougher for Jen than for me. She needs some spiritual guidance. She tells it this way:

CHRISTIAN'S DAD SENDS ME A BEAUTIFUL VINTAGE ENGAGEMENT-TYPE RING THAT I'VE KEPT FOREVER. WE LOVE EACH OTHER, BUT I'M STILL NOT SURE ABOUT THIS DECISION. CHRISTIAN IS ABOUT TO BE SENTENCED, AND HE COULD BE GONE FOR NEARLY TEN YEARS. I TELL MY UNCLE, PASTOR CHRIS SWAIM, ABOUT MY INDECISION, AND HE SAYS, "WHY NOT READ A PROVERB AND SEE WHAT THE LORD SAYS?" "YEAH, BUT THERE ARE THIRTY-ONE PROVERBS; WHICH ONE?" I ASK HIM. I PICK THE DATE, WHICH IS THE EIGHTEENTH, AND I PICK MY AGE, WHICH IS TWENTY-TWO. PROVERBS 18:22 SAYS, "HE WHO FINDS A WIFE FINDS A GOOD THING, AND OBTAINS FAVOR FROM THE LORD." THAT'S GOOD ENOUGH FOR ME, AND RIGHT THEN I REALIZE THIS IS WHAT I'M SUPPOSED TO DO.

WHEN WE GET MARRIED, I'M WEARING A WHITE DRESS WITH FLOWERS, AND CHRISTIAN IS IN AN ORANGE JUMPSUIT AND HAND-CUFFS. I ALWAYS (JOKINGLY) TELL PEOPLE IT WAS THE MOST ROMAN-TIC WEDDING EVER. ON OUR WEDDING DAY WE FIND OURSELVES IN THE COURTROOM WITH THE SAME JUDGE WHO OFFICIATED CHRIS-TIAN'S CASE INITIALLY.

I'M A COUPLE INCHES TALLER THAN CHRISTIAN, AND WHEN I PUT ON MY WEDDING SHOES, I TOWER OVER HIM. I REMOVE MY SHOES AT FIRST, SO IT WILL LOOK LIKE WE'RE ON THE SAME LEVEL. BUT CHRISTIAN'S SO CONFIDENT IN EVERYTHING THAT HE DOESN'T CARE, AND I END UP PUT-TING THEM ON AGAIN. HE DOESN'T HAVE THAT SHORT MAN'S COMPLEX WHERE HE HAS TO HAVE A SUPER LIFTED TRUCK OR ANYTHING.

AT FIRST MY FAMILY DIDN'T LIKE CHRISTIAN, BECAUSE HE WAS SUCH A BAD INFLUENCE ON ME—AND HE REALLY WAS. BUT WHEN THEY BEGIN SEEING ALL THE CHANGES IN OUR LIVES, BOTH BEFORE THE WEDDING AND AFTER, THEY START TO BELIEVE.

We're married in court on June 19, 2001, just before my sentencing. The Lord has confirmed our marriage to us both, in spite of the fact that I'm facing eight more years. Pops is there, sketching the whole thing, so we've got a good record. At the wedding, the judge goes to the podium and says, "All right, we're doing a Christian wedding." He reads from I Corinthians 13 and gives a speech to us. After he performs the actual ceremony, he smiles and says, "You may kiss your bride." Later my attorney tells Jen that it was the first time he'd seen that judge smile in his courtroom in seventeen years. I believe he was joyful in that union because he knew he

FEDERAL COURTHOUSE. WEDDING AND COURTROOM SKETCHES BY POPS. © *IVAN HOSOI.*

Judge Glenn C Kay

M. Brewer
esQ

COUT. = 94 91 (COURT DATE)

in courtroom
waiting for Judge C Kay
H
6/29/01

was involved in something that God was a part of, and something that was good. That was a kiss I will never forget!

I don't have a job during my first year inside, so there's nothing to do other than study the Word, play cards, play chess, and watch a little TV. I'm glad I don't have a lot of distractions, because all the Bible reading I do that first year, lying in my bunk, helps me build a solid foundation.

Jen proves her love to me by hanging in there with me the entire time. I mean, here she is, a beautiful young woman of twenty-two when we marry, giving her life to a thirty-something man who will be in his forties the next time we're together. Realizing her sacrifice, I'm doing all that I can to make it out while I'm still in my thirties.

For starters, I'm building a file of character reference letters to present to the judge. My behavior has changed so radically since I've been inside that people are speaking up for me. I have tons of letters, most from people I don't even know! They all say pretty much the same thing: that I can do more good on the outside, helping keep kids out of trouble and out of jail and off drugs, than I can do in here. Even my old rival Tony Hawk writes a letter that he sends to me along with a donation.

After an interview with me runs in *Thrasher* magazine, the editors post my address and I receive over 250 letters. There are letters from all sorts of people, even from six sheriffs in the prison system. They're saying how I'm a model inmate and an awesome worker. Imagine that! (Not bad for a guy who's never had a real job.) But that isn't the reason I behave so well, or work so hard; I'm on a mission, and for the first time in my life, I'm representing more than myself. I read my Bible, write to kids, and speak in the Scared Straight program whenever they come in. One of the sheriffs brings his whole church in for me to speak to them.

I eventually do every job there is in prison, but my favorites are to hand out toilet paper and distribute library books to the inmates. If I were in my old shoes, I'd think that doing this sort of work was lame. I was once on top of the world, and now I'm handing out toilet paper to prisoners? Instead, though, I think how great it is. I can cover the entire prison on this job, visiting everyone in every cell. It's my opportunity to be a light and offer a little encouragement. I look through the bars and say, "God bless you; have a good day." The inmates know I'm in the same situation they are, but they can see that I'm content. I try to get the guys the best books available. It keeps them occupied so time moves faster and easier for them.

INMATE ETIQUETTE

There's always a chance that a race riot will kick off. There will be ten Southsiders, ten blacks, twenty whites, and twenty Border Brothers, all just doin' their own thing. If the Southsiders and the Border Brothers get together, the odds are in their favor. But things don't work like that in prison. It's all done politically. There's always talk of riots, but that will get quashed unless there's something legitimate to riot about. If an inmate causes a riot or fight and thereby causes the group or gang he's affiliated with to have a problem, he has become a problem himself. In jail or prison, problems get dealt with one way or another.

Other prisoners don't stop anything like a riot in prison; there are certain rules we all have to abide by. I never actually experience a riot, but I see beat-downs all the time. These are commanded by the shot-callers. The shot-callers are the highest ranking gang member in that particular cell. Every cell has one. They take orders from the lifers in the hole. They hear about an issue and decide what to do about it when it comes to serious matters. Beat-downs are always ordered by them. When there's a beat-down, everyone just sits back and watches like it's a reality TV show. When it ends, you wait for the next episode to see who's rolling it up.

In addition to these beat-downs, there are often fights between inmates. And sometimes one fight causes another. After all, if someone gets beaten by someone else, you can't just say it's cool and walk away, cuz then it will happen all the time. The fights can get heavy. People get stabbed and the guards come in with pepper spray.

Usually, though, if somebody's gonna fight, they wait for the guards to walk past first. Everybody's like, "Nobody jump in." When the coast is clear, there might be a full-on brawl in the middle of the tank, lasting until one dude gets knocked out or they both get too tired and quit. Most times guys have no idea of how to fight, though. They're in there wrestling around without knowing how to throw punches. I grew up watching kung fu movies and ultimate fighting on TV. This isn't like that; it's more like something you'd see in junior high, only with grown men.

Everybody bets on the outcome of a fight. I don't bet on the fights, but I do play pinochle and spades where the loser does pushups. Though the guys take some pretty hard shots, we all hope nobody will get hit in the eye or the mouth. If the guards see a guy with a black eye, or blood on his mouth, an investigation goes down. They look at everybody's knuckles, have guys lift their shirt for bruises and scratches, and try to figure out who else got into the fight. If the fighters are caught, those two dudes get rolled out to the hole.

But the shot-callers usually get things in order before it gets too crazy. They're the ones who decide if the green light is on or not. Once the green light's on, you know there's gonna be bloodshed, but both sides have to decide if it's really worth it. Usually it's talked out and there's a truce.

The "etiquette" of life inside is so much more elaborate than it is on the outside, and in some ways that system works better than the one we use out here. When I was a kid, Venice was basically like that. It was a ghetto, but it was a family, and people looked out for their own. County jail was like that. You've gotta be thankful, polite, and respectful. You step out of that and you're done. �֍

POPS IN A "FREE HOSOI" T-SHIRT. WHOM THE SON SETS FREE WILL BE FREE INDEED. SEE JOHN 8:36. © CESARIO "BLOCK" MONTANO.

DOING LIFE

In or out of prison, if you're not
serving God, you're just doing time.
—JACK "MURF THE SURF" MURPHY

Christian getting
out of prison was a miracle.
—CESARIO "BLOCK" MONTANO

CHAPTER 21

> *I'm bounced around from jail to jail, prison to prison, until eventually I'm sent to Nellis Federal Prison Camp. Nellis, which is located on the outskirts of Las Vegas, Nevada, will be my home for two years. At least once a month Jen leaves Huntington Beach long before dawn and drives through the desert for hours to visit me. Talk about dedication! Visitations are first come, first served, and she's always first in line. Those visits are among the best memories in my life to that point. We hang out from eight in the morning until three in the afternoon, talking and praying. Watching her arrive is as joyful as watching her leave is difficult.*

I know that some people think I'm faking Christianity and hiding behind the Bible to get better time. It happens all the time, but I'm not a poser and never have been. Besides, that sort of pretense doesn't work very well in here. In here, your only chance of survival is to pick a side and make your stand.

My stand is firm and I don't look back. I mean, we're housed right near the ultimate party town, Las Vegas. In the past I did my share of celebrating there, but I've completely lost my taste for all that. I'm not thinking about the bright lights or endless parties; I'm concentrating on knowing God better and staying close with my family.

I work busing tables and washing pots and pans. A lot of inmates know who I am, but for the most part I'm just another guy in a khaki uniform—and I'm *certainly* a long way from $500 belts and $800 boots. This is exactly what I need, the best place in the world to get broken down so that God can build me back up. It takes that sort of breaking to realize that I'm no more important than anyone else and that there's no partiality with God. Still, a day doesn't pass that people don't remind me about my past as a skater. That's cool, but it doesn't mean nearly what it used to.

Although the trophies and the groupies have become insignificant, I still long to skate. Any skater will tell you that when they look at structures, all they see is places to skate. You see a banked wall, you think of skating it. You see a ditch, you think of skating it. You see a pool, you just hope it's empty so you can ride it. A skater will look right past Notre Dame Cathedral to those flying buttresses, which seem perfect for skating!

You're constantly scoping out every curb, ramp, or swimming pool, even tracing water pouring down a streetside gutter to see if it leads to a pool being drained.

In prison I see so many things I want to skate. I look at the bars on the triple-decker bunk beds and think about how hard I could grind on them. The picnic tables are made of metal and would be killer to skate. The ditch by the rec yard would be a perfect jump ramp; I see myself doing ollies over it. I mentally skate everything, all the time.

It's just dreaming, though. The only time I actually touch a skateboard is when I'm in the San Bernardino County jail. A woman who works there tells me she has two of my boards she wants signed. She says that if I do that, she'll get me whatever food I want. I think about sushi but end up getting an In-N-Out burger for myself and one for this Southsider friend of mine, because that's what he wants. I sign her two Black Label Hosoi boards, then stand on one of them and ollie on the carpet—and that's the extent of my skate time for the duration.

Like everything else, prison is what you make it. I take advantage of the time and finally graduate from high school. Jen comes to visit on graduation day, and I still remember the beautiful dress she's wearing. The only other woman in my life, my mom, is really stoked that I finally graduate.

FINALLY, THE RIGHT LAWYER

All the legal work I need done gets expensive, and we're having a tough time financially. Suddenly God busts open the doors with Pony shoes. The opportunity comes through Block:

CHRISTIAN AND I HADN'T SPOKEN FOR A WHILE WHEN I WORKED OUT THIS DEAL WITH PONY. I WAS SHOOTING AN AD CAMPAIGN FOR THEM ABOUT FAMOUS ATHLETES THAT HAD DIFFICULTIES IN THEIR LIVES. ONE OF THEIR MAIN GUYS WAS BASEBALL STAR PETE ROSE. THE ADS WERE LIKE, WHATEVER HAPPENED TO PETE ROSE? GAMBLING TOOK HIM OUT. THEY HAD SOME OTHER GUYS TOO. WHEN I TOLD THEM THEY NEEDED HOSOI, THEY WENT FOR IT.

I fit right in with Pony's program, and they sign me to a two-year deal for 50 grand. Every six months we'll get paid like 12 grand. Before the two-year contract is up, Pony informs us that they're dropping the program. I'm like, "Okay, thanks for the money." Money for nothin'! If that's not God, I don't know what is.

Dave Duncan raises a lot of money too, and he gets a lot of pro skaters to put up funds. It says a lot about him and my other friends that they'll go to bat for me like that. It also says a lot for my wife and the rest of my family, the way they keep fighting to get me released, even when things look impossible.

Chicken has been busy too; he's been printing FREE HOSOI stickers and T-shirts, and he's told me where those have been sent. A bunch of us inmates are hanging out one day, watching an awards show on TV. The Chili Peppers are about to play, and I tell some of the guys that I've heard that the Chili Peppers have been wearing FREE HOSOI shirts. One of the guys in the TV room is like, "Yeah, right—whatever, dude." They naturally think I'm trippin'. When the band comes on, though, there's the front man, Anthony Kiedis, and sure enough, it says FREE HOSOI on his shirt. All the other band members are also wearing FREE HOSOI shirts, except for Flea. Flea never wears a shirt for shows, so he's got FREE HOSOI painted on his chest! The other inmates can't believe it; they're like, "What; you really do know those dudes?"

I've had four lawyers before we hire the right one, Myles Breiner. All our earlier lawyers either lie to us or say, "There's nothing we can do for you." *So tell me why we're paying you again?*

At my sentencing it's immediately apparent that the judge is on our side and wants me released. Problem is there's only a small window of time when he can reduce my sentence. It's all because of a legal case, *Butler v. the United States,* in which mandatory minimum sentences

HOSOI FAMILY COLLECTION.

were stricken down as illegal. But the law is about to be changed, and then the judge's hands will be tied. He can see that I've been rehabilitated and he wants to give me so-called downward departures—that is, incremental steps toward a lesser sentence than would ordinarily be granted.

On one hand, things look good; on the other hand, the prosecutor isn't having any of it. He objects, saying that I'm a danger to society and that in any case we should wait until the law on minimums is settled. The judge tells him, "Look, you do your job; I'll do mine. I'm gonna give him what I'm gonna give him." When the judge gives me downward departures for post-offense rehabilitation, the prosecutor goes nuts, shouting, "We *object*, your honor!"

The prosecutor argues that post-offense rehabilitation is supposed to be for extraordinary circumstances. The judge then addresses everyone in the court, asking, "Has anybody in this courtroom—have *you*, sir," speaking to the prosecutor, "ever had a sheriff write a letter on an inmate's behalf?" The prosecutor is silent as the judge reads such a letter that came for me, and he says, "I think this is an extraordinary circumstance."

Bottom line, I get points down—court lingo for specific items that count toward a reduced sentence—and I'm now facing only seventy months. Including the time I've already served, that means only three and a half more years. After just a year, though, I get a letter saying that the prosecutors have appealed my case and had it overturned. Again, it looks like I'll be doing the entire ten years. Ironically, I tell my wife nearly the exact same thing she said to me in that first prison phone call: that God has a plan, and that he's in control and we have to trust him. Maybe God needs me in prison for a while to help some people.

Around that time a lawyer calling himself David Goldstein contacts me. Goldstein says he can help with my case by qualifying me for what, in the sentencing world, is called safety valve. This would untie the judge's hands regarding length of sentencing. All I have to do to qualify is get my earlier misdemeanor drug charges set aside. I'm thinking, Sick, we've got a chance. I tell Myles Breiner about it, and he's like, "Yeah, this sounds great."

But first things first: it's time to get baptized. In prison you don't just find some water and get dunked; everything there has to be done in an

orderly fashion. You have to sign up. Somehow I missed out when the list first came around, and now they say I'll have to wait until the next time, or I won't get a certificate of baptism. I've been cooperative in every way, but not this time. Now I say, "I don't need a certificate; I'm getting baptized right now!" I'm the last person in the tank, but I make it. I jump in and get dunked as a symbol that I'm dead to myself and alive in Christ.

I've made a lot of progress in my faith, but that couldn't have happened without great mentors. One guy I'm blessed to have as a mentor is Bill Kennedy. We're an odd pair for sure. He's an older gentleman, in his fifties, and nothing like the skaters I grew up with. While we were on our skate-and-destroy street missions, he was a conservative and successful businessman. Still, we hang out all the time at Nellis; rules are laxer there, and we walk to chow together, pray together, walk to the movies or church, often talking about spiritual matters.

Bill says this about our time in prison together:

WE WOULD MEET FOR ALMOST AN HOUR EACH DAY. THEN I WOULD GIVE CHRISTIAN MEMORY VERSES AND HE MEMORIZED THEM ALL. HE WAS SO STEADY AND ALWAYS THE SAME, NO MATTER WHAT HAPPENED. YOU COULDN'T TELL BY LOOKING AT HIM IF HIS SENTENCE HAD BEEN IN-CREASED OR REDUCED. I MISSED HIM WHEN HE WENT BACK TO HA-WAII. THEN WHEN I HEARD THE MIRACLE, THAT HE WAS GETTING OUT EARLY, I WAS AS HAPPY FOR HIM AS IF IT HAD BEEN MY OWN DAY.

Bill has been in prison for eight years by the time I get to Nellis and meet him. Prior to that he ran a big company. Somebody cooked the books and he took the rap for it. He was told to lie on the stand to convict somebody the DA wanted in prison. He refused to lie and got twenty years because of it. He's one of the people in prison who doesn't belong there, but he serves his time patiently and with dignity.

I tell Bill about the lawyer who has contacted me about safety valve. He warns me, saying, "Christian, you've gotta be careful. There are con artist lawyers who will take your money and run. Make sure this guy's for real." He asks the lawyer's name and I tell him David Goldstein. Bill doesn't say anything at the time, but he does suggest that I have my attorney, Myles Breiner, check him out. I call Breiner and say, "Make sure this guy's legit." He calls Goldstein and gets back to me, saying, "Oh, he's totally legit," confirming that Goldstein is okay. My family pays Goldstein $5,000 from money that's been donated to us by my mom's friend Tevis. A week later, the FBI informs Jennifer that the lawyer who has taken that money is actually named *Harold* Goldstein, not *David* Goldstein. Turns out Harold Goldstein isn't so legit after all.

Goldstein has taken our money, and now he's been busted for running a scam. On the phone Jen's crying, asking, "What are we gonna do now?" I tell her, "Our first lawyer"—this is before she jumped to her death— "is friends with people at the court right there in Orange County, where my misdemeanors happened. Call up and see if she can get my charges dismissed, as Goldstein suggested." Jen calls her and discovers that the woman is still practicing law. She does right by us this time, getting the judge to sign off on everything. Now my priors are all set aside and dismissed, leaving me eligible for safety-valve sentencing.

We send everything to Breiner and he's like, "Done! You're gonna get safety valve, no problem!" So we're back up again, optimistic, right? Yes, but only temporarily.

I'm flown back to Hawaii to face court again, and the adventure continues.

Traveling on a plane as a prisoner is kind of a trip. You're in the back row, cuffed to a waist belt next to a marshal who's guarding you. The Hawaiian marshals take one handcuff off so you can eat and drink, but they won't allow you to have Coke or coffee or anything with caffeine in it. (I guess they're afraid you'll get all hyper on them.) The L.A. marshals don't take a cuff off, but they let you have caffeine; you have to eat by leaning down toward your food because of the waist belt holding your wrists. The Hawaiian marshal lets me have a Coca-Cola. It's the first one I've had in years, and man, is it good.

I'm in the courtroom for resentencing and my lawyer's like, "Great news! You're gonna get released, Christian." My mom has flown out to Hawaii from the East Coast, and my dad is already there, of course. They sit with Jen.

My lawyer makes a motion to release me right then, but the judge says he can't do that. The judge considers his paperwork and says, "Looks like everything is dismissed and you can get safety valve; I'll give you extra points down." Looking at my attorney he says, "I'll give him forty-one months." I'm thrilled! That's a lot better than the seventy months I was assigned in 2001.

The prosecutor objects like crazy, saying he's been on leave and hasn't had time to prepare a case against me. The judge is clearly leaning our direction, but the prosecutor asks for more time. The judge grants him a week. During that time one of my cell mates, a guy who frequents the law library, finds a case law saying that set-aside and dismissed cases can still be used against defendants in federal court. I know that the prosecutor will find that case law if he has a week.

I go back to court at the assigned time, and the prosecutor's sitting back in his chair, kicked-back style, looking cocky. I know he has *something*. My lawyer, on the other hand, enters the courtroom with a downcast look. The prosecutor then offers the very case I was hoping he wouldn't find and argues that my priors can't be expunged.

The judge wants to release me, but there's only so much he can do. He tells us all to come back in two months' time for another appearance, at which time he'll hear from both sides and render a judgment. In the end an entire year will pass before I return to get sentenced again.

During the intervening months, my lawyer tries to convince the prosecutor that he should give me credit because he's going to testify against Harold Goldstein, the attorney who ripped us off. Breiner used to be a DA himself, and seventeen years earlier he worked with the guy prosecuting my case. The two of them are talking, shouting, battling it out, trying to out-lawyer each other with how much they know about the law. Neither one of them will budge. My lawyer comes back, sits next to me, and says, "Christian, you didn't turn anyone in. Now they're going to use you as an example."

My attorney tries to get everything expunged but there's no way they'll do it. Another year passes before I return to get sentenced again. Right before I go back to court, I call my wife and it sounds like she's jumping up and down, ecstatic over something. "They're giving you credit for your lawyer and us helping with the Goldstein case," she shouts. My lawyer filed a bad-faith motion. Once the DA receives it he agrees to give me credit.

MIRACLE ON JUDGMENT DAY

We're in the courtroom again, finally, and the DA agrees to reduce my sentence. He wants me to be taken down only three points, though—which is equivalent to about thirty-six months—which means I'll still do another year. Not bad, considering I'd been looking at four more years. The judge says, "Yeah, okay, I know the law says downward departures aren't applicable here, but I'm gonna read them off anyway." He reads all the downward departures that he tried to give me the first time, and he reads one of the letters from a sheriff again.

It also states in my file that the arresting detectives called me a courier, or a mule. The judge says, "That right there says he's not in a manager's role, so that's another point down." The prosecutor isn't happy with any of this, but to my surprise, he doesn't object. The judge proposes that everything be applied to my case and he asks the prosecutor how he pleas. He stands up and I'm thinking, Of course he's gonna object. To my surprise, he says, "No objection, your honor." I look back at my wife as I hear the judge then conclude, "That puts you in the fifty-six-to-seventy-month bracket." He says, "I'm giving you fifty-six months." He looks down and reads something, then says, "It looks like you've served fifty-seven months already, plus six months good time, so you're already seven months over."

My lawyer requests that I be released from the court right then. The judge replies that I'll have to be processed out, which will take a few days. Nonetheless, I've gone from sitting in the courtroom thinking I'm gonna do a few more years, to heading home in a few days. Nobody can believe it's happening, but I know that God has a plan.

Two days later—June 4, 2004—they kick me out the prison door. My lawyer drives me straight to his office, where I meet up with Jen. I squeeze and hug her, and kiss her like never before. My dad is there also, and so is Block, filming it all for his upcoming documentary on my life. Jay Adams hands me a Big Mac. That's something you can't have when you're in prison, and it tastes unbelievably good.

I had done an interview with *Sports Illustrated* earlier that year, and it

. . . .
(ABOVE) **JUST RELEASED HOURS AGO. SUSHI DINNER WITH**
(LEFT TO RIGHT) **MY LAWYER, MYLES BREINER; JENNIFER, MY WIFE;**
BLOCK; ME; AND CHUCK KATZ. HOW STOKED AM I?
(BELOW) **JEN AND ME.** *HOSOI FAMILY COLLECTION.*

comes out right as I'm released. My attorney has the magazine in front of him. He opens it up to my story and says that the prosecuting attorney wants me to sign it for him. Despite our differences, I do: I write, "God bless you; thank you for everything."

That night my wife and I eat sushi and begin our honeymoon. What a night! I felt like a virgin all over again. The first full night of our life as husband and wife! The next day I go to a Honolulu skate shop called APB. They set me up with a board and I skate a park in Hawaii Kai with my original skate heroes Jay Adams and Shogo Kubo. Jeff Hartsel, a friend I met years ago in Hawaii, is also on hand. This is a day I'll never forget!

I've had a bad knee for a while and I haven't skated for four and a half years. I'm not sure how I'll do, but when I get on that board it all comes back. I just roll into the park, do an axle stall over the bowl, and drop right into a rock 'n' roll. I pull into a layback, then I ollie up these gaps. Dang, it's unreal to skate again, especially being clean and sober. I'm not 100 percent, but in a short time it's almost like I never stopped.

Skateboarding is awesome, but the best things in my life have nothing to do with it. It's all about my family and spreading the love and joy of my faith. I've learned a lot about ministry in prison, much of it from my mentor in Nellis, Bill Kennedy. Bill had a hunch all along that the attorney calling himself David Goldstein was really Harold Goldstein. He didn't tell me that right away, however, because he had a feeling that God was telling him not to say anything about it. What he did was right, as it turns out, because if he'd said anything about the guy or if my lawyer had found out the guy was crooked, I would have done the whole time and wouldn't have been released for years.

An Unusual Suspect

One of the unlikely suspects God has used in my life and in the lives of thousands of others is the actor/producer Stephen Baldwin. He's one of the most interesting people I've ever met. His family is big-time in the Hollywood scene, and Stephen was on his way up in the film world when he got saved. Not long after his salvation he attended a Christian festival where he saw skaters doing a demo. That's how he got the idea for *Livin' It*, a DVD where he tells God's story through skateboarding. That all

happened while I was in prison, where I heard talk of it in its early stages.

Turns out Stephen and I know a lot of the same people. One of them is our friend Marcos, who grew up with me going to clubs and break dancing. It's cool how they supported me when I was in prison, showing up together at a fund-raiser for me, on Harleys. Stephen came to one of our fund-raisers when I was in prison, and he met my wife there. Stephen and I had been aware of each other for a long time before that, though—since long before my drug use got bad.

I'll let him tell you the story of how he first got to know me:

I WAS A "SIDEWALK SURFER" AND TOOK A SKATEBOARD EVERYWHERE WITH ME IN MY YOUTH. AROUND 1987 I WENT TO L.A. TO KIND OF KICK IT WITH MY BIG BROTHER, ALEC. HE INVITED ME TO ONE OF THOSE SEEDY HOLLYWOOD INDUSTRY PARTIES. WE COME TO THE DOOR AND I BUMP RIGHT INTO WINONA RYDER AND ROBERT DOWNEY JR. MY BROTHER INTRODUCES US, AND THEY'RE LIKE, "OH HEY, WHAT'S UP?" I'M LIKE TWENTY OR TWENTY-ONE, AND DOWNEY'S GIVING ME THE TOUR. HE SAYS, "DUDE, COME WITH ME. I REALLY WANNA SHOW YOU SOMETHING FRICKIN' CRAZY."

HE LEADS ME DOWN THE HALLWAY UNTIL WE GET TO THIS ROOM WITH FLUORESCENT LIGHTS AND MAHARAJA MUSIC PLAYING. I LOOK IN AND IT'S LIKE THE MAHARISHI, THE GURU OF THE BEATLES, WITH HIS FOLLOWERS. THERE'S THIS DUDE SEATED UP AGAINST THE WALL IN RIPPED JEANS, A VEST, AND NO SHIRT. HE'S GOT LONG HAIR DOWN TO HIS WAIST AND THERE ARE LIKE SIX GORGEOUS CHICKS ON EITHER SIDE OF HIM. WE TIPTOE CLOSER TO THE DOOR AND ROBERT WHISPERS, "DO YOU SEE THAT DUDE?" AND I WHISPER BACK, "YEAH." HE GOES, "DUDE, DO YOU F--KING KNOW WHO THAT IS?" I GO, "NO," AND DOWNEY REVERENTLY SAYS, "THAT'S HOSOI." THAT WAS MY INTRODUCTION TO CHRISTIAN. DOWNEY CALLS OUT, "DUDE," TO CHRISTIAN, AND ALL OF A SUDDEN CHRISTIAN TURNS HIS HEAD MAYBE A CENTIMETER AND NODS A LITTLE BIT.

. . . .

(LEFT) SECOND DAY OUT. FIRST SESSION. HAWAII KAI SKATEPARK.
© CESARIO "BLOCK" MONTANO.

I WOULD BE AT PARTIES WITH HOSOI TWO OR THREE TIMES A YEAR AFTER THAT FOR THE NEXT FIFTEEN YEARS. WE KNEW A LOT OF THE SAME PEOPLE, BUT I NEVER REALLY KNEW HIM AT THE TIME; HE WAS JUST THIS COOL GUY HANGING OUT AT THE BEST PLACES.

MY JOURNEY OF FAITH LED TO MY GETTING INVOLVED IN A SKATE-BOARDING MINISTRY. IT WASN'T LONG AFTER THAT WHEN I HEARD THAT CHRISTIAN HAD BEEN BUSTED. IN SMALL TALK SOMEBODY SAID, "IT MIGHT BE COOL TO GET A COPY OF OUR *LIVIN' IT* VIDEO TO CHRIS-TIAN IN PRISON." I HAD A WEIRD INTUITION THAT THERE WAS A CON-NECTION THERE. I SOUGHT OUT JEN AND TOLD HER I WAS A CHRISTIAN GETTING INVOLVED IN A SKATEBOARD MINISTRY AND WANTED TO SEE WHAT GOD MIGHT DO WITH CHRISTIAN AND ME TOGETHER.

IT'S LIKE A HOLY SPIRIT THING. I CAN'T EXPLAIN IT; I JUST KNEW I WAS SUPPOSED TO BE THERE. CHRISTIAN AND I HAVE SIMILAR HEARTS AND SIMILAR PASSIONS TO HELP CHANGE THE YOUTH CULTURE WITH THE GOSPEL.

In the first week after I get out of prison, Stephen flies to Hawaii to visit me. I'm staying at my aunt Kuipo and uncle Dennis's house, and he moves in with us for a while. Everybody's wondering, What's Stephen Baldwin doing here? We are strategizing on how we can do skate ministry. Since then I've participated in several outreaches with him, and we've seen tens of thousands of people give their lives to Christ as a result.

I'm using my faith in other ways too. A few weeks after my release, my family and I fly back to California. I'm invited to participate in a big stadium outreach called the Harvest Crusade. The organizers have requested that I skate a ramp for their event at Angel Stadium in Anaheim. Skate a vert ramp in front of forty thousand cheering spectators! What could be better than that? Even the flight to California is awesome—no marshal, no shackles, no handcuffs.

Once I finish the demo, the MC asks me on the microphone how it all feels, and I say, "Man, it's awesome to be free in Christ!" The crowd just goes off, and I feel a tremendous rush of love.

It's kind of like the old days where I skate to the roar of the crowd, only this has a deeper meaning. While I was high for all the demos I did in the years just before prison, *this* time I'm not high or scanning the crowd for girls to hook up with. And I feel real love pouring in from everyone. But the love I feel on that ramp has nothing to do with my performance on a skateboard. It's a love that *anybody* can have, offered freely to winners and losers. ✺

FIRST SESSION. ME WITH MY FIRST MENTOR, SHOGO KUBO, AND POPS HOSOI. HAWAII KAI SKATEPARK. © CESARIO "BLOCK" MONTANO.

ALL '80S ALL DAY VERT CHALLENGE 2008: ME, LANCE MOUNTAIN, AND TONY HAWK.
© CESARIO "BLOCK" MONTANO.

THE PRICE OF ADMISSION

CHRISTIAN IS A PHOENIX RISEN FROM THE ASHES. I STILL ENJOY WATCHING HIM SKATE. HIS STYLE STILL SHINES CLEAR. WHEN HE FIRST CAME BACK TO THE SCENE I HADN'T SEEN HIM SKATE, AND I WAS SKEPTICAL THAT HE COULD STILL PERFORM. THEN WE HAD THIS '80S SKATE JAM THROUGH QUIKSILVER WHERE ALL THE PROS FROM THE '80S WERE INVITED. YOU HAD TO DRESS IN '80S CLOTHES AND DO '80S TRICKS. CHRISTIAN SHOWED UP LOOKING JUST LIKE HE USED TO. HE HAD THE HAIR, HE HAD THE CLOTHES, AND HE SKATED LIKE HE USED TO. THAT WAS WHEN I SAID, "WOW, HE'S BACK!"

—TONY HAWK

CHAPTER 22

We settle down in Huntington Beach, where Jen has been living. Life for me now consists of family, church, skating, and catching up with friends. I finally get another shot at fatherhood and have another son. I plan to do better this time. Classic was born to Jen in 2006, and Endless two years later. Rhythm is eight by the time I get out; we share our time with him and his mom, Kim.

Some years ago, I was on MySpace when a girl wrote to say that her boyfriend, James, was my son. She said he was going through difficult times and thought that I was the only person who could get through to him. She sent me his phone number and I called him immediately. Right away, Jennifer mentioned that we should have him flown to our house. He agreed to that and we picked him up at the airport. It was mind-boggling, like looking into a mirror—the rings on his fingers, the hat, the necklaces. Without ever knowing me, he had all the same mannerisms, characteristics, and style. That first night we were together we caught up and spoke about his life and mine, up to that point. I showed him my *Rising Son* documentary. After that, I shared my relationship with the Lord with him. He opened his heart, just as I had mine, and invited Jesus in. He moved in with us and lived with us for about four months. During that time, a strong relationship was built between him and the rest of our family. We have a strong father-son bond, and I'm so thankful that God has allowed me this blessing. He's a great kid and I love seeing him whenever I can. I've missed out on so much with my two eldest boys by not being there over the years. I love and cherish them now.

I've been with so many women that I'm not sure how many I've gotten pregnant and how many abortions I'm responsible for. Three or four for sure. Society acts like it's no big deal, but it always leaves me cold.

My last three kids all have the first name Christian. It's not some George Foreman thing; I just want them to always know that they're Christians. I mean, who knows how long I'll be around; tomorrow isn't promised to anyone. I want them to have every possible spiritual marker in their lives—to realize that their parents want them to stay the course and finish the race. This is a personal message from us to them.

Our kids are all called by their middle name, and they all have a Hawaiian name as well. My grandmother is Hawaiian, and she chooses the Hawaiian names. Rhythm is Christian Rhythm Kealii Hosoi. Kealii means "royal blood" in Hawaiian. Classic is Christian Classic Kamea Hosoi. Kamea means "one and only" in Hawaiian. Then there's Endless Kealoha Hosoi. Kealoha is a highly revered name in Hawaii, with some great surfers bearing it. Kealoha means "love" in Hawaiian, so his name is Endless Love.

All my kids skate, and I love to cheer them and the other kids on from the sidelines. Classic is really into skating, Rhythm enjoys it but is more into supercross, and even Endless (at two) shows a lot of interest in getting

THE HOSOI FAMILY: JENNIFER, CLASSIC, ENDLESS, ME, RHYTHM AND JAMES.
HOSOI FAMILY COLLECTION.

on a board. James is a musician. I don't push them into anything, but I tell them, "Some pros don't start skating until they're seventeen; you've still got time." I'm rollin' the dice that one of them will be a pro skateboarder.

My family is one of my greatest accomplishments, intimately linked with my faith. The way I love my wife, with great depth and commitment, reflects how much I love God. And I love her so much. Life is all about dying to self and giving to God. I've experienced the truth in what the

279

apostle Paul says in Philippians 1:21: "For to me, to live *is* Christ, and to die *is* gain." It's really strange how so many people want to go to heaven but act like there's no such place. Jesus said, "Whoever seeks to save his life will lose it, and whoever loses his life will preserve it" (Luke 17:33). It's as simple as that. The coolest thing is that when you give your life to Jesus, he gives it back to you—not all broken like it was, but restored, like some old car with new paint, newly upholstered seats, rebuilt engine, everything replaced, until it's better than new. Of course we can mess it all up again, if we don't do the homework, research, and maintenance.

REENTRY

Within days of being back on the mainland, I see many of my old friends. I haven't seen my main rival, Tony Hawk, since I did that demo with him in Japan years earlier. I finally run into him in 2004 at the X Games, the event I once worked so hard to avoid. I thank him for his donation and the letters he wrote to the court on my behalf, and I congratulate him on all of his accomplishments. I studied the magazines while I was in prison, keeping up on him and everyone else in skating, and I'm truly proud of him for what he's done for skateboarding.

MOM, I WILL SEE YOU AGAIN. I LOVE YOU TOO MUCH! *HOSOI FAMILY COLLECTION.*

STANDING ON THE WORD. *HOSOI FAMILY COLLECTION.*

It's my first year at the X Games—I'm watching, not skating—and my old friend and team rider Danny Way takes out the gold. The ramps are many times higher than when I last competed, and on Danny's winning run he tips his hat to me by doing the world's highest Christ Air to date. Danny is one of those skaters who come along once in a lifetime—both stylish and athletic. He recently reminded me that he first saw me skate back at the Del Mar Skate Ranch when I was battling it out with Tony Hawk and he was around eight or nine years old.

Danny says I met him at the time, but I don't recall that. He was just another stoked grom—a kid—getting stickers from the older guys. By the age of ten, however, he rode for my team. He had made a big impression on our mutual friend and my team manager at the time, Dennis Martinez. Dennis saw Danny skating in Mission Beach and signed him up immediately for Team Hosoi.

Danny talks about those early days:

THE FIRST FREE BOARD I EVER GOT WAS THROUGH HOSOI. GETTING A BOX AT MY HOUSE FOR FREE WAS SUCH A BIG DEAL TO A LITTLE KID. MY FIRST SKATE TRIP WAS ALSO WITH THE HOSOI TEAM. MY MOM DROPPED ME OFF AND I WAS SUDDENLY BEING PICKED UP BY HOSOI

DANNY WAY AND ME AT HIS MEGARAMP IN KAUAI. © RAY IBE.

TEAM MANAGER DENNIS MARTINEZ. I WENT ON TOUR WITH ALL THESE GNARLY GUYS. I HAD BEEN HIRED AS A STREET SKATER, BUT I WAS ALSO A VERT SKATER. CHRISTIAN SAW ME RIDE A RAMP ONE DAY AND HE WAS SURPRISED. HE DIDN'T KNOW I COULD SKATE VERT.

DANNY WAY AND ME AT THE WOODWARD MEGARAMP OPENING. © THEO HAND.

It's like that joke about the pope being Catholic when you ask if Danny skates vert. We soon find out that he rips at all types of skating and he gets better and better, really fast. When Dennis got lost in his addictions and became ineffective as team manager, there was nobody there to keep Danny going. He moved on, and our team lost an amazing skater. That sucked for Hosoi Skateboards.

By the time Danny was fourteen years old, we met up in competition, and he was already a threat in street and vert. In one event at a high-air contest he flew higher than I did. But, typical of Danny's humility, he makes an excuse for me, saying that I wasn't really on my game that day and that's why he beat me. I don't know, but one thing's for sure: I don't want a rematch with a guy who jumps the Great Wall of China just for fun! That and other legendary achievements on a skateboard put him in a class all his own.

It's a great privilege to have helped give Danny his start. Even though I wasn't much of a role model, I supported him when he was a kid. He'd seen all sorts of drug and alcohol abuse as a kid and wanted nothing to do with any of it. I respected that, and if someone was doing drugs anywhere near him, I'd tell them to leave him alone. They always did, and look at the results!

Danny Way's shoe company, DC, is a really big help; they give me all the skate shoes I want. Quiksilver's Mark Oblow and Black Label's John Lucero are also there for me. Now I'm covered for shoes, clothing, and boards, but I have no income. Things are getting tight when all of a sudden I land a paid sponsorship from Vans. Next I set up sponsorships with Quiksilver and with Nixon Watches.

I'm just as stoked on skating as ever and get on a board whenever I can. Between church, work, and family, I don't have much time to skate. I wish I still had the spring and resilience of my teens and early twenties. Still, the enjoyment and gratification of being able to continue with a career in a sport I love outweighs all the accolades and highest achievements from back in the day. It's also cool: skating keeps me connected to the youth, and that's right where I can be an effective role model and mentor.

RONNIE FEIST, JAY ADAMS, AND ME. *HOSOI FAMILY COLLECTION.*

CLASSIC AND ME. *HOSOI FAMILY COLLECTION.*

X TO THE FIFTEENTH POWER

It's been fifteen years since the X Games began, and they've become one of the biggest events in sports. I've been a commentator for a while, but never a competitor. That changes when I enter the Grand Masters division in 2009. For those who have difficulties relaxing the night before a big event, try watching *Cars 2* for the thousandth time. I'm sitting in the front room with my wife as our kids run in and out, Classic crawling all over us, bringing little presents and asking Daddy and Mommy to pick him up.

A lot of things have changed in skating since I first began thirty-five years ago, but standing on that ramp at the X Games, ready to drop in, I feel exactly the same as I did that *first* time I stood on a ramp and looked down. Whether it's being televised live on ESPN for six million viewers, or watched by six skaters in a backyard pool, it's still the same. I drop in, and above

CLASSIC. *HOSOI FAMILY COLLECTION.*

the crowd all I can hear is my son Classic screaming, "Go Daddy! Go Daddy, go!" I launch a frontside air and am intoxicated with adrenaline as I pull my routine. Since I'm not high on any other substances, my reflexes are great, making up for my

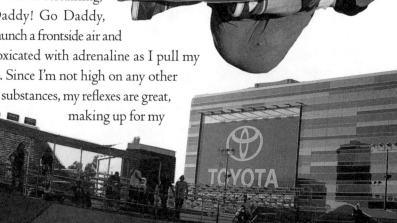

ME WARMING UP BEFORE THE 2009 X GAMES. © RAY "MRZ" ZIMMERMAN.

ME AND ENDLESS. *HOSOI FAMILY COLLECTION.*

advanced years. I'm eighteen again and moving fast. Dave Duncan is an-
nouncing over Classic's screaming, but my focus is on the board as I do a
grind over the big gap, then some back-to-back airs. The next thing I know
I'm standing on the stage and hearing, "Christian Hosoi has just won gold!"
The crowd is calling my name, cheering for me. Many of them know what
I've been through. My phone blows up with text messages and my e-mail
inbox overflows with love from some of the world's top skaters, including
Danny Way and many others who know me. The feeling on that stage is
beyond what I've felt at winning any other event, because my faith, wife,
and kids are all present.

TRANSFORMERS

As I mentioned earlier, one skater who took a radical left turn into drugs is
my old team manager, Dennis Martinez. Dennis has long since retired from
skateboarding and is now a frontline warrior in the fight against drugs. In
1977 he was the World Freestyle Champion; then, like me, he disappeared
after meth got the best of him. He did something few live to tell about,
surviving a twenty-year meth addiction, sixteen of them on the needle. He
went from paying cash for new cars and anything else he wanted to living
beneath a freeway bridge. He's such an amazing and giving guy now that
it's hard to imagine this, but he got so bad he would hold people up at gunpoint and play Russian roulette, just for the rush of it. Today he's running a
rehab facility called the Training Center in San Diego, where he works with
convicts with addiction problems and tries to orient them back into society.

One of the world's first pro skateboarders, Bruce Logan, also fell to a meth addiction, his lasting forty years. Like Dennis, Bruce ended up living beneath a bridge. I had the privilege of praying with Bruce and watching him accept Christ a few years ago while filming the movie *D.O.P.E. (Death or Prison Eventually)*. The movie stars Bruce, Dennis, Jay, and me and is all about our rise, fall, and redemption.

Redemption has come to some other friends as well. Eddie and Duncan came to visit me in jail. There we spoke through the thick glass that's

JAY "ALABAMY" HAIZLIP, TONY "MAD DOG" ALVA, AND ME.
HOSOI FAMILY COLLECTION.

used to separate inmates from the people outside. I confirmed Eddie's suspicion that I'd died—not in the physical way, of course—when I said, "Christian Hosoi's dead, and he's never coming back." They understood that I was speaking in spiritual terms.

They're still among my closest friends today, and at their core they're tenderhearted guys. They've made up since their fallout at Focus years ago, and now they occasionally attend the Sanctuary—the church in Huntington Beach where, since 2004, I've served as the outreach pastor. At the end of one service, when I first spot them there, I scurry over and put a hand on each of them, telling them I've been waiting for this moment. Little by little I watch their lives change.

Eddie was born in Peru, and when someone says they're going down there to build ramps for poor kids in the inner city, he volunteers to go with them. They visit the most dangerous parts of the country, building skate ramps for the poorest of the poor, working with fellow hard-core Christians. According to Eddie, "Those guys don't care if they die in service for the Lord; they know where they're going." Eddie helps lots of kids' lives, and he continues making great progress personally.

Jay Adams has been on quite a journey. Tattooed on the back of his neck is 100% SKATEBOARDER. He's that and a whole lot more. He's always been radical, but now that can work in his favor. What he suggested in his letters to me years ago has come to pass, and we've done outreaches to kids together. Jay isn't always perfect in his walk, but when he's going strong, it's an amazing testimony to God's power.

Of all the salvation stories I've witnessed, one of my favorites is that of my childhood friend Aaron Murray. To this day Aaron is one of the most radical guys I've ever met, and I'm amazed and thankful that he's lived to tell the story. Our lives were bound together from those early days when we'd reach for something above us in the trees, to the opening of the skateparks, to our involvement with drugs (me) and alcohol (him). We've done it all together.

I haven't seen him for a while, and when I do, I see a desperate, unchecked addictive personality holding him down. He has drug problems like we all did, but I know that alcohol is his main thing and that it's finally getting the best of him. When he drinks, you can be pretty certain he'll start a fight. He tries and tries to quit drinking, but he just can't stop on his own. Even back in the day we'd all tell him he shouldn't drink. He'd manage to give it up and wouldn't drink for like a month or so. The next thing you knew, though, he'd be drunk or in a fight and blacking out on the way home from a party.

Pastor Jay, the lead pastor at the Sanctuary, remembers seeing Aaron out in front of the church looking like he'd just been beaten up. Jay says that Aaron appeared so angry and wasted that he could have been arrested just for the way he looked. He was still drunk from the night before. Still, he agreed to come inside. I'm not sure if he got much from that first service, but he continued coming each week after that, and it's evident that changes began happening in his life.

A few months pass and we're doing a group baptism in a park. It's in a horse trough in Huntington Beach. I ask Aaron to ride along with me to the baptism. He doesn't say much on the way there, and once we arrive, he sits quietly, watching and listening. After we baptize the last person I turn around and there's Aaron, standing in the water—pants, shoes, and all. I'm like, "Whoa, bro—what are you doin'?" He says, "I wanna get baptized." I say, "Okay, why don't you take your shirt and shoes off?" His answer reminds me of something Peter the apostle might have said: "Nope, I want it all; I want everything baptized." This dude is serious, and I gladly baptize him. He comes up from the water and we're both crying and hugging each other.

He doesn't change completely overnight, but something good is born in his heart that day. At this point, 2012, his entire life is different. He's been

attending church and been sober for five years now. His wife, Marissa, has a similar background, and now she's right there with him.

The Murrays have two sons, a six-year-old and a three-and-a-half-year-old, along with Aaron's two teenage stepsons. Their kids are a little older than ours, but they all love hanging out and playing together. His family recently moved to our town, and now we all hang together all the time. Aaron's an extreme guy, very passionate and emotional. When he reads the scripture he really looks into it and wants to squeeze all he can from it. Given his experience, he has a unique gift: he can present the gospel to people from a life of experience and a place of total surrender, describing a life that was radical and fragmented but is now committed, solid, and whole. I believe he's going to be used powerfully in the coming years. He and his wife are taking college Bible classes and are getting excellent grades. They also serve at the church. They're *definitely* committed.

I'm a Christian, but make no mistake: I'm not religious. To me religion is a *program*, comparable to the regimen of those old teams of skateboarders in the '70s, performing the same tricks in the same uniforms. That approach may work for some people, but I want nothing to do with it. I understand why it's so repellent to most skateboarders and anyone else who is used to being hard-core and doing things their own way. While many skaters are lost, I think it's the responsibility of those of us who know the truth to reach out and preach the gospel and love them. ✸

THE ONE AND ONLY

> The devil don't play by the rules. They don't call him the father of lies for nothing!
>
> —CHRISTIAN HOSOI

CHAPTER 23

> *Some people call Pastor Jay Haizlip "Alabama Jay" or simply "Alabamy." Because Jay's from Alabama, the nickname makes sense, but pastor? Nobody would ever have expected a druggie with his past to lead a church, unless maybe it was some whacked-out congregation that did drugs and partied all night. But Jay is the senior pastor of the Sanctuary, a thriving church in Huntington Beach with a vibrant mixture of skaters, punkers, street people, and drug addicts, most of whom have cleaned up, but some of whom are still in transition. Not only is Jay an awesome pastor, he's one of the most dedicated and radical men of God I've ever seen.*

PASTOR JAY AND ME. *HOSOI FAMILY COLLECTION.*

I relate deeply to Jay because our lives have run on parallel courses in many areas. His mother raised him. She was like Pops in a way—a product of the '60s who grew up thinking that getting high was normal. Friends of the family once thought it was cute to pour the kid drinks and blow pot smoke in his face, ignorantly getting him drunk or stoned way back when he was still in kindergarten. They had no idea that they were creating a drug addict and that his upbringing would nearly destroy him. By the age of twelve Jay was dealing bags of pot. At age fifteen he split for California, where his landlady got him into coke. He crashed on Tony Alva's family's couch for a while.

Years later, as an adult, Jay is just another strung-out crackhead looking to score. It's a Friday night in 1990 and he's off to meet his connection, when he encounters a man with something more to offer. After some

HOSOI CO-WRITER CHRIS AHRENS, JAY ADAMS, AND ME. © T-ROC.

intense conversation the man leads Jay in a simple prayer of salvation. Jay never does meet his connection that night, and he never uses drugs again. Instead he starts the Sanctuary Church, here in Huntington Beach in 2002. Two years later, I join him there.

I've seen many broken lives put back together at the Sanctuary, but there's so much more to be done. We drive down the street and gather our congregation up—pick up some homeless addicts, get them food, and preach the gospel to them—but then we drop them back off at the dumpster

ALEX OLSON, RHYTHM, ME, DOM DELUCA, AND STEVE OLSON.
HOSOI FAMILY COLLECTION.

they're living behind or the bridge that shelters them. It's heartbreaking leaving them there on the street. What's more, I know that it's only the grace of God that has kept me from being this guy or that guy. Without Christ there's no difference between me, the addict on the street, the guy in the penthouse suite at Trump Tower, or Trump himself. They're all gonna stand one day before the God who created them. As the Bible teaches in Philippians 2:10–11, ". . . at the name of Jesus every knee should bow, of those in heaven, and of those on earth, and of those under the earth, and *that* every tongue should confess that Jesus Christ *is* Lord. . . . "

None of these people started off in the gutter; in fact, many of them had good homes. In almost every case drugs or alcohol destroyed everything they had. Lots of them initially bought into the idea that drugs would benefit their lives. By the time they realized that wasn't true, it was too hard to pull themselves out of the trap. I can honestly say now that drugs were nothing but a dead-end road that cost me nearly everything and could have cost me my life. All drugs ever did for me was keep me from thinking straight. When I smoked weed I didn't think about responsibilities or my purpose in life—just girls, skating, and more weed. When you're smoking another joint, doing another line, or blowing another glass pipe with a torch, life blows by and suddenly you're a middle-aged druggie with no skills to support yourself.

Drugs, money, fame, sex—it's all an illusion. Through those means we grab at the wind, not knowing what's at stake. As a society we've set the bar so low that we actually *expect* our kids to try drugs, to do them at home and not in the street. We've quit warning our kids not to follow a risky path. Instead, we tell them to be safe while they experiment with the poisons they've chosen. The fortunate ones get in and get out of the drug world quickly, but one day they too regret wasting the best of their lives.

WEAPONS OF WARFARE

This next section should come with a warning like the one they give on movies. It could scare some people. It's about demon possession. I realize that not everyone is comfortable discussing that subject. This is by no means the main part of my ministry, but I can't leave it out. All I know is that this is what I witnessed:

The Sunday night service is over. Some of us are hanging around, talking with friends and praying with those who've requested it. From out of nowhere a woman says, "I hear voices." She looks like your average Orange County woman, only with a background in punk rock and raging. But something's different here—a glossy glow in her eyes and an indescribable darkness. She says she's feeling sick. Pastor Jay puts his hand on her head and begins praying. As soon as he says the words, "In the name of Jesus," her head snaps back, her eyes roll back in her head, and her tongue shoots out like a snake. If I didn't know better, I'd think she was having convulsions.

As we pray she's spitting up, almost vomiting. Then she shouts, "His claws are in my back. Get this thing *out* of me. Get him out of me—get him out, get him out!" Pastor Jay and I are both there, yelling, "In the

name of Jesus, come out of her." All of a sudden I sense the authority that Jesus gave his followers in Luke 10:19: "I give you the authority to trample on serpents and scorpions, and over all the power of the enemy, and nothing shall by any means hurt you."

She's here with her boyfriend, who has a painfully jacked-up shoulder. He's standing in the front row, and since everyone around him is raising their hands, he raises his own hands. Just like that, his shoulder is healed. That's at nearly the same moment his girlfriend gets set free.

I'm spending a relaxing evening at Pastor Jay's house when he gets a call from Brian Sumner and Richard Jefferson, two hot skaters from the Sanctuary. They've been out skating with a friend who's a hard-core ultimate fighter. Out of nowhere the guy starts acting really strange. That's when they call and ask Jay what to do. His advice is simple: "Cast the devil out of him." They reply, "We've never done anything like that before."

It's ten at night; Jay is locked down for the evening with his family. He looks over at me and asks, "Do you want to go down there?" I agree to do it and head out alone. At the time I was renting a warehouse for Hosoi Skateboards, and I tell the guys to meet me there. By the time I arrive, the guy's lurking in the bushes and Brian and Richard are waiting by the door. The guy glares at me as if he's a wild predator.

"Let's go inside," I suggest. He follows us into the office. There's a recliner in the middle of the room, and I point him toward it. "I'm going into the bathroom for a moment," I explain. "Sit down and relax, and when I return we're gonna pray for you." In the bathroom I pray, "Lord, I don't want to be here for hours on end; let's cast this devil out and go home. You're all powerful, and this guy's innocent."

When I return from the bathroom he's still standing up. I say, "Hey, sit down in that chair." I ask Brian and Richard if everything's right between them and God. They both reply that they're fine. I tell them, "All right, stand on either side of him and hold his arms down." This guy is a trained ultimate fighter, remember: if he gets loose, he'll do a lot of damage. I look right at him but talk directly to the devil, saying, "In the name of Jesus, you are *not* gonna move from this chair." Then I talk to the guy, saying, "Hey, we're gonna pray for you right now, and Jesus is gonna free you.

Are you ready?" A low growl comes from him as I set my hand on his forehead and say, "In the name of Jesus." Right then his body stiffens, his tongue shoots out, and he hisses like a cobra ready to strike. His eyes are glassy and have a distant look. Richard and Brian are holding him down, but because of our prayer he's not going anywhere.

I address the demon again: "In the name of Jesus, I have all authority over you. In the name of Jesus, come out of him." The demon answers, "I'm not comin'; I'm not comin'." I say, "Devil, this is a vessel of God, and you have no right to be in there. Come out of him." For ten or fifteen minutes I command the demon in that manner. He tries to combat me and put fear into me, but I don't listen. He's yelling, "You can't *do* this. He's mine; he's mine!"

"Kid, can you hear me?" I ask the guy. He nods his head yes. I say, *"You're gonna have to tell this devil to get out as well."* I walk the kid through a renouncing prayer—we say the words together—and I tell him to take a deep breath. At first he can't breathe deeply at all. Then I tell him, "You need to *fight* for this." He finally forces a deep breath and I shout, "Okay, now blow it out." We can smell a dark cloud filling the room as he exhales.

He's screaming hysterically. Then his eyes come back into focus, his shoulders drop, and he smiles. After a moment he laughs joyfully. "It's gone!" he says, hugging each of us. He exclaims over and over how good it feels to be free. This major life change takes only twenty minutes through the authority and power of Jesus Christ.

We see physical healings at the church too. One day a man comes to the church. He's not what I'd call super saved. He comes up front and says, "I've got only a few months to live, and I'll try anything." There are tumors all through his body apparently, though none is visible. He tells me he wants as much prayer as possible. We pray for him on two occasions. When he returns to the doctors the next time, they check him out and are shocked. "What happened?" they ask him. He says, "What do you mean?" They say, "There's no trace of cancer in your body." As far as he can tell, there's only one way to explain that. He tells them, "Jesus healed me!" Then he repeats: "Jesus healed me; Jesus healed me." He keeps coming to church and is soon traveling all over the place giving his testimony. The cancer never does return.

These are dramatic accounts of spiritual and physical healing. The events described aren't everyday occurrences at the Sanctuary. What we *do* see every day is evidence of God's love for each and every person—not just those we currently serve, but those who are still waiting to learn about Jesus's redeeming sacrifice. Every day, in conversations all across town, we hear about the many ways that God has blessed—and continues to bless—those who give their lives to Jesus.

PRO SKATING REVISITED AND REVISED

I now own 100 percent of Hosoi Skateboards and have just launched the company again in order to put something together for the future. Our new models are flying off the shelf. I hope to support my family with this work, but I also want my company to offer more than profit. I want it to influence the world and give something back.

I believe that this is the reason God allowed me not to OD or lose my mind when I was running the streets on drugs. I can't account otherwise for the fact that my heart didn't stop at those times when I was up for days in a row, blowing clouds of smoke—good dope, bad dope, it didn't matter—every single day for years. Drugs are the trap that got me, but they're not the only ones out there. Even being cool can ensnare you. Unfortunately, good is *not* cool; bad is cool in the world that *I* came from. I always *wanted* to be a good guy, but felt I needed to have a foot in the dark side. You can see where that can take you.

I didn't make a lot of good choices as a kid, but in the long run it all worked out for good. Pastor Jay, Aaron, Jen, and anyone else walking closely with God will tell you the same things about their lives. Everything Pastor Jay and I have done, good and bad, is now used to spread the gospel, and because of our background we have a chance to minister to a lot of people with radical backgrounds.

THE NEW AFTER HOURS

It's a Sunday night. We're finished with church at the Sanctuary; we've prayed with people, eaten something, and skated long into the night. Now we're hanging out at the local 7-Eleven like a couple of stoked skate

JENNIFER, ENDLESS, AND ME. © CESARIO "BLOCK" MONTANO.

groms when I see this girl I know. I can tell she's on drugs. She used to attend church with us, but I haven't seen her there for a while. I have a chance to encourage her and pray with her before she disappears into the darkness—or, hopefully, into the light.

Right as she drives off, a kid skates up. It's now two in the morning, and I can see he's a hard-core skater. I also imagine he's high on something—he has that look—but I can't judge him for that, cuz if he'd done half what I've done, he probably wouldn't be alive right now. We strike

SPORTS

Sunday, April 11, 2010 • www.daltondailycitizen.com

SUNDAY SHOWCASE

Making a difference

Professional skateboarder Christian Hosoi, right, autographs the skateboard of 11-year-old Nick Tucker, who is from Chattanooga, during an appearance at the North Georgia Skateboard Center in Tunnel Hill on Saturday. Hosoi lost his fame and money to drugs but has turned his life around after a four-year prison term.

MATT HAMILTON
The Daily Citizen

Hosoi turns from addiction to preaching

BY ADAM KROHN
adamkrohn@daltoncitizen.com

Fifteen-year-old Christian Hosoi became a professional skateboarder in 1982 and quickly gained fame, earned corporate sponsorships, made thousands of dollars and saw his face plastered on magazine covers. But he couldn't handle that success.

In time, Hosoi slipped into the dark world of drug addiction and watched as his fame and money evaporated. In January 2000, he was arrested for possession 1 1/2 pounds of crystal meth and eventually served four years in prison

INSIDE SPORTS
► Black wins Dogs' spring game, **2B**
► DGCC tennis tourney results, **3B**
► Complete Masters scoreboard, **4B**
► Taylor: A true student-athlete, **6B**

in San Bernardino (Calif.) Central Detention Center.

Sober for 10 years now, Hosoi has turned his life around, discovered Christianity and serves as pastor at The Sanctuary church in Westminster, Calif. He also has returned to professional skateboarding — he won a competition at last year's X Games — and

travels the globe making speeches about his life experiences.

On Saturday, Hosoi was in Tunnel Hill to deliver his message to young skaters at the North Georgia Skateboard Center.

"I wanted to come here and see if I could make a difference in people's lives in this community and influence them to do something positive to steer them away from the trials and tribulations I've gone through," said Hosoi, now 42. "It's about making the right choices, knowing good life skills and being good members of society rather than going down

the dark roads that a lot of kids don't make it out of."

Hosoi was impressed with the NGSC, which recently moved from downtown Dalton to a much larger facility off North Varnell Road. The expansion of NGSC reflects the growing popularity of skateboarding in this area and Hosoi sees that as a positive.

"If I was a kid, I'd be ecstatic," he said. "Like I was in heaven. When I look at this place, it can breed professional skateboarders.

➢ Please see **HOSOI, 2B**

up a conversation and talk about life for a while. I end up leading him to the Lord, right there in the parking lot.

Another girl I know pulls up while we're still sitting here, and I'll minister to her if she gives me the chance. It's going to be a long night, I can tell—almost like those sleepless marathons I did on meth. The difference is that this has a purpose to it.

My ministry is far-reaching, both through the Sanctuary and through skate events. Whatever the forum, I do all I can to spare kids from a life filled with addiction like mine was. I speak at high school assemblies when I can, and anywhere else they'll let me talk about the dangers of drug abuse, and preach at churches around the world. Kids these days are all told that weed is harmless, but I need them to know that pot and every other drug not only never helped me, but set me on a course that could have taken my life.

I can't say for sure, but my hope is that this ride called life is still far from over for me. Again, as the apostle Paul said, "For to me, to live *is* Christ, and to die *is* gain." There's a great deal of work left to do; and no matter what, I plan on burning hard and shining brightly until the end.

Years ago, as you've seen in these pages, I invented a skateboarding move called the Christ Air. My name is Christian, I've worn crosses most of my life, and people used to call me Christ. I used to think that I was the man and that being called Christ was cool. Now I know that Jesus Christ is more than a rad-sounding name; it's the name above all names. It's my hope and my prayer that you will learn to understand the meaning of that name for yourself—no matter how good or bad you think you are.

You don't have to be a professional skateboarder or a drug addict. Just confess your sins, ask Jesus to forgive you, invite Jesus into your heart, and tell someone about it. That's all there is to it. That's what I did, and all my guilt, all my hurt, and all my shame fell off my shoulders. I was finally free—and I've been free ever since. *You* can be free too. My family and many of my friends have been launched into the adventure of an eternal lifetime. They called me Christ, but that was just a nickname and one I could never live up to. My hope and prayer is that you also meet the One and Only. I promise you this: if you do, you'll never be the same again. ✺

NAME: CHRISTIAN ROSHA HOSOI

BORN: OCTOBER 5, 1967, LOS ANGELES, CALIFORNIA

WORK HISTORY: SKATEBOARDER, 1977–PRESENT

- 1ST IN 1979 OPEN GOLD CUP SERIES
- INVENTED HAMMERHEAD SHAPE SKATEBOARD, 1984
- BROKE TEN-FOOT BARRIER, HOLIDAY HAVOC, ANAHEIM CONVENTION CENTER, 1985
- 1ST IN 1985 NSA SUMMER SERIES 5 (CANADA): PRO VERT
- 1ST IN 1985 NSA
- INVENTED CHRIST AIR, 1986
- INVENTED ROCKET AIR, 1986
- 2ND IN 1986 EXPO '86 (CANADA): VERT
- 1ST IN 1987 THRASHER SAVANNAH SLAMMA I: STREET
- 2ND IN 1987 VISION RAMP N RAGE DOWN SOUTH: VERT
- 1ST IN 1988 VISION SKATE ESCAPE: VERT
- 2ND IN 1988 OHIO SKATEOUT: STREET
- 1ST IN 1988 RAMP RIOT (AUSTRALIA): VERT
- 1ST IN 1988 TITUS WORLD CUP (GERMANY): VERT
- 2ND IN 1988 TITUS WORLD CUP (GERMANY): STREET
- 2ND IN 1988 VISION BLUEGRASS AGGRESSION SESSION: VERT
- 1ST IN 1989 NSA SAVANNAH SLAMMA III: ARENA STREET
- 2ND IN 1989 NSA GOTCHA GRIND: VERT
- 1ST IN 1989 JAPAN SLAM JAM (JAPAN): VERT
- 3RD IN 1990 DISCO IN FRISCO: STREET
- 3RD IN 1990 NSA ALL PRO MINI RAMP JAM HAWAIIAN STYLE: MINI RAMP
- 1ST IN 2008 10TH ANNUAL TIM BRAUCH MEMORIAL CONTEST GRANDMASTERS EVENT

RESUME

- 1st in 2008 Etnies GVR Skull Bowl, Masters division
- Overall Best '80s in 2008, All '80s All Day Vert Challenge
- 1st in team event, 2009 Ultimate Boarder
- 2nd in 2009 Pro-Tec Pool Party, Masters division
- TransWorld Legend Award 2009
- 1st in 2009 X Games 15 Skateboard Park Legends contest
- 2nd in 2009 11th Annual Tim Brauch Memorial Contest Grandmasters Event
- 1st in 2010 X Games 16 Skateboard Park Legends contest
- Named one of the most influential skateboarders of all time by *TransWorld Skateboarding* magazine, December 2011

ACKNOWL

THANKS TO ALL MY CHILDHOOD
SKATEBOARDING MENTORS, INCLUDING: JAY ADAMS,
SHOGO KUBO, TONY ALVA, DENNIS "POLAR
BEAR" AGNEW, AND PAT NGOHO.

THANKS FOR CONTRIBUTING YOUR WORDS:
CESARIO "BLOCK" MONTANO, AARON MURRAY,
ROBERT RUSLER, STACY PERALTA, TONY HAWK,
DANNY WAY, CHRISTIAN FLETCHER AND THE
FLETCHER FAMILY, LOUANNA RAWLS, MAX PERLICH,
STEVE OLSON, DAVID HACKETT, STEPHEN BALDWIN,
POPS HOSOI, SERGIE VENTURA, JENNIFER HOSOI,
DAVE DUNCAN, EDDIE REATEGUI, JAY "ALABAMY"
HAIZLIP AND THE SANCTUARY FAMILY, KIMBERLY
BAIRD, BILL KENNEDY, DENNIS OGDEN, STEVE
CABALLERO, LANCE MOUNTAIN, GRANT BRITTAIN,
JEFF GROSSO, AND SCOTT OSTER.

THANK YOU TO THE LATE FAUSTO "V" VITELLO
AND THE VITELLO FAMILY. THANK YOU, STEVE VAN
DOREN AND FAMILY. THANK YOU, JIM GANZER, FOR
GETTING ME ON MY FIRST SKATEBOARD AND ALL
THE THINGS YOU'VE DONE TO HELP ME OVER THE
YEARS. THANKS TO JOEL RICE, WHO HELPED WITH
THE INITIAL STAGES OF THIS BOOK PROJECT AND
INTRODUCED ME TO HARPERONE. THANK YOU, CHRIS
AHRENS, FOR THIS AMAZING JOURNEY THAT WE

DGMENTS

TOOK TOGETHER FOR THE PURPOSE OF TOUCHING THE HEARTS OF PEOPLE AROUND THE WORLD WITH THE LOVE OF GOD THAT WE SHARE. I AM SO THANKFUL THAT GOD COULD USE YOUR WRITING AND MY STORY TO IMPACT THOSE THAT WILL READ IT. THANKS TO YOUR WONDERFUL WIFE, TRACY, WHO KEPT US FUELED DURING LATE NIGHTS AND LONG HOURS WITH HER AWESOME HOME-COOKED MEALS, HOT TEA, AND COFFEE. THANKS TO MY LITERARY AGENT, CLAUDIA CROSS, AND CHRIS'S AGENT, SANDRA BISHOP. THANKS TO MY FABULOUS MANAGEMENT TEAM, DARRYL FRANKLIN AND RAY IBE.

THANKS TO HARPERONE FOR BELIEVING IN MY STORY AND GIVING ME THE OPPORTUNITY TO WORK WITH SUCH AN INCREDIBLE PUBLISHING HOUSE AS HARPERCOLLINS. SPECIFIC THANKS TO JAMES IACOBELLI AND HARPERONE'S SUZANNE QUIST AND TERRI LEONARD FOR ALL YOUR HELP IN DESIGNING AND PRODUCING THE WONDERFUL INTERIOR OF THE BOOK. THANK YOU, MICHELE WETHERBEE AND FACEOUT STUDIO, FOR AN AMAZING COVER. THANKS TO HENRY LEUTWYLER FOR TAKING JUST THE RIGHT COVER SHOT. THANK YOU, JULIE BURTON, MOLLY BIRCKHEAD, CLAUDIA BOUTOTE, AND LAINA ADLER, FOR YOUR TIRELESS EFFORTS TO PROMOTE THIS BOOK.

A HUGE THANKS TO MY EDITOR, ROGER FREET, FOR THE LONG HOURS, ATTENTION TO DETAIL, NUMEROUS LATE NIGHT CALLS, AND GOING ABOVE AND BEYOND TO MAKE THIS BOOK A REALITY. KNOWING THAT YOU ONCE BROKE TWO ARMS SKATEBOARDING AND STILL TAKE TIME TO SKATE WITH YOUR SON, JARED, PROVES YOUR COMMITMENT AND DEDICATION. I COULD NOT HAVE HAD A BETTER EDITOR OR COUNSELOR.

THANK YOU TO TONY HAWK FOR WRITING THE FOREWORD. THANKS ALSO FOR YOUR CONTRIBUTIONS TO SKATEBOARDING AND YOUR CONTINUED LOVE AND INSPIRATION TO FURTHER OUR SPORT FOR THE NEXT GENERATION. THROUGH THE TONY HAWK FOUNDATION, KIDS EVERYWHERE HAVE GREAT SKATEPARKS. THE WAY WE HAD IT!

THANK YOU TO PHOTOGRAPHERS CESARIO "BLOCK" MONTANO, GRANT BRITTAIN AT THE *SKATEBOARD* MAG, JEFF HIGGINBOTHAM, MORIZEN "MOFO" FOCHE, IVAN HOSOI, JENNIFER HOSOI, TRACY "T-ROC" AHRENS, MARK OBLOW, *THRASHER* MAGAZINE, GLEN E. FRIEDMAN, AMBER STANLEY, MELINDA KIM, TED TERREBONNE, CHUCK KATZ, RAY "MRZ" ZIMMERMAN, AND THEO HAND.

THANK YOU, ALL MY SPONSORS, FRIENDS, AND FAMILY, WHO HAVE SUPPORTED ME AND MY FAMILY THROUGH FORTY-FOUR YEARS OF MY EXISTENCE IN THIS WORLD, AND FOR BEING

THERE DURING MY THIRTY YEARS OF
SKATEBOARDING PROFESSIONALLY.

THANK YOU TO AUNTIE KUIPO (RIP) AND
UNCLE DENNIS AND THEIR CHILDREN FOR ALLOWING
ME TO STAY IN THEIR HOME AFTER BEING RELEASED
FROM PRISON. THANKS TO GRANDMA BECKY
FOR HELPING CHOOSE HAWAIIAN NAMES FOR MY
CHILDREN. THANKS TO THE ALO FAMILY AND
EVERYONE IN THE HOSOI FAMILY. THANKS TO MY
FATHER-IN-LAW, MITCH "POP" MITCHELL, AND
HIS FAMILY. THANKS TO ALL AUNTIES, UNCLES,
COUSINS, NEPHEWS, NIECES, GRANDPARENTS, GREAT-
GRANDPARENTS, AND ALL OTHER OHANA.

A SPECIAL THANKS TO MY MOTHER, WHO TAUGHT ME
TO BE HONEST, SINCERE, AND KIND. I WILL SEE YOU
AGAIN IN HEAVEN. I LOVE YOU TOO MUCH! THANKS TO
MY FATHER FOR YOUR SACRIFICIAL LOVE IN RAISING
AND SUPPORTING ME WITH YOUR GUIDANCE TO BE
ORIGINAL. THANKS TO MY BEAUTIFUL CHILDREN THAT
THE LORD HAS BLESSED ME WITH. ENDLESS, CLASSIC,
RHYTHM, AND JAMES. YOU ALL HAVE TAUGHT ME HOW
TO LOVE LIKE A FATHER SHOULD LOVE HIS CHILDREN.

THANKS TO MY LOVELY WIFE, JENNIFER, WHO
STUCK BY MY SIDE THROUGH THICK AND THIN.
THANK YOU FOR BEING AN AMAZING MOTHER AND
A WONDERFUL WIFE. EVER SINCE WE MET IN 1999,
MY HEART AND LIFE HAS BEEN FOREVER CHANGED

THROUGH THE LOVE OF GOD THAT WE EXPERIENCE
TOGETHER NOW AND FOREVER. LIKE PROVERBS
18:22 SAYS, I FOUND FAVOR FROM THE LORD WHEN HE
BROUGHT YOU INTO MY LIFE. I LOVE YOU WITH MY
WHOLE HEART, MIND, BODY, AND SOUL.

MY FINAL THANKS TO MY LORD AND
SAVIOR JESUS CHRIST, WHO CAME INTO MY LIFE
AND CHANGED IT FOR ALL ETERNITY.

IVAN "POPS" HOSOI ART.

MY RECENT ART PIECE OF JESUS CHRIST.

SKATEBOARDS

HosoiSkateboards.com

www.facebook.com/ChristianHosoiPage